SHADES OF GRAY

Books by Barry Siegel

A Death in White Bear Lake
Shades of Gray

SHADES OF GRAY

ORDINARY PEOPLE IN EXTRAORDINARY CIRCUMSTANCES

BARRY SIEGEL

BANTAM BOOKS
NEW YORK TORONTO LONDON SYDNEY AUCKLAND

SHADES OF GRAY

A Bantam Book/March 1992

For permissions, please see page 288.

Book design by Joseph Rutt.

Library of Congress Cataloging-in-Publication Data
Siegel, Barry.
Shades of gray / Barry Siegel.
p. cm.
ISBN 0-553-08115-2
I. Title.
AC8.S54425 1992
081—dc20 91-31159
CIP

Published simultaneously in the United States and Canada

Bantam Books are published by Bantam Books, a division of Bantam Doubleday Dell Publishing Group, Inc. Its trademark, consisting of the words "Bantam Books" and the portrayal of a rooster, is Registered in U.S. Patent and Trademark Office and in other countries. Marca Registrada. Bantam Books, 666 Fifth Avenue, New York, New York 10103.

PRINTED IN THE UNITED STATES OF AMERICA

BVG 0 9 8 7 6 5 4 3 2 1

For Ally
who is my girl

CONTENTS

INTRODUCTION

Virtually all of these pieces appeared originally, although in somewhat different form, in the pages of *The Los Angeles Times.* They grew out of a proposal I presented in late 1979 to Bill Thomas, then *The Times*'s editor. What I had in mind was a roving national correspondent's assignment that involved no fixed beat as to subject or site, no relation to breaking news and no time or space constraints. By then I had been working as a *Times* staff writer for three years, and it's fair to say I'd grown restless with daily newspaper journalism. I admired and enjoyed the energy and immediacy of newspapers, but I wanted to write about events without telescoping information or rushing to judgment.

What interested me most was not what had happened—legislators passing a law, townsfolk adopting a policy, jurors reaching a decision—but rather, how it had happened and why. There were people behind these events, after all—some triumphant, some anguished, some puzzled. Exploring what they'd been through, and the ideas with which they'd wrestled, seemed as illuminating and intriguing as even the most penetrating report of the outcome. I did not at all mind the notion of coming late to an event, even by a matter of weeks or months, for people then were much more willing to talk and hand over documents, and I was after what was enduring, not immediate. I regarded such stories as a form of continual, subterranean news about how people and communities actually lived and functioned day in and day out, so I thought they merited a place in the newspaper.

Trying to describe all this to Bill Thomas one morning, I felt wary, for I knew he was prone to telling people they were talking nonsense when that was his opinion. At one point, studying his expression, I thought he was about to hustle me out the door. Instead, when I finished, he shrugged and growled out his blessing. This response wasn't altogether surprising, to tell the truth. Although it is unusual for a daily newspaper to accommodate the type of articles I was describing, both because of their nature and their length, *The Times* over the years had always provided an imaginative and encouraging environment for all sorts of writers.

So at the start of 1980 I found myself casting about for something that I could only vaguely describe to others. I wanted to find stories that weren't so conventionally newsworthy that they already were being well covered. I wanted to find stories about people caught up in conflict and wrestling with provocative ideas. I wanted to focus on individuals who should be well known, rather than those who were. Above all, I wanted to begin with the particular—a specific event or circumstance or conflict—rather than an abstract notion or theme. Beyond that, I could not say.

A good many of the stories I was after emerged from scanning the back pages of small-town newspapers and obscure journals, where all manner of news briefs fairly screamed for amplification. A one-sentence item about the monetary value the Environmental Protection Agency placed on a human life in its cost-benefit analyses set me in search of the specific EPA risk manager who makes the choice between dollars and lives. A one-paragraph report about a federal research vessel plying the waters off the coast of Peru, studying an unexplained one-degree rise in water temperature there, raised the question of why one degree would matter so much. A short item about an odd petition drive in southern Georgia aimed at impeaching three federal appellate judges led me to ask just what had made those people so angry.

Questions like these took me to all corners of the nation and beyond—from the dirt-poor towns of Donalsonville and Willacoochee in Georgia to Callao, Peru, and Rio Frio, Costa Rica; from Charleston, South Carolina, to the Amish region of southern Indiana; from New Orleans to the Pacific Northwest, the gulf coast of Florida, the upper peninsula of Michigan and the farm country of southern Minnesota. The more I traveled, the more intrigued I became with how things worked. I also began noticing how often critical events appeared to arise out of random twists of fate or petty jealousies or raw ambition. A young, inexperienced defense attorney forgets to subpoena a witness and a man is sentenced to Death Row. A scientist tries to head off a competitor and inadvertently leads him to a luminous discovery. More than once my flagging interest has been revived by someone who interrupts an extended explanation of his accomplishments to deliver a sly, halting confession about a particularly egregious piece of nastiness or foolishness he'd committed on the way to his triumph.

The more complex the story, the better. Two sides to a conflict or two levels to a tale were not enough—I wanted three or four or five. Only then did I sense I was getting it right. Most situations have nuances, after all, and most people are a shaded mix of qualities, and most issues yield several understandable points of view. Stories that did not reflect such layers left me suspicious. When a prosecutor insists that the accused murderer is "evil incarnate," my eyes glaze over. On the other hand, when a neighbor allows that she sort of likes the defendant even if she's guilty, and thinks there's good in the bad people she knows and bad in the good, I sit up straight. There is a necessary and understandable pressure in daily newspaper journalism to boil it down, to get to the point, to characterize what has happened or will happen, but I can't help wondering whether a "stunning victory" will look like a "crushing defeat" from a perspective of time and distance. Is it really the mood of the country or the thoughts of the three guys next to me in a bar? Is it a national trend or a sociologist's study decorated with half a dozen anecdotes? Is it malfeasance or human fallibility?

My favorite stories offered more than complexity, though—they left me feeling torn by the issues they raised. A federal judge hostile to corporate America once returned my phone call by pretending to be a representative of the oil lobby. "Why do you want to talk to that judge?" he snarled, before finally identifying himself and setting me to chuckling. Here was a judge to cheer, for he was insisting upon justice for unfortunate victims in a situation where his brethren had failed to act. After burrowing into his tale, however, it seemed clear that he was achieving his goal by disregarding certain valuable, fundamental principles of the law. What if he was pursuing a less honorable cause? Did the end justify his means?

Questions without clear answers were the topics I most warmly embraced: Ambiguity, not absolutes. Most of these stories are about people who have had to make choices amid uncertainty, or find design amid disorder. I do not think such experiences are rare. In pursuit of them, I found myself returning time and again to matters of law, medicine and science, and the natural world. This happened not by design, but simply because courtrooms and laboratories offer much the same attractive elements: intriguing characters, twisting plots, subtexts, ambivalent issues and a very human search for transcendence. Where the lawyers pursue justice by means of a sometimes brutally unfair adversary system, the scientists reach for order and meaning through an often petty and ruthless competition. Best of all, though, such stories offer—hidden within a mountain of transcripts, reports, journals and exhibits—a wealth of detail.

Details are wonderful things. They are more interesting than opinions, and they thoroughly cripple ideology. Details reveal how something really is, not how we want or believe it to be. A Death Row inmate finally comprehends his fate when authorities come to measure him for his burial suit on the night before his scheduled execution. An unconventional scientist shuns the society of others, preferring to sit alone in his darkened living room or practice *tae kwon do,* the ancient Korean martial art. A disabled man planning to kill himself collects canes in a brass urn by his bedside so as to mask the rifle hidden there. I was forever looking for items like these. Whenever I interviewed people I asked mainly for memories of where they sat and what they told the other fellow and just how they figured it out. Armed with the answers to these questions, I felt certain there at least would be a tale to tell.

And that, finally, was what mattered most—a tale to tell. It would be misleading to suggest that I began to work on each of these pieces because they fit a grand, preconceived scheme. The truth is, sometimes I jumped at a story simply because instinct said it was worth pursuing. The only lure necessary was the hope that I'd find people wrestling with something interesting—something that lifted a curtain on how they lived or how their communities worked.

Such stories matter even if they are not individually important in an obvious way. In deciding to break up a family, to help a relative die, to abort a deformed fetus, to punish a passionate judge, to reward an ambitious scientist, to rescue or condemn a Death Row inmate, people are laying down some rules about what's right and wrong. And combined, these choices send signals about our values, signals that guide and empower the institutions that most affect our lives—governments, courts, legislatures, schools, corporations. Most of the time, prosecutors, regulators, politicians and directors of marketing tread only where they sense the public will allow them to go. Although I would not want to describe these pieces as anything but good yarns, I don't think it goes too far to say that in them, individuals are wrestling with something important. The moral choices we make and the meanings we impose on events, after all, taken together form the character of our communities.

AUTHOR'S NOTE

While researching and writing these articles, I often was looking at circumstances that continued to evolve after I left the scene. Later events have altered the outcome in some of the stories, and in others, developments have simply rounded out the tale, or carried it to a new and still continuing phase. I have not tried to incorporate these recent twists within the articles themselves, for that would make them different pieces entirely. Instead, the reader will find brief updates at the end of those stories that seemed to call for them.

During the decade in which I worked on these pieces, I benefited greatly from a number of *Los Angeles Times* editors' attention, indulgence and advice. Above all, I thank Bill Thomas, who gave me my job and put most of these pieces in the newspaper. My debts are also large to Dennis Britton, Mike Miller, Stan Burroway, Linda Mathews, John Foley, George Cotliar, and Bill Thomas's successor, Shelby Coffey III.

A number of my fellow writers at *The Times* have provided encouragement and, by the example of their own work, more than a little inspiration. Among them are Richard E. Meyer, Barry Bearak, Bella Stumbo, Robert A. Jones and Robert Scheer. Nina Green, the *Times* national correspondents' splendidly talented research assistant, graciously assisted with the preparation and updating of several articles.

Marti Devore supplied helpful advice and unwavering support. At Bantam Books, Ann Harris, confronted with a manuscript already worked over by other hands, generously provided an additional dose of elegant and meticulous polishing. My agent Kathy Robbins—I wish I'd known her since I was in kindergarten!—as always contributed wisdom and warmth.

A special thanks is due Tim Rutten, who as a *Los Angeles Times* assistant national editor for more than four years oversaw my work on many of these pieces. Rather than rub his own thumbprints over his writers' pages, he preferred to force them into the habit of good thinking, out of which he believed good writing would naturally develop. Always stimulating, always challenging, Rutten understood what I was after even when I did not.

I

Matters of Justice, Matters of Law

Monstrous Mischief

December 1984
Minneapolis

As U.S. District Judge Miles Lord drove along Highway 7 at dusk on the evening of February 24, 1984, heading toward his home on Christmas Lake, thirty miles west of Minneapolis in the outlying suburb of Chanhassen, he knew he should feel satisfied. After weeks of sometimes bitter wrangling, the A. H. Robins Company, manufacturers of the Dalkon Shield intrauterine contraceptive device, that day had agreed in a pretrial settlement to pay $4.6 million to seven women who claimed they'd suffered infections, sterility, miscarriages and other health problems because of the IUD. Lord knew this corporate capitulation was unusual, because for over ten years A. H. Robins had been fighting, and winning, dozens of Dalkon Shield claims. Lord knew also that his rulings—most particularly, his decision to reopen long-closed discovery proceedings—were the primary reason why the giant pharmaceutical company had backed down. Almost single-handedly, the judge had to admit, he'd brought this conglomerate to its knees.

All the same, Lord was not entirely pleased. A settlement alone did not seem nearly good enough to the judge. During all the pretrial legal wrangling—in fact, throughout years of litigation in courts across the country—A. H. Robins's top officials had never admitted that they even knew their product was harming anyone, or that more than ten thousand Dalkon Shield lawsuits had been filed against their corporation. It seemed to Lord that they should acknowledge this. He wanted to talk to those executives, even though he had no authority over them. He wanted them never again to say they did not know. He wanted them to look in the mirror and take responsibility. In short, Judge Lord wanted the A. H. Robins executives to confess and repent, right in his courtroom.

Reflecting on these matters as he drove, Lord decided to compose the speech he intended to deliver to these men if he ever could get them into his courtroom. He reached for the tape recorder he kept at the ready in his car, and turned it on.

"It is not enough to say, 'I do not know,' 'It was not me,' 'Look elsewhere,' " the judge said into the recorder's microphone. "Time and again each of you have used this kind of argument in refusing to acknowledge your responsibility and pretending to the world that the chief officers and directors of your gigantic multinational corporation have no responsibility for the company's acts and omissions. . . . The accumulation of corporate wrong is in my mind a manifestation of individual sin. . . . Your company in the face of overwhelming evidence denies its guilt and continues its monstrous mischief. . . . This is corporate irresponsibility at its meanest. . . . Confession is good for the soul, gentlemen. Face up to your misdeeds."

Lord paused, then turned off the tape recorder. He knew perfectly well there had been no trial in his courtroom, and thus no verdict. The three men he planned to address, in fact, were not technically even parties to the lawsuit. He could not force them into his courtroom. His signature was not, for that matter, needed on the settlement agreement. Denouncing the corporate executives under such circumstances could cause a federal judge considerable trouble.

Lord drove on for a while in silence. Then he flipped the switch on the tape recorder, and resumed his dictation.

The unconventional and precarious decision to reprimand publicly A. H. Robins's executives was only the latest episode in the singular history of sixty-four-year-old Miles Lord. For better or worse, he is a legendary figure in upper Midwest legal circles. Everyone agrees that Lord is outspoken, folksy and opinionated, but, after that, thoughts divide over whether the judge is a Trumanesque champion of the underdog or an out-of-control judicial zealot. He has been named the outstanding federal judge of the year by The Association of Trial Lawyers of America within months of being named in an *American Lawyer* survey as the worst federal judge in the Eighth Circuit and one of the eleven worst in the country. He has been praised as an innovative jurist able to cut through legal obfuscation, and he has been removed by the Eighth Circuit Court of Appeals from a landmark pollution case because of what the appellate panel called "gross bias."

Lord does not hide his belief that legal procedures often are an obstacle, rather than a tool, in achieving justice, so he does not behave in court as most other judges do. He is determined not to let formal procedures and language obscure what he believes actually is going on. A lawyer reciting points of law or legal precedents is likely to be interrupted with a wave of the arm and told by the judge to "just give me the facts." A prosecutor outgunned by a team of high-priced defense lawyers can expect Lord to offer advice and take over questioning of witnesses. Not even his most ardent supporters would suggest the judge is a patient scholar. He favors action, and results. More than a few who know Lord call him "the last breath of frontier populist justice." It is an indication of the ambivalence he inspires that some offer this description derisively, others admiringly. Lord's twenty-year career on the bench, besides spawning rich courthouse lore, has regularly forced others to consider just how far a judge can and should bend the rules in order to make a cumbersome legal system arrive at truth and justice.

He is a wiry five-foot seven-inch man with a partiality for perch fishing and Copenhagen snuff. He can match stern glares with any federal judge, but more often than not displays the devilish expression of a young boy who knows he is misbehaving. He often tilts back in his chair and listens with a mischievous expression as a lawyer laboriously explains his case in formal legal terms, then leans forward and rephrases what was said in a brief, blunt sentence. Speaking in his chambers one day late in the spring of 1984, he said, "I think my job as a judge is to see that justice is done. The whole object is to get at the truth, and I try to do that. I worship the truth. If you just don't read the lawbooks, you can get lots done. Judges tend to use precedents instead of figuring things out themselves. You can find a precedent for anything. That's one of the real difficulties with the law."

Because they are appointed by the president on the advice of U.S. Senators, federal judges tend to come from large, affluent, politically connected law firms. Lord, instead, is the eighth of nine children of an impoverished lumbering and farming family from northeastern Minnesota's Iron Range, a region of the state that produces, along with iron ore and taconite, a tradition of liberal politics, unionism and intense identification with underdogs. A featherweight Golden Gloves boxer who worked his way through the University of Minnesota Law School at his mother's urging, he has never practiced privately for more than a year at a time. He quit his first job as an insurance adjuster after three months because "they criticized me for paying an old lady four hundred dollars for a broken knee when she would have taken fifty dollars." He then ran unsuccessfully for a seat in the Minnesota State Senate, he said, "not because of the call of the electorate but rather the howl of creditors. . . . It was also a way to meet people."

Among the many state Democratic Farmer-Labor party officials he met was a young fireball orator who had recently moved from the mayor's office in Minneapolis to the United States Senate. Hubert H. Humphrey became one of Lord's closest political cronies and fishing companions. As they traveled together across the state, Lord regularly enjoyed suggesting to Humphrey that he was more popular among the people of Minnesota than was the senator. One afternoon while the two were journeying through the Minnesota Boundary Water District in the northeastern reach of the state, they came upon a traffic jam, a prime opportunity for the ebullient Humphrey to work a crowd, as often was his wont. Lord jogged on ahead, boarded a bus, and warned the passengers that there was a man coming up behind him who was pretending to be a United States Senator. "He's harmless," Lord advised, "but he'll sponge a drink off you and talk a lot. Humor him along, but don't lend him any money." Humphrey, arriving a moment later, was dismayed to find himself rebuffed when he tried to press the flesh.

Lord, by nature a raconteur and backslapper, felt comfortable in the world of Minnesota politics, and did well there, three times getting elected state attorney general during the 1950s. In 1961 he was named U.S. attorney for Minnesota by President John F. Kennedy. In 1966, President Lyndon B. Johnson appointed Lord to the federal bench at the strong urging of then-Vice President Humphrey, who proudly proclaimed his pal "the people's judge."

Lord took with him to the bench a passel of passionate beliefs he has never tried to disguise. Above all, he has little patience for wrongdoing by large corporations and insists that top executives be held personally accountable. "Why is it that if you plot in the barroom, it's a crime, but if you plot in a boardroom, it is not?" he likes to ask. "The evils committed in the name of the corporation become the responsibility of no one. When a person is allowed to have a corporate charter by merely laying down seventy-six dollars, any number of people can get together and operate as a single entity and, except in very rare instances, the conspiracy laws do not apply. . . . I'd say eighty-five percent of what's done in this country is by corporations. When you talk of what's wrong, you've got to talk about corporations. They're running things."

Lord acted on his beliefs as well as talked. For example, in December 1983, after the Sperry Corporation was allowed to plead guilty in his courtroom to overcharging the Defense Department $325,000 on an MX missile contract, Lord denounced the federal prosecutors because "it hasn't been called to my attention that any individual has been punished. I just have a view that this will never stop until the officers of a corporation are held accountable for the conduct of their subordinates." Before formally accepting the plea bargain, Lord called a hearing mainly to make public a report that showed Sperry actually had overcharged the government $3.5 million, not $350,000. "I just wanted their shareholders to know," he explained afterward, winking.

Lord also feels strongly that the discovery process that underlies the civil legal system is little more than a charade. He has long argued that objective, court-appointed special masters should be responsible for producing documents, not the lawyers involved in the case. "Lawyers' self-interest, their economic interest, their fundamental loyalty and the rules of ethics dictate that they do only those things which are in the interest of their client," he told an American Bar Association seminar in April 1984. "But what of those federal rules which require that documents be produced by that same client, and, worst of all, the lawyer is responsible for seeing that they are produced? These documents may involve some of the client's most horrible secrets. . . . I pose a question—is there not inherent in this situation a horrible and irreconcilable conflict of interest? We refuse to see what is so apparent."

Lord's admirers tend to be plaintiffs' attorneys, his detractors criminal and white-collar defense lawyers, and because of these groups' disparate interests, they are capable of placing quite different values on the judge's actions. In fact, when *American Lawyer* called Lord the worst judge in the Eighth Circuit, it cited his role in the very same antitrust antibiotics case that won him top honors from the plaintiffs-oriented Association of Trial Lawyers.

It was, everyone agreed, a tangled piece of litigation. In 1976, months after he'd forced through a fifty-million-dollar settlement with five drug companies who'd been fighting price-fixing charges for years, the judge found himself still presiding over the federal government's suit to recover overcharges paid by the Veterans Administration. During the trial, one government attorney particularly tried Lord's patience by examining a single witness for three months—"He never got an answer out of him," Lord later recalled, "because the witness was a lawyer." Lord finally told the two sides to settle or else he would declare a mistrial. When the government refused the drug companies' offer of seventy-six million dollars, Lord proved good to his word.

Lord has found himself in trouble on more than one occasion with the U.S. Eighth Circuit Court of Appeals, but it was his involvement in a complicated pollution case against the Reserve Mining Company that caused him the biggest problem. In 1974, Lord ruled that Reserve Mining's discharges into Lake Superior from its taconite processing plant were creating pollution and possible health hazards. The ruling was upheld by the Eighth Circuit, which ordered Reserve Mining to find a suitable alternative dump site and at the same time directed Lord to stay out of negotiations between the company and the state over where that site would be. Almost two years later, however, those negotiations were still dragging on in November 1975, so Lord, growing impatient, summoned state officials to an uncommon series of hearings. The scene was vintage Lord. He called his own witnesses and even testified himself. At one point, he said flatly: "I have dispensed with the usual adversary proceeding here, because I simply do not have time to spend, as I did, nine months in hearings, six months of which was wasted by what I find now . . . to be misrepresentations by Reserve Mining Company."

Two months later, in January 1976, the Eighth Circuit Court of Appeals ordered Lord removed from the case because of what it described as his disregard "for the mandate" of the appellate court. In removing him, the appellate judges said: "No one can doubt that Judge Lord does have deep convictions in this matter or that such convictions largely influence his actions. . . . [But] Judge Lord seems to have shed the robe of a judge and to have assumed the mantle of the advocate."

It was in late December 1983, eight years after the ignominious Reserve Mining rebuff, that twenty-three Dalkon Shield cases were first placed on the calendar of Miles Lord. By then, he was, because of seniority, chief judge of the U.S. district court for the District of Minnesota. Over time, he had tried to moderate his ways, partly out of respect for the wishes of his family. The Dalkon Shield cases, though, stirred Lord's lifelong passions. Here, once again, was a corporation behaving in a way he felt was abominable. Here, once again, was a legal history that Lord felt consisted mainly of evasive discovery, ineffective judges and unnecessarily protracted litigation.

At the very least, the history was byzantine.

A. H. Robins, a multinational corporation based in Richmond, Virginia, that reported $563 million in sales in 1983, had bought the design for the Dalkon Shield in June 1970, and had sold four and a half million of the IUDs between 1971 and 1974. The first lawsuit claiming injury from a Dalkon Shield was filed in 1972, and dozens followed during the balance of that decade. Evidence introduced in court during the adjudication of these cases suggested that the design of the IUD's stringlike tail displayed what are called "wicking qualities"—that is, acting like a wick, the tail tended to absorb and draw bacteria from the vagina through the cervix into the relatively sterile uterus. This wicking tendency, the lawsuits claimed, caused dangerous infections, pelvic inflammatory disease, miscarriages, sterility and seventeen deaths.

The evidence also suggested that A. H. Robins executives knew of these problems almost from the start of marketing. Eldrin Wayne Crowder, a former Robins quality control supervisor responsible for monitoring production of the Dalkon Shield, testified that he pointed out the flawed design in the summer of 1971. It was not until 1973, however, that the company first notified the Food and Drug Administration about the troubles and complaints connected with the Shield. In mid-1974, at the FDA's request, A. H. Robins voluntarily stopped distributing the IUDs and sent a letter to all doctors, hospitals and birth control organizations advising them of the problem. Six more years passed before Robins recommended to doctors that they remove the Dalkon Shield from women still using the device. Finally, in August 1983, the FDA warned in a bulletin that "due to increased risk of pelvic inflammatory disease, the Dalkon Shield should be removed from any woman wearing one."

A. H. Robins, however, never had issued its own recall or actively sought to contact all women who had purchased the Dalkon Shield. The company was not required by law to do so, and the company's president, E. C. Robins, Jr., in 1983 explained why he was not planning such an action: "A. H. Robins' position is that the greater weight of the medical evidence shows that the infection rate associated with the Dalkon Shield is not statistically different from infection associated with other IUDs. There is substantial medical doubt that any IUD causes pelvic infection. . . . Neither this company nor its people, now or in the past, would be a party to the manufacture or marketing of any product known to be defective."

During most of the 1970s, A. H. Robins appeared to prevail within the legal system. Indeed, the company used the system as a form of protection, settling thousands of claims for minimal amounts while keeping a cloak of secrecy around the central facts about the Dalkon Shield's development and flaws. The A. H. Robins attorneys' basic strategy was to keep cases spread through various jurisdictions and treat them as separate, individual lawsuits. Even for a combined multidistrict discovery proceeding in 1977 that was intended to create a record for all subsequent cases, the company produced few corporate documents related to the Dalkon Shield, claiming most were "privileged" because they had passed through the hands of their attorneys. In addition, as part of settlement negotiations, Robins regularly requested that opponents' attorneys agree not to pursue any other Dalkon Shield lawsuits. By early 1984, A. H. Robins had gone to trial in just thirty-six cases, losing seventeen and winning nineteen. The company had settled 6,900 claims out of court for $197 million, and at least 3,800 cases were still pending.

"They were putting out individual brush fires before they combined to form a giant blaze," one Minnesota lawyer observed later. "They fragmented the cases so no one lawyer or judge ever had all the information. Most judges' eyes would just blur over at the idea of undertaking major discovery for just one single case."

Miles Lord, however, responded differently. In January 1984, two Dalkon Shield plaintiffs' lawyers, Dale Larson and Michael Ciressi (partners in the Minneapolis law firm of Robins, Zelle, Larson & Kaplan) appeared in his courtroom with motions they had vainly submitted earlier to other judges. They wanted to consolidate all their twenty-three cases, and they wanted to reopen discovery. Lord, who understood perfectly well what they were after, promptly granted both their requests.

The Robins-Zelle lawyers began taking new depositions from A. H. Robins executives that same month. The deposing at A. H. Robins headquarters in Richmond dragged on, however, because A. H. Robins executives, as in previous cases, had difficulty remembering much about the Dalkon Shield. In a conference call among all parties on January 23, 1984, the plaintiffs' attorneys reported to Judge Lord that they were making little progress. In particular, they said, the deposition of board chairman E. C. Robins, Sr., was stalled by his inability to recall any conversations at all concerning the Dalkon Shield.

This report angered Lord. Before the conference call ended, the judge had ordered A. H. Robins officials to produce the minutes of its board of directors meetings; perhaps the minutes, he said, might stimulate the chairman's memory. When company attorneys responded the next day by turning over only certain excerpts from those minutes, claiming the rest was privileged, Lord promptly ordered that all the minute books be produced in Minneapolis for him to examine in chambers. He would decide what parts were privileged, he said. He would decide what parts should be provided to the plaintiffs.

In his chambers on January 25, with A. H. Robins's attorney Alex Slaughter and plaintiffs' attorney Roger Brosnahan present, Lord began to read through the minute books. As he did so, he grew increasingly angry.

"Well, there is some discoverable stuff in here," he said. He turned several pages. "There is some impeachable stuff in here," he growled. He read on. "Shit, there's some sanctionable stuff here!" he finally thundered.

To Lord, the minutes made it clear that E. C. Robins, Sr., and his son, president and chief executive officer E. C. Robins, Jr., had not only attended nearly every board meeting, but also had demonstrated a detailed knowledge of the corporation's affairs. The minute books also suggested to Lord the existence of countless documents relevant to the Dalkon Shield that the company had never produced during the multidistrict discovery proceeding, including results of testing, communications from doctors about problems with the IUD and periodic reports addressed to the company's top management from the in-house attorney who had directed the company's defense in the 1970s. In one 1974 report, that company attorney, Roger Tuttle, had advised against a recall of the IUDs because it would be tantamount to an admission of liability. "We ought to let it die slowly," the lawyer had written.

When he finished reading the minutes in his chambers, Lord turned to A. H. Robins lawyer Alex Slaughter. "Do you think it would be helpful if I flew down to Virginia, Alex?" the judge asked.

· · ·

When Lord arrived at the A. H. Robins headquarters in Virginia early the next morning, he seized an executive's office and set out to provide his personal supervision, and acceleration, of the deposition and discovery process. In the small, hot room the company provided for depositions, Lord noticed with irritation that the chairs were positioned so that the attorneys for the deponents sat shoulder-to-shoulder, knee-to-knee with their clients. A nudge by an attorney could—and did—silence the deponent without notice in the official record. By the time E. H. Robins, Sr., appeared for his deposition, Lord felt the need to say something to the elderly executive, whom doctors had said wasn't well enough to travel to Minneapolis. "Because your doctor said your health may be in jeopardy," Lord began, "I have invoked every kind of protection for your health. Now should someone have done that for the women who were wearing this Dalkon Shield device . . . ?"

A. H. Robins's hospitality soon waned. Halfway through the judge's planned two-day sojourn, Alex Slaughter formally objected to Lord's power to issue orders in the state of Virginia. The judge, now more irked than ever, soon after departed for Minnesota.

Lord's retreat did not matter much—once the discovery doors had been reopened, they could not be shut so easily. Armed and encouraged by Lord's rulings, plaintiffs' attorneys began making repeated requests for more documents. After all, if evidence existed that proved company executives knew of the Dalkon Shield's problems years ago, plaintiffs could claim not just direct compensation, but also sizable punitive damages. In response, A. H. Robins sent an ever-growing and changing team of attorneys into court with assorted briefs arguing against producing the documents. Here Lord rolled up his sleeves and, not without some relish, began hand-to-hand combat.

One morning the judge, counting seven A. H. Robins attorneys at the defense table and "more back in the wings," as he put it, announced that he wanted all out-of-town lawyers "to take a little oath that they'll agree to abide by the rules and regulations of the Court here in Minnesota, will voluntarily subject themselves to the jurisdiction of the State Board on Ethical Practices, and that they'll not contest the jurisdiction of any Minnesota tribunal to take such steps, the same steps against them as they could take against anyone who is admitted to practice in Minnesota." The A. H. Robins team, Lord pointed out, kept moving people in and out, so he could not control them and did not know who they were. He wanted this matter resolved, he said, "before we have argument from people I have never seen before and may never see again." Otherwise, he said, he would not be able to take action, as required by law, against attorneys "doing specious and frivolous things."

When an A. H. Robins attorney asked for one day to prepare a response to this oath request, Lord said, "You don't need all day to talk that out. We'll recess for lunch and I will see you at one-thirty P.M." When the out-of-state lawyers returned and said they could not sign the oath, Lord ordered them from the courtroom and instructed the company's local Minneapolis attorney to proceed with the case alone. When that attorney said he was not authorized to do so, Lord threatened to enter a default judgment against A. H. Robins. In time, though, after emotions calmed and everyone agreed that a single attorney from each firm would identify himself as responsible for his firm's behavior, Lord dropped the oath requirement.

Another morning, Lord first railed against an A. H. Robins brief that he considered, in its opaque incoherency, to be an "abomination," then grew even more outraged when no one from the A. H. Robins team could say who had written the offending document. The unfortunate Minneapolis attorney representing A. H. Robins that day allowed that although he'd signed the brief he didn't know who'd written it, and had not even read the documents toward which it was directed, since the work emanated from Richmond. When it turned out the lawyer from Virginia also did not know who had written the brief, Lord promptly issued an order saying that every brief submitted to the Court from that day on had to bear the signatures of every person who had contributed to its composition in any way. "I cannot preside over an enigma wrapped in a fog surrounded by a mystery where once in a while they raise a curtain and let me peek under that," Lord fumed. "I want some responsibility here."

So it was not entirely surprising that after several more days of such wrangling, Lord on February 8 issued the order that of all his actions most likely had the most sweeping and the most lasting effect on A. H. Robins and the Dalkon Shield litigation. Lord that day told A. H. Robins to produce every single company document that fell within ten broad categories, which he spelled out in detail. Lord also appointed two special court masters to sort out and determine which among them were privileged and which should be made available to the plaintiffs. Lord made it clear that his eyes were not only on the few cases before him. He told the lawyers: "Certainly what I am attempting to do here and give herald to is a system whereby some five thousand cases—which threaten to tie up the federal courts if they try each one of them for three months—can be resolved. . . . This additional discovery will aid the resolution of all these outstanding cases, and it is not so drastic an undertaking when considering the massive scope of the litigation."

On February 9, A. H. Robins's attorneys appealed the judge's order to the Eighth Circuit Court of Appeals. A week later, the company went further—it filed a motion asking that Lord remove himself from the case because of an "unprecedented degree of hostility and bias toward Robins. . . . In short, the trial judge has put on a cloak of partiality and has injected himself into the proceedings not as an unbiased arbiter, but as a partisan advocate."

The wording pointedly echoed that used by the Eighth Circuit when it removed Lord from the Reserve Mining case in 1976. So did the judge's written response: "As the arguments against production of the documents exhaust themselves, the tribunal itself becomes the target. This court has tasted of this cup before; it has had its fill."

Lord was not required to taste again. On February 23, the appeals court upheld his document production order. That same day, Lord declined to remove himself, and A. H. Robins's attorneys decided not to pursue the matter further.

Instead, the company's lawyers, anxious to stop the continuing examination of the corporate documents by the special masters, rushed to settle the cases remaining in Lord's court. There were not, as it happened, many left—feeling anxious and pressured by the reopened discovery, A. H. Robins had gradually been settling as many of the original twenty-three cases as it could throughout January and February. Now, near the end of February, only two remained to be tried.

"The judge had them on the run," said one lawyer who was watching the proceedings from the sidelines. "It became a race for time. The masters were down in Richmond, going for documents. A. H. Robins kept raising the settlement offers, which made for incredible tension, because the plaintiffs' attorneys were hanging by the skin of their teeth. They had to settle if the offers were good enough, but if they settled, the discovery would stop. It became a matter of physical endurance. Lord was going twenty hours a day. They all were being run into the ground."

Eventually, Lord's special masters turned up no fewer than 120,000 documents never before presented to any court. A. H. Robins by then was ready to agree to any terms. Besides the two remaining cases before Lord, the company offered to settle five other cases not even connected to that litigation—cases that also happened to be represented by the Robins-Zelle law firm. On February 28, A. H. Robins agreed to pay $4.6 million in those seven combined cases—which was more than the plaintiffs originally had requested in their lawsuits. A. H. Robins also agreed to several other nonfinancial conditions: The company would not try to transfer pending cases in Minnesota out of state, a practice it had pursued previously; the documents described in Lord's February 8 order would be numbered, inventoried, maintained and preserved in a library, with a distinction made between those the company claimed were privileged and those that were not; the Robins-Zelle law firm would have the right to examine the documents not claimed as privileged, and to ask for a court ruling on those that were claimed; and the Robins-Zelle law firm could use those documents in pursuing the cases of the three hundred other Dalkon Shield plaintiffs it represented.

On the afternoon of Friday, February 24, three attorneys from the Robins-Zelle law firm and Alex Slaughter from A. H. Robins appeared in Lord's chambers to inform him that they were on the brink of settling the last of the cases. If the exhausted lawyers were happy at what they'd hammered out, however, Lord was not.

He worried that the settlement might benefit only the three hundred or so litigants represented by the Robins-Zelle law firm. In this sense, it seemed to him that A. H. Robins had won, because the settlement required new court orders from other judges whenever any of the thousands of other Dalkon Shield litigants sought those documents. He also worried that some documents might somehow get "lost"; privately, he was convinced that A. H. Robins was destroying piles of paper. Above all, though, Lord was bothered by the failure of A. H. Robins's top executives to recall the Dalkon Shield, or to admit knowledge of and accept personal responsibility for their company's actions. To Lord, the truth remained obscured.

Accordingly, even though the four lawyers sitting in his chambers had all agreed to the settlement's terms, Lord was not inclined to acquiesce passively. He told the attorneys he wouldn't accept a settlement without the presence in his courtroom of A. H. Robins's three top officers: president and chief executive officer E. C. Robins, Jr., vice-president and general counsel William Forrest, and senior vice-president for research and development Carl Lunsford. He wanted to ensure, he said, that the signatories to the settlement would have sufficient authority to bind the company to an agreement that could have far-reaching effects on thousands of cases pending in other courts.

Sitting in the judge's chambers, Alex Slaughter and the Robins-Zelle lawyers looked at each other blankly. None of them knew what Lord had in mind, but he was a federal judge. Okay, Slaughter agreed. The A. H. Robins executives would appear in Lord's courtroom the next Wednesday, February 29, 1984.

That weekend, Saturday and Sunday, February 25 and 26, the judge toiled for hours on his speech, first dictating into his car's tape recorder, then showing early drafts to his law clerk Roberta Walburn, who urged him on. On Monday and Tuesday, he showed a more polished version to three other federal judges, who gave him much more mixed responses.

In his courtroom on Wednesday morning, Lord at first simply handed copies of his prepared remarks to the three A. H. Robins executives, and asked them to read the document privately. But then, as they leafed through the pages, the judge began to question the three and offer his comments. "Is this the first document you have ever read in connection with the Dalkon Shield?" Lord demanded of E. H. Robins, Jr., at one point. Later, he ordered the men not to leave: "I want you folks to stay here. I want you to read that document. . . . And if that doesn't change your ways, when you see what your lawyers have been doing in the name of Robins—when you have the stamp of three generations on that company, you've got to have some personal feelings about what's going on, something besides the bottom line as your beacon and the low road as your route."

A. H. Robins's defense attorney Carl Socha objected at several points, saying that the proceedings were in excess of the court's jurisdiction and constituted an abuse of the court's discretion. He pointed out that Lord's approval was not necessary for the settlement agreement. Socha asked that the proceeding be stayed while he either sought a formal ruling from a higher court, or at least arranged a telephone conference with the Eighth Circuit. Lord denied that request. At one point, when A. H. Robins senior vice-president Lunsford said his attorneys had instructed him not to answer the judge's questions, Lord held up the settlement agreement and acted out the motions of tearing it in half. Socha, wanting that nonverbal threat reflected in the written record, asked the judge what he was doing. "I don't intend to tear up anything," Lord finally replied. ". . . I agreed that I would hand this document to them and I thought I could visit with them about it in a rather superficial way just to be sure they had read it."

Then he announced his change of plan: "I am going to read the whole speech, my appeal to these gentlemen." His first words were the very same ones he had dictated in his car on the way home the previous Friday evening. After calling upon the executives to acknowledge their responsibility and confess, he continued, speaking for one full hour.

> None of you have faced up to the fact that more than nine thousand women have made claims that they gave a part of their womanhood so that your company might prosper. . . . You state that your company has suffered enough. . . . Well, when the poor and downtrodden in this country commit crimes, they too plead that these are crimes of survival and that they should be excused for illegal acts which helped them escape desperate economic straits. . . . Until such time as your company indicates that it is willing to cease and desist this deception and seek out and advise victims, your remonstrances are indeed hollow and cynical. . . . If every judge is terminated as soon as he catches on to what's going on, if you settle the case and flee the jurisdiction, that leaves no one to follow up to make any cohesiveness to this. . . . If a judge were to wait until all the cases were over before he spoke out on the evils he sees inherent in the system and in the trial tactics, then no one would ever speak out. There is a time when measures must be taken . . . to see that fair play and ethical standards apply to the disposition of all the cases that are to come in the future. . . . Were these women to be gathered together with their injuries in one location, this matter would be denominated a disaster of the highest magnitude. The mere fact that these women are separated by geography blurs the total picture. . . . These matters of which I speak are not matters about which I speculate. They are matters contained in the evidence that has gone before me. . . . I do not have the power to order you [to recall the Dalkon Shield]. . . . I must therefore resort to moral persuasion and a personal appeal to each of you. Would you believe it, gentlemen? I am not angry with you. I don't dislike you personally. I am not happy with some of the things you have done. I would really like to talk you into doing this. . . . You've got lives out there, people, women, wives, moms, and some who will never be moms. . . .

> You are the corporate conscience. Please, in the name of humanity, lift your eyes above the bottom line.

When Lord finished, A. H. Robins's attorney rose and objected to the judge's remarks. "You have become an advocate for the plaintiffs' position," Socha said.

It was Lord's response to this comment that would cause him the most trouble with the Eighth Circuit. "I certainly have," Lord said. "At the end of this case, after reviewing thousands of documents, looking at the briefs, reading the depositions . . . I have concluded that the plaintiffs are right and that the things I say are based—they are my judgment based on the record. . . . You don't have to argue that I am prejudiced at this point. I am."

Then the judge wrote the words "so ordered" on the settlement document, and signed his name.

To the lawyers, Lord's earlier actions in consolidating the twenty-three Dalkon Shield cases and reopening discovery were easily the judge's most important and influential actions against A. H. Robins, but it was his courtroom reprimand on February 29 that garnered the attention of the national news media and the general public. The responses to his speech were varied, and passionate. For weeks, hundreds of letters of admiration and support flowed daily into Lord's chambers. One came from a justice sitting on the supreme court of another state, offering legal assistance and praising Lord for "the eloquent execution of your moral and legal duties." Another, from Wayne Crowder, the former A. H. Robins supervisor who warned his superiors of the Dalkon Shield's wicking tendency, commended Lord's "combination of courage and integrity."

Lord's action, however, also aroused some more complicated, and less enthusiastic, reactions. There were those who grudgingly admired his impulses but still preferred a cumbersome and even ineffective legal system over a judge who, in reaching for his goals, at times put himself above the law. Those who felt this way—among them certain lawyers within the Minnesota legal community who'd faced Lord in his courtroom—occasionally referred, by way of argument, to the wording used in the Eighth Circuit Court of Appeals order removing Lord from the Reserve Mining case: "Our system of government is premised upon subservience to the rule of law. If a judge in the exercise of judicial power loses sight of these principles, the result is autocratic rule by lawless judicial action."

A. H. Robins, of course, tended to side with the judge's critics. Lord's comments, the company said in a statement issued the day after the courtroom reprimand, "constituted a gross abuse of judicial discretion and power." General counsel William Forrest also defended the company's legal tactics, saying "I don't think [we] can be faulted for doing what is necessary to defend the company." A. H. Robins, though, was concerned with more than a judge's stinging verbal rebuke. In writing the words "so ordered" on the settlement agreement, and signing it, Lord was hoping to make a legally binding official document out of the company's private commitment to produce a library of Dalkon Shield papers. So on March 30, the company filed an appeal asking that Lord's signature and the words "so ordered" be expunged from the settlement agreement.

A. H. Robins executives were not finished—they also took aim at Lord himself. On April 24, the company filed with the Eighth Circuit Court of Appeals two complaints against the judge under the rarely used four-year-old federal Judicial Conduct and Disability Act. The first complaint noted that Lord "openly conceded he was biased against Robins and was acting as an advocate for the plaintiffs. . . . Lord also violated his ethical duty to refrain from making public statements about litigation still pending in other courts." The second complaint charged that by compelling the presence in his court of Robins's three executives on February 29, although they were not parties to the lawsuits and had not retained individual counsel, he had subjected them "to public scorn and ridicule" and "grossly abused his office, thus bringing the courts into disrepute and prejudicing the administration of justice."

A. H. Robins's complaints were serious ones—if the Eighth Circuit found Lord guilty of misconduct, it could reprimand him, ask him to retire or even ask Congress to impeach him. The company, however, was not just trying to counter Lord's public rebuke with one of its own—it also had a more practical motive. Because Lord's speech was in the public record, it could be used by plaintiffs' attorneys seeking punitive damages in thousands of other Dalkon Shield cases all across the country. At the heart of A. H. Robins's misconduct complaint was a request that Lord's speech be expunged from the record.

When the Eighth Circuit's investigatory panel convened in St. Paul on July 9 for a two-day hearing into A. H. Robins's charges, it was hard not to sense that the role of judges, and the character of justice itself, was as much on trial as was Miles Lord. Both sides had retained former U.S. Attorneys General to represent them—Griffin Bell for A. H. Robins, Ramsey Clark for Lord. At Lord's request, the normally confidential hearing was opened to the public, and the judge was in his element.

He'd been warming up for days, in fact. A throng of print journalists as well as camera crews from all three television networks had rushed to Minnesota the weekend before the hearing was to start, and although Lord's lawyers had instructed him not to talk to the press, he could not resist when the network crews pitched camp outside his home Sunday evening. "I'm pretty hard to tame, but this proceeding will have a chilling effect on other judges," he told the cameras. Speaking privately in his Minneapolis chambers on the eve of the hearing, Lord added a good deal more. "What is a fit role for a judge?" he asked visitors. "To just lay low? Let discovery take years? People lose that way. It honestly wouldn't cause much damage, I guess. People would just sit home, shiver and cry and hurt. I could be popular. I could be called upon by the chief justice of the United States to make speeches."

The investigatory panel consisted of Donald Lay, chief judge of the Eighth Circuit; appellate judges Myron Bright from Fargo, North Dakota, and Richard Arnold from Little Rock, Arkansas; and U.S. district judges Albert Schataz from Nebraska and Howard Sachs from Missouri. On both days of the hearing, a 150-seat courtroom in the downtown St. Paul federal courthouse was filled to its limits, with many turned away at the doors. Lord sat in the front row with his four children. On the morning of the second day, before the panel took the bench, he strolled the aisles of the crowded courtroom, and again he could not resist commenting. "Gee, with such a nice crowd, I should make a speech," he said. The crowd applauded enthusiastically.

In their written briefs and oral arguments, the two former attorneys general presented arguments that essentially asked the appellate panel to choose which was more important: making the legal system work effectively, or protecting at all costs the constitutional rights guaranteed everyone, including corporations and individuals such as the three A. H. Robins executives. Griffin Bell argued that Lord had interfered without justification in a settlement of private litigation, made public statements designed to affect lawsuits and violated the due process rights of the A. H. Robins officers. Ramsey Clark, in turn, cited example after example of earlier Dalkon Shield cases in which trial judges, in firm but less flamboyant fashion than Lord, also had criticized A. H. Robins's courtroom methods. He presented an affidavit from U.S. District Judge Frank Theis in Wichita, who had presided over the earlier Dalkon Shield multidistrict discovery litigation. Considering A. H. Robins's ten-year history of apparently hiding documents and delaying proceedings, Theis had said, "Judge Lord's remonstrance was mild punishment indeed."

On the second day, the appellate panel's members peppered both sides with equally challenging questions.

Judge Lay, speaking to Griffin Bell, said: "[Ramsey] Clark's argument is that judges are human, we're not robots. You were [a] judge yourself. You shouldn't be just of the frame of mind that it [being a judge] does not have compassion. . . . As I sense what Mr. Clark is saying . . . this matter had reached a point of settlement and it was now over with, and although Judge Lord had not tried the case, he had lived with it, gone back to the depositions, he had read all these depositions, and he'd come to an opinion that there was a moral responsibility, a legal responsibility of the company, and he wanted to express his opinion on it. . . . As I understand Clark, he says that's not only the right of a judge, but he used the word an obligation of a judge. Well, I'd appreciate your comments."

Griffin Bell answered bluntly: "I think I've never heard anything as outrageous as that in any court in my entire career as a lawyer. That you could call in any American citizen, accuse him of high crimes and misdemeanors without giving him a notice, without giving him an opportunity to be heard, without giving him a lawyer, without following all the due process reasonings. I do not understand in this case why somebody doesn't say we should have given these people their rights. . . . Judge Lord purported to say 'speak out' on the 'evils' he saw 'inherent in the system.' His statements, however, are entirely different from a judicial opinion reached following a trial. . . . Judge Lord took one side's unproven allegations and, without more, stamped with them the imprimatur of his judicial office in a way calculated to harm the opposing side in other lawsuits pending in other courts. . . . Judge Lord considers all American corporations to be evil. . . . It was like an accident waiting to happen. He finally got one of these evil corporations into his court."

Later, Judge Bright addressed Ramsey Clark: "Well, you may have a great point, and it may well be that the system we have for dispute resolution in massive product liability cases is not a very good system. . . . It may well be that the system doesn't work very well for these cases. But that's the only system we've got right now—"

Clark interrupted: "Well, I think that's where Judge Lord came in. The change."

Judge Bright responded: "Then it was his prerogative to change the system for these cases?"

Clark did not hesitate: "It was his prerogative to use the power for discovery in a proper way. He tried to get these cases moving. It was his prerogative . . . to consolidate the cases. . . . It was his prerogative to go to Richmond. . . . He had a sense of obligation . . . of responsibility to move these cases."

This time Judge Lay interrupted: "Doesn't the judicial system have to remain detached from taking sides and to assure . . . equal justice to both sides?"

Clark's answer: "I believe that law involves a passion for justice or it's a danger to society. . . . The judiciary has an affirmative responsibility to achieve justice. . . . The Constitution directs—and public interest compels—the judiciary to pursue justice with a vital activism. . . . This is especially true where, as in the present case, a federal judge is confronted with abuse of the court's own process. Federal judges must stand up to—and repel—these assaults. Only then will justice be served."

At twenty minutes past noon on Tuesday, July 10, the disciplinary hearing ended. Judge Sachs thanked all the parties involved, noting that they "have given us some important issues to resolve."

By the next morning, however, the investigatory panel of judges had decided it would not—or could not—resolve those issues. The backpedaling was rapid. Within hours, the Eighth Circuit's fourteen-member Judicial Council, to which the investigatory panel was to report, suspended the misconduct proceedings before final briefs could be filed or deliberations begin. The appeals judges did not want to explore the role of judges or the character of justice after all. The judges wanted A. H. Robins to pursue its complaints against Lord through the conventional appellate process, rather than through the Judicial Conduct Act.

To help the lawyers along this path, the Eighth Circuit's chief judge, Donald Lay, signed an order calling for an expedited hearing on A. H. Robins's long-dormant effort to remove Lord's signature and the words "so ordered" from the settlement agreement. Lay asked all attorneys to file supplemental briefs in that appeal on "whether the trial court committed error in using the reprimand, and if so, what judicial remedies would lie to correct it." Lay also gave Judge Lord the opportunity to intervene in the appeal by submitting his own briefs. Finally, Lay said he himself would head a three-judge panel that would hear the appeal in Kansas City, Missouri, on September 14, 1984.

That one-day hearing proved to be somewhat puzzling, and not a little unsatisfying. All sides thought the three-judge panel intended to hear arguments on the propriety of Judge Lord's remarks in court the previous February, but when Chief Judge Donald Lay took the bench, he announced that the panel had already heard all those arguments at the aborted misconduct hearing. They now wanted only to hear arguments on the appeal's original issue—Lord's signature and the words "so ordered" on the private settlement. At the day's end, all parties left the hearing feeling uncertain about what next would happen.

In a sense, it did not matter. A. H. Robins's extended confrontation with Miles Lord had already produced a number of irreversible repercussions. Armed with the knowledge, revelations and documents unearthed by Lord's pressure, more and more Dalkon Shield victims now were rushing to file lawsuits, and they no longer were willing to settle for relatively small amounts of cash. Plaintiffs' lawyers were aggressively seeking unreleased corporate documents. Judges other than Lord, previously reluctant, were ordering additional discovery. More than four thousand Dalkon Shield claims were still pending, and new lawsuits were being filed against A. H. Robins at the rate of five hundred every three months. The National Women's Health Network had sued A. H. Robins and petitioned the Food and Drug Administration, seeking to force a formal recall. On June 4, 1984, the Colorado Supreme Court had upheld a record $6.8 million Dalkon Shield judgment. In early September, a Miami jury had awarded $4.5 million to another woman. In the second quarter of 1984, A. H. Robins had reported a seventy percent decline in net income, even though revenue had climbed thirty-six percent. The reason for this, the company explained, was a 430 percent increase in its legal expenses associated with the Dalkon Shield litigation.

By the fall of 1984, when Alex Slaughter and other A. H. Robins lawyers started meeting with plaintiffs' lawyers Dale Larson and Michael Ciressi to hammer out the final settlement of all their remaining three hundred Minnesota cases, both sides knew the pharmaceutical company was up against the wall. Within three days, everyone agreed on the issue of dollars. The balance of the eight-week-long exchange involved what the lawyers called "non-economic" provisions. Larson insisted that A. H. Robins recall all Dalkon Shields that women were still wearing. Slaughter at first resisted, but in the end, he had little room to maneuver.

On October 29, A. H. Robins made a public announcement that startled the business and legal communities. In a series of press releases and a three-week-long paid advertising campaign, the company revealed that it planned a program to get all women still using the Dalkon Shield to have it removed. The company would pay the cost of all medical examinations and removal procedures. "Extended use of the Dalkon Shield and other IUDs may—I repeat may—increase the risk of infection," said E. C. Robins, Jr. "It is not now our purpose to debate the merits of these arguments. Our effort grows out of our concern about the adverse publicity our company and the Dalkon Shield have received in recent months. . . . We hope [this action] will bring to a conclusion the Dalkon Shield episode."

A. H. Robins, in other words, was taking the very action Judge Lord had so passionately urged in his controversial courtroom speech the previous February.

Five days later, on Friday, November 2, the Eighth Circuit Court of Appeals finally released its decision in the appeal heard six weeks before in Kansas City. It was a day of some irony, for within the formal rules of the legal system, A. H. Robins won a virtually unqualified victory. Just as the company had asked, the federal appeals court struck from the record Lord's hourlong public reprimand, and removed from the settlement agreement the judge's signature and words "so ordered."

The appellate judges also took direct aim at Miles Lord. Lord's action, they said in their written opinion, was "a violation of due process. . . . The truth or falsehood of plaintiff's claims, and the propriety, legal or ethical, of the actions of Robins and its employees are not the point here. The point is that the facts are to be determined only after notice and an opportunity for a hearing. A court must hear before it condemns. . . . Many people will champion what Judge Lord has done in the conduct of the Dalkon Shield litigation because of their deep convictions about the substantive issues involved. However, these people overlook the proper role of a judge in the administration of justice. The judicial branch of the government is not and should never become an advocate for private causes."

Despite these harsh words, though, the appellate panel appeared disinclined to punish Lord formally, as A. H. Robins had requested. The panel did not indicate what would happen to the suspended disciplinary proceeding, but in its written opinion said: "It is far more desirable for this issue to be addressed in the normal appellate process than in the extraordinary context of a disciplinary proceeding."

After ten long years, the bitter and enormously expensive Dalkon Shield proceedings were drawing to a slow but definite finish. On Saturday, December 22, 1984, lawyers for A. H. Robins and more than two dozen plaintiffs met in a federal courtroom in Richmond to discuss the possibility of a class action motion and other legal aspects of the cases. That same month, A. H. Robins lawyers said they were ready to discuss so-called "global settlements," in which all cases being handled by a particular plaintiffs' lawyer are settled at one time. Not everyone was ready just yet to accept such offers, since the prospect of sizable punitive damages now seemed likely—Wall Street analysts estimated that wrapping up the Dalkon Shield litigation could cost as much as half a billion dollars over the next five years. All in all, though, this moment was clearly the beginning of the end.

Left unanswered, of course, were the critical questions raised by Judge Lord's actions. Had the system worked? Or was justice finally achieved in spite of the system, by a person willing to twist and bend its fundamental principles? Was such a person required, or could the same result have been achieved otherwise, by people more dedicated to following the letter of the law? Were the judge's means justified by the end? In other words, was Miles Lord a menace, or a champion?

On December 26, 1984, a judicial panel of the Eighth Circuit Court of Appeals delivered a mixed answer to those questions. The appeals judges officially dismissed the misconduct disciplinary proceedings against Judge Lord. In handing out that written ruling to the news media, however, they made a point of attaching to it fresh copies of the opinion they had released the month before, in which they had soundly criticized the judge and struck his speech from the public record.

As a result, Miles Lord found himself spending most of the day after Christmas on the phone with reporters, who still were unsure which side had won and which had lost.

UPDATE

A. H. Robins, overwhelmed by Dalkon Shield claims, filed for Chapter 11 bankruptcy protection in August 1985. Under the bankruptcy reorganization, through which the company eventually was acquired by

American Home Products in December 1989, a $2.4 billion trust was set aside to compensate women for injuries caused by the Dalkon Shield birth control device.

By then, Miles Lord was no longer sitting on the bench. On May 19, 1985, five months after the disciplinary proceedings against him were dismissed, Lord announced his retirement as chief judge of the U.S. District Court for the District of Minnesota. After an extended career of public service and government salaries, Lord at age sixty-five intended to open the lucrative private law practice that could provide his family with financial security. "It has indeed been satisfying and rewarding to work with so many wonderful people in helping shape the direction in which our beloved state and nation has traveled, and in making government more responsive to the needs of people," Lord said in his farewell announcement.

Six years later, however, the fundamental questions raised by Judge Lord's uncommon actions once again became a matter for critical scrutiny and uncertain answers. In April 1991, *The Journal of Clinical Epidemiology* published a new scientific paper challenging the validity of the original medical research that a decade before had condemned the Dalkon Shield and fueled the litigation leading A. H. Robins to bankruptcy. In this paper Drs. Richard A. Kronmal and Coralyn W. Whitney at the University of Washington argued that the original research, titled the Women's Health Study and sponsored by the National Institutes of Health, had "showed an almost complete disregard to epidemiologic principles in its design, conduct, analysis and interpretation of results." Many violations involved the way the original researchers had selected the women used for purposes of scientific comparison, Kronmal contended. The Dalkon Shield indeed did have a higher risk than other IUDs for pelvic infection, Kronmal allowed, but he believed there was no way to determine whether the higher risk was due to a cause-effect relationship or to selection and other biases.

Kronmal and Whitney's connection to the Dalkon Shield, as it happened, stretched back many years, for they had been consultants to the A. H. Robins Company and had served as expert witnesses on its behalf during court proceedings. In openly acknowledging this past connection, they explained that they'd waited all these years to publish their findings so it would not look as if A. H. Robins had hired them to write the paper. They hoped the paper could now get "a fair reading from scientists."

What it got was a mixed reading. Some medical experts vouched for

Kronmal and Whitney's credentials, others suggested that a disinterested third party should look at the same data, and Dr. Ronald T. Burkman, the chief author of the Women's Health Study, called Kronmal's paper "replete with factual error, misrepresentation and overstatement." Digesting all this, the trustee administering the $2.4 billion set aside to compensate women harmed by the Dalkon Shield said the new report "may play a role" in how future claims are settled.

Voices from the business and legal communities, meanwhile, remained conspicuously silent. Spokeswomen for A. H. Robins and its parent company said they would have no comment, as did the spokeswoman for A. H. Robins's former Richmond law firm. Speaking to reporters, all three cited the advice of counsel for their silence, but offered another reason as well: They could not put their hands on the relevant files. They no longer had the records of what transpired during the tortuous Dalkon Shield debacle.

An Easy Target in Adams County

February 1981
Adams County, Indiana

Dan Sigler, the prosecutor for Adams County in northeastern Indiana, was asleep when the phone in his bedroom rang at 10:40 P.M. on August 31, 1979. It was the dispatcher over at the sheriff's office, saying something about a death in the southern part of the county. Sigler was needed right away. What kind of death? the prosecutor wanted to know. An Amish baby had been killed, the dispatcher said.

As he dressed, Sigler, a trim and athletic-looking twenty-nine-year-old, tried to figure out what this was all about. He knew very little about the Amish who lived in the countryside. He figured it might be some kind of accident, like the time a few years ago when a car hit an Amish buggy. When he had been elected prosecutor of Adams County in November 1978, he'd asked to be called at home whenever the sheriff encountered a homicide or any death under peculiar circumstances. Until now, there'd been no such call—Adams County, after all, only has a murder every six years or so. That was one reason Sigler had moved from Chicago to Decatur, Indiana, five years before, even though he knew he'd be something of an oddity in the small town.

Most of the twenty-seven thousand people who live in Adams County were born there, are of German-English-Swiss extraction, are

Catholics, Lutherans or Methodists, and work as farmers, metalworkers or carpenters. All but a few are white, and the average salary is $227 a week. Adams County is homogeneous, but in no way ominous. It is not uncommon to see a handful of regulars greet one another over cans of beer at nine or ten in the morning at the Rheinelander bar and restaurant on Route 27, even on particularly wintry mornings. It is also not uncommon to see dark-clothed Amish men with wild, untrimmed beards, plain black garb and wide-brimmed hats riding through the countryside in open horse-drawn buggies. A motorist might think he has slipped into a time warp: there are as many hitching posts as parking slots. Adams County is home to more than fifteen hundred Old Order Amish, part of the twenty-five thousand Amish in the United States, all descendants of the breakaway Mennonite sect that fled Europe for America in the early 1700s.

Generally, the locals take the Amish for granted, since they have lived and farmed in the countryside for more than one hundred years. Only an outsider's eyes are startled by repeated images reminiscent of eighteenth-century America. Members of the Old Order are the most conservative of all the Amish, eschewing cars, electricity, phones, buttons on clothing and covers on buggies. "Be not conformed to this world," the Bible instructs the Amish, and so they are not. They live by their own rules in their own self-preserved world, and hold back time. But all that keeps getting more and more difficult to do in Indiana.

In recent years, the Amish there have faced state demands for photos on driver's licenses, for polio immunizations and for milk-pasteurization standards that would require electric refrigeration. Each time, legislators have shielded the Amish, but not because the Amish fought the measures or campaigned for assistance. They do not even vote. They say that any event, be it blessing or tragedy, is God's reward or punishment and is not to be avoided.

If the Amish and non-Amish communities of Adams County did not seem to embrace warmly, they also did not seem to bother or offend each other. That is, they didn't until August 31, 1979.

At nine-thirty that night, a twenty-seven-year-old Amish carpenter, Levi K. Schwartz, was guiding his one-horse buggy north on Tile Mill Road at ten miles per hour, taking his wife and six children home from a visit with his brother-in-law, Jay L. Wickey. The older children—Wilma, Marie, Clara, John and Daniel—were riding in the back. Levi sat up front on the right. His wife, Rebecca, sat on the left, holding their sleeping seven-month-old baby, Adeline.

A loud and rough-sounding pickup truck approached, heading south. As it passed, just in front of Esther Striker's home, an object thrown from the truck hit the lantern-lit buggy, causing what Levi Schwartz would later call "one ge-bang." Rebecca screamed; something had hit her left wrist, she said, and it really stung. Adeline, still asleep in her mother's arms, made no noise but stretched twice, "kind of like when they dream," Rebecca said later. Levi turned and looked at the retreating pickup, noticing that the right taillight was burned out.

Once home, Rebecca handed the baby to the oldest daughter, Wilma, eight, who took her upstairs and laid her on a bed. Not until Wilma lit a lantern did she see the blood on Adeline's head. She screamed. "We couldn't believe it till we came in there and worked on her, you know, looked at her, that she was dead," Levi said later. "When she was stretchin', that's probably when she was taking her last breath."

Levi rushed to the house of his non-Amish neighbor, Royce Huffman, to summon an ambulance. He did not intend to get the sheriff involved. But in Adams County, an emergency call for an ambulance at ten in the evening is a bit unusual. Deputy Sheriff Kerry L. Uhrick reached the Schwartz home at 10:16 P.M.

He checked the baby for a heartbeat and found none. She was ash white, cold, with blood oozing from her right ear. An autopsy would later reveal that a massive skull fracture had cut into her brain. Levi could tell Uhrick only that the pickup was old and noisy and had a burned-out right taillight. Although he was distraught, his strongest words were, "I feel so bad about this." The deputy sheriff would recall those words clearly months later, for he was especially struck by the Amish father's lack of anger.

Uhrick had received a call thirty minutes earlier from another Amish man, Eli A. Weaver, who'd complained about someone in an old red International pickup throwing objects at buggies. So now the deputy sheriff radioed this combined description to all area law-enforcement units. Gary Bollenbacher, a deputy marshal from the nearby town of Geneva, heard the sheriff's bulletin. Minutes later, at eleven o'clock, he saw a vehicle going north on County Road 000 while he was heading west on 218. He couldn't tell what kind of truck it was, but he noticed it had dim headlights. He knew enough about old Internationals to know they have a six-volt electrical system and usually have dim lights, so he turned south on 000 and passed the vehicle. It was a red International with a burned-out taillight. He whipped his car around, flipped on his police lights and stopped the truck in front of the Berne Veterinary Clinic.

Inside were four local men: Lynn A. Rich, eighteen; Kevin Scott Rehm, nineteen; Linn Burkhart, nineteen; and Thomas Scott Wilkins, eighteen. All were recent graduates of Adams Central High School and sons of what people in Adams County call "good families." They all lived with their parents. Wilkins's father was an engineer for Magnavox in Fort Wayne; Rehm's had retired after years at International Harvester; Burkhart's was a prosperous farmer. Rich worked at his uncle's Phillips 66 service station, Rehm for a printing company, Wilkins at a grocery store. None had criminal records.

Bollenbacher ordered them to get out of the truck and spread-eagle against its side. Looking inside, Bollenbacher found thirty-three white rocks, ten ears of field corn and ten pieces of red tile. When he radioed for help, some twenty law-enforcement officers and CBers responded.

Dan Sigler couldn't believe the scene when he pulled up: police cars everywhere, lights flashing, people running around. Quite a circus. Part-time volunteer cops from all over the county had come out for this one. In charge was Adams County's young sheriff, twenty-nine-year-old Tom Coolman. Usually, Coolman is a self-assured, even cocky sort who particularly enjoys talking about the importance of the "disciplined family unit" and of his own "social counseling" in controlling Adams County crime, half of which involves juveniles. But this night he was a bit anxious. Most of his work, after all, involves sitting in a small brick building in Decatur, taking reports over the phone from farmers about knocked-over mailboxes.

Within hours, all four young men had signed written statements acknowledging that they'd been driving around, throwing rocks and tile at the Amish. They said they had not realized one rock had struck and killed an Amish baby.

Looking over the statements given that night, Sigler felt the base of his neck tighten. In Adams County, the elected prosecutor's job is a part-time affair—Sigler maintains a private practice and handles county business out of his law firm's offices. From the moment he'd been called, he had known this case would be tough. He would have to decide; it would be up to him. How would he prosecute these boys? Was it a stupid prank or murder? What was he willing to do? What to call this?

▪ ▪ ▪

Those would prove to be quite the questions. The local reaction to Adeline Schwartz's death could fairly be described as ambivalent. Most people emphasized that they "in no way condoned" what the four young men had done. They were "horrified" by the tragedy. But virtually no one felt the attack had been motivated by racial or religious bigotry or involved any particular feeling about the Amish. "The Amish just happen to be the best and easiest target for these boys," said Sheriff Coolman, echoing many others. "In their buggies, the Amish are slow-moving targets, and young people know they won't retaliate by chasing them or filing charges." There was a feeling among many that the death had been the result of "kids fooling around," of a "prank"—usually called "a stupid prank"—that went awry. Certainly "the boys" had not intended to kill anyone.

The night Adeline died, Sheriff Coolman—on Sigler's recommendation—jailed the four on preliminary charges of criminal recklessness, which is a misdemeanor. Bail was set at ten thousand dollars each, and within forty-eight hours, bonds were posted by their families and all were free. Sigler tried to explain to local journalists that the minor preliminary charge was simply a way to hold the four until an investigation could be completed. But the original news accounts that spread across the nation didn't dally over such fine points. A baby had been killed, the articles reported, and the four alleged to be responsible had been charged with misdemeanors.

Within days, Sheriff Coolman was swamped with phone calls and letters from outraged people across the country who demanded stiffer punishment for those involved. The FBI's Fort Wayne office even sent a man down, on orders from Washington, to see if there were racial overtones. Coolman had never before received so many envelopes and message slips bearing out-of-state addresses and phone numbers. Just what, the outsiders asked, was going on in Adams County? "Contrary to what you may have heard," the sheriff took to telling them, "I do not have an uprising against the Amish going on here in Adams County."

Also sitting on Coolman's desk, though, was a folder that grew fatter by the day. It contained the police reports and personal statements made in connection with the investigation of Adeline Schwartz's death. Much was put together by the deputy sheriff, who interviewed more than fifty people. The file was not a public document, since it had not been introduced in court, so few in Adams County knew of its contents.

People were missing some interesting reading. The file indicated clearly that three of the four men apprehended the night of August 31 had done much the same thing on several previous nights. It also indicated that these four were by no means the only ones in the county guilty of attacks on the Amish, and that not all of the attacks could, by any stretch of the imagination, be called "prankish."

Levi Schwartz, when questioned, had reluctantly acknowledged that such attacks "have been going on for some time. They throw at buggies, windows, mailboxes. There's trouble on the school bus. It's gone on for as long as I can remember." Other Amish came forward to confirm this. It turned out that they simply had never reported these incidents, since they didn't believe in retaliation and didn't want to get involved with the government and courts. Sheriff Coolman eventually estimated that thirty percent of the high school students at one time or another might have thrown objects at the Amish.

In a written statement signed the night he was arrested, Kevin Rehm said he, Rich and Burkhart "had done this three or four times before." Rich admitted the same. It was in these statements that the word *clape* first emerged in the case as a derogatory term for the Amish. "We began talking about going out and getting some clapes," Rehm told the sheriff. At first, not everyone in Adams County allowed that they knew what the word meant. Then gradually, people started admitting that they'd been hearing it for years. Two schoolteachers and a state trooper said it was "in common use" among the young. Rebecca Schwartz finally provided an explanation: It was a contraction of *clay* and *ape*—the Amish being farmers who worked the clay earth.

It also emerged in the statements that the four young men's activities on August 31 were more planned than haphazard. At five that afternoon, Scott Wilkins had finished with his work at a neighbor's farm and stopped by the service station in Berne where Lynn Rich worked. "He said something about getting together that night," Wilkins later recalled in a sworn deposition. "He asked if I wanted to go with him. . . . He said something about, well, throwing stuff—'claping' is what he said." Rich picked up Wilkins at eight, and they drove to Burkhart's house, getting there by eight-thirty. Along the way, Wilkins recalled, Rich "told me what we were going to do and what it was like." Burkhart and Rehm were painting a pickup when the others arrived. Wilkins, Burkhart and Rich filled a fifty-pound nylon feed sack with ten pounds of rocks and pieces of tile from a nearby construction site, then threw the sack into the back of Burkhart's red International pickup. By the time they drove off, night had fallen and the country roads were pitch-black.

They first passed Jerry J. Girod's buggy; a rock thrown from the pickup tore a hole in its back. They passed Eli Weaver's buggy and threw more rocks. At 9:20 P.M., objects started hitting Andrew Hilty's house, and he heard someone yell "get moving." Another rock broke a window and screen door and struck Mary S. Shelter on her right shoulder as she sat in her living room. A rock hit Jake J. Byler on his left hand, forearm and knee as he rode in his brother's buggy.

Overall, during an estimated forty-five-mile ride that night, the youths threw at four buggies, nine homes and an Amish school. At one point they took a break, stopping at a car wash in Berne to fix the float on the pickup's carburetor. Across the street at Hook's Drugstore, they bought cinnamon gum, cigarettes and chips. At no time during the evening were they drinking or using drugs.

"What is the purpose in throwing objects at Amish?" Sheriff Coolman asked Burkhart at 2:10 A.M. the next morning.

"I don't even know."

"For fun?"

"No, not really, I . . ."

"You don't really have an answer for that question?"

"No, I don't."

Sergeant Robyn Wiley, a detective with the Indiana state police, questioned Rich the same night. Wiley later said Rich "advised me that he didn't want to sound like he was trying to make excuses, but if there were more things to do in Adams County, he and his friends wouldn't have to find their own entertainment."

There was even more surprising information in Sheriff Coolman's files. Signed statements by three of Kevin Rehm's co-workers at Economy Printing in Berne said that Rehm—a beanpole at six feet one and 145 pounds—regularly came to work on Mondays bragging about how many Amish he had attacked over the weekend. "One thing that stands out in my mind," said Lois E. Bedford of Geneva in her statement, "is when he was telling me about when he threw a corncob out the window of a car at an Amish buggy and hit a kid in the face, he busted his face up. He said blood went all over, and he just rolled back and laughed." Another co-worker, Rita Lilly of Berne, stated that when Rehm was warned that he might hurt or kill someone, "he'd say, 'So what—they're just clapes.' " Rehm talked like that, Lilly said, "for at least a year, since I've known him . . . before a number of people at work." Jim Jones, a co-worker from Decatur who grew up and went to school with Rehm, said Rehm once talked about driving down a road at seventy miles per hour and throwing a three-foot-long, two-by-four plank at an Amish man walking by. "It was a regular thing," Jones told police. "Like, some people go to the show every weekend. He went out and got Amish."

Such revelations were not widely distributed around the county—the co-workers' statements did not carry the legal force of court testimony or sworn depositions—but those who were privy to the information expressed shock. "We didn't know all this was happening," said Sheriff Coolman. "It turned out that some Amish had just stopped going out at night to avoid attacks. It makes it hard for us to enforce the law if they won't tell anyone what's happening."

Even Joyce Wilkins, Scott's mother, sounded surprised. "I don't fully understand what the boys' intent was," she said one afternoon some months after Adeline Schwartz's death. "We used to play with the Amish when I was growing up here. The Amish should not have to put up with this. I never realized there is so much hostility toward them." Of the Amish habit of turning the other cheek, she said, "It's a good practice if everyone holds to it, but they don't."

The notion that adults in Adams County harbored no ill feelings toward the Amish gradually seemed to lose its foundation, however. When questioned at length, a good number of people eventually expressed "irritation" at what they sometimes called the Amish "hypocrisy." They referred to the Amish habit of asking non-Amish neighbors for the use of their phones or rides in cars when the destination was too distant or the mission too urgent to use buggies. "The Amish disdain material possessions," one prominent citizen confided privately, "which is sort of an implicit criticism of our life-styles and values. But when they need to, they will use our phones and ride in our cars. Some here think that's hypocritical. I hear bitching about that."

The Fort Wayne attorneys representing Rich and Rehm—both lawyers were former federal prosecutors—also detected this feeling in the county. John Wilks, Rich's lawyer, understood the sentiment. "We have an Amish girl who works as a maid in our home," he said. "When I try to call home, my phone is always busy because she's talking on it, or she's listening to rock and roll. And she doesn't mind taking the car ride in from the country."

It was apparent that such feelings were not the direct cause of the harassment that led to Adeline Schwartz's death, but they did go partway toward explaining the general community reaction to the event. Coupled with that was an even stronger impulse: the simple desire to preserve the county's good image and, finally, to preserve one's own self-image.

When parents got an inkling of how widespread the attacks on the Amish had become, they realized their own children could easily have been involved. "Everyone wants us to be tough," said Sheriff Coolman, "until it involves their own kids." Dick Heller, publisher of the *Decatur Daily Democrat,* was one of those who had suggested early on that the August 31 incident was "no big deal—just kids fooling around"; only later did he acknowledge that a relative had recently been stopped by police while driving around with a crowd that was throwing firecrackers. By then, several adults in the county had started admitting to activities that could have put them in the very spot now occupied by the four accused young men. One of the defense attorneys thought back to when he'd thrown things at the milkman who rode around in an open van; this could have been me on trial, John Wilks told himself. Even Dan Sigler had memories to deal with—while growing up in Chicago Heights, a poor, ethnic section of Chicago's South Side, he'd had his moments. His father, an ordained Baptist minister, had run a neighborhood house for the underprivileged, mostly blacks. Sigler had never gotten into real trouble, but for a while in high school, he used to get a perverse pleasure from throwing eggs at cars parked on lovers' lane.

This type of thought finally was voiced publicly in an editorial in the *Berne Triweekly.* Editor Geral Gerig aroused little objection when he wrote: "Before we become angered over what is taking place, let us be honest in admitting that the objects have changed but not the incidents. One man confessed to this writer . . . that when he was young, he was a party to throwing tomatoes at the Amish. Now it is tile."

There was also much talk of "compassion" for the four young men's parents. Joyce Wilkins, it was noted with approval, had required her son, Scott, to help pay for his lawyer and to go to Levi Schwartz's house and apologize. "This was not just a prank, and I've been hard on Scott," Mrs. Wilkins said, blinking back tears. "But I don't think he should go to jail."

If any group in Adams County agreed with Joyce Wilkins, it was the Amish. Soon after Adeline's death, some Amish suggested that the best punishment for the young men would be for them to attend her funeral. They didn't, but still the Amish sought no revenge. "We wouldn't push for jail. We just hope they never do it again. That's all," said one Amish leader, David L. Schwartz (a distant relation of Levi's), speaking hesitantly in his blacksmith shop.

A talk with Levi Schwartz one snowy, wind-whipped, bone-cold morning yielded similar sentiments about the young men. Schwartz politely welcomed a visitor into his farmhouse and seated him next to the potbellied stove that warmed his bare front room, despite the fact that the uninvited and unexpected stranger was interrupting their meal. He spoke softly and haltingly while his wife, Rebecca, sat in a corner off to the side of the room. "I can't say I feel hate or anger," he said. "If I saw the boys who did this, I would talk good to them. I would never talk angry to them or want them to talk angry to me. Sometimes I do get to feeling angry, but I don't want to have that feeling against anyone. It is a bad way to live. Their punishment is not up to us. We didn't want to file charges."

Schwartz looked uncomfortably surprised when told that the sheriff and prosecutor expected him to testify at the trials. "I don't know about that. I let them do an autopsy and gave them a statement, like they asked. I thought that was enough. I was just hoping this could be taken care of without me. I will have to think about this. If I testified against them, I would just feel I have an enemy."

It was up to prosecutor Dan Sigler, finally, just as he knew it would be. Most of the pressure came from within, for he wanted so much to make the right choice. He'd quickly dismissed the possibility of charging the four with first-degree murder. No way—the death had not been premeditated. He could charge them with manslaughter (second-degree murder in many other states). But that would still mean they had intended to kill someone. The next choices down the line were involuntary manslaughter and reckless homicide. Both are Class-C felonies calling for a maximum five-year prison term. Sigler studied the legal definition of reckless homicide: It meant the accused did not intentionally kill, but that a death was caused as a direct result of his reckless conduct. That, Sigler decided, was the most fitting description of what had happened. He would charge the four with reckless homicide. The usual five-year sentence could be reduced to two or stretched to eight, depending on the circumstances, or the judge could suspend all or part of the term.

Since Sigler had to make sure Levi Schwartz's family would testify, he arranged for Levi, Rebecca, their daughter Wilma and their bishop,

Moses Schmidt, to stop by his office one morning about ten days before the trial. He wanted to check Wilma's memory, and he needed the bishop to help convince the Schwartzes to cooperate. Levi arrived in a tall black hat, blue shirt and black pants; Rebecca wore a black dress and a black bonnet. It was the first of five times that Sigler would deal face to face with these Amish. He started by talking tough: "You may not expect to testify," he told them, "but I need you, so I'm going to subpoena you. That's the way it is. You really have no choice." Then, aware that the Schwartzes were mostly concerned about being perceived as seeking retribution, Sigler explained that they'd be testifying only to tell what had happened. It would be up to the government to seek retribution. The Schwartzes still weren't happy, but they agreed to cooperate.

Afterward, Sigler realized he had not found the meeting at all unpleasant. Even though they acted gentle, there was something very strong and sturdy about these people, he thought. Sigler started wondering what the mood in the county would be if it had been two outsiders who had thrown the rocks. Or if a non-Amish baby had been killed instead. He sensed that some people felt a single baby wasn't very important to the Amish because they had so many. But he couldn't avoid noticing the tears in Levi's eyes whenever they discussed the case.

Soon after, the attorneys for Rich and Rehm—John Wilks and Charles Leonard—drove out to Bishop Moses Schmidt's home to discuss the possibility of the young men doing farm work for the Amish in lieu of a jail term. That made for quite a scene: the two Fort Wayne lawyers, in coats and ties, wheeling up in Leonard's 1978 white Corvette to where a group of Amish men were busy building a hog barn. They located the bishop, identified themselves and started explaining what they wanted. The other Amishmen, curious, put down their tools and straggled over. They all listened for a while, then began talking among themselves in a form of German that sounded to the lawyers like a strange dialect. Finally, the bishop just shrugged and told the lawyers, in English, "Well, we really don't care. It's not up to us to decide."

The trial for Kevin Rehm and Lynn Rich—the two who rode in the back of the pickup and threw most of the objects—began June 24, 1980, in the Adams County circuit courthouse. At the request of the defense attorneys, who feared local pressure, Circuit Court Judge Hermann Busse of Fort Wayne presided. Both defendants pleaded not guilty. Most of the first day was spent picking a jury and wrangling over a complicated defense motion that would have prevented Sigler from introducing much of his evidence. Sigler finally won that battle.

The courtroom on June 25 was filled with friends and family of the defendants; no Amish were present. The lawyers delivered their opening statements. Then, suddenly, the defense attorneys asked for a recess. Retreating with Sigler into a conference room, they asked point-blank: "What can you do for us?" They wanted to deal.

The best he could do, Sigler replied, was not make a recommendation or introduce evidence at the sentencing hearing if the defendants pleaded guilty. There would be no plea bargain, though, and no prior agreement about the sentence.

The defense attorneys conferred with their clients' families, but only briefly. Having already lost their battle to keep out Sigler's evidence, they were not inclined to fight. Okay, they said. We'll switch the pleas to guilty.

The defense strategy was nothing if not shrewd. The idea was to keep out of the court record evidence suggesting that the events leading to Adeline's death were not unique, that such harassment had occurred on several occasions. The defense attorneys, for example, were not particularly anxious to have Sigler introduce the testimony of Rehm's co-workers. The prosecutor may not have been allowed to use it in the trial, but there was some chance he could have worked it into a sentencing hearing. By striking a deal with Sigler, the defendants would probably have to do some time, but not the maximum.

Sigler had his reasons to bargain as well. He was afraid the jury, drawn from the community, would be sympathetic to the young men. If he made the deal, he would really only be giving up the stuff about Rehm and the past incidents. In looking at those statements by Rehm's co-workers, Sigler had recalled his own youth, when he would sometimes bring things up, act tough and brag when he didn't really mean it. These youths had done a terrible, malicious thing, but it had not been an intentional murder. Would jail rehabilitate them and protect society? What would lots of hard time do to Rehm and Rich? If he made the deal, they would admit what they had done, and the community would not have to rehash all the terrible events. Rehm and Rich would still get at least two years, Sigler figured, and in return, he wouldn't go after every square inch of their hides.

The lawyers went to tell the judge there would be no trial. Minutes later, when the recess ended and the jury was called back into the courtroom, Judge Busse announced a deal had been made. "You jurors don't have to decide this issue. . . . The monkey is now on my back, and I have got a broad back." A sentencing hearing was set for July 29, one month later.

At that hearing, a presentencing report from the county probation department was presented to the judge. It contained no references to past or recurring incidents. There were, instead, praiseworthy letters of reference from employers, school officials, neighbors, Sunday-school teachers and ministers. There was a notation that the Levi Schwartzes "held no malice" and recommended only that the young men reimburse them for funeral, doctor and related expenses. There was a letter from the Schwartzes' bishop stating that the boys had done wrong, "but I also feel that the boys have had quite a bit of punishment already." All the Amish community wanted, he added, was "that it does not happen anymore." Sigler, holding to the deal, said nothing and submitted nothing.

Hermann Busse is known as a crusty, cantankerous but straightforward judge. He despises the news media—he has announced from the bench that he won't let most newspapers into his home, let alone their reporters. He is perhaps most famous for once telling a rape victim, in court, that she had been "out trolling" that night. After all the lawyers were finished giving speeches, Busse talked from the bench for a good five minutes. He knew the Amish, he said, and thought they were good people. He knew their way of life, that they were not interested in vengeance or punishment. It was too bad most people weren't like that. It was in the spirit of the Amish, the judge explained, that he had decided what to do.

He was sentencing Rich and Rehm to five years in prison and five-thousand-dollar fines each, he said. But he was suspending both prison sentences and placing the young men on probation for five years. They would only have to pay their fines, plus restitution to the Schwartzes. They would spend no time behind bars.

Sigler was shocked, just plain shocked. This was not at all what he had expected from the guilty pleas. There was nothing he could do now, though.

When the trial for Linn Burkhart—who had been driving, not throwing objects—came to court on August 22, 1980, there was no point in fighting. Sigler let him plead guilty and draw three years' probation and a three-thousand-dollar fine. That December, Scott Wilkins pleaded guilty to criminal recklessness and drew a two-year suspended sentence and a two-thousand-dollar fine.

The reaction in Adams County was predictably split between those who were satisfied and those few who went about muttering that the defendants had gotten off. For the most part, though, people were just relieved that the whole matter had been settled. There was no uproar—time had softened all the intense feelings. And the Amish, of course, were content. Levi Schwartz was happy he didn't have to testify.

It was Dan Sigler who ended up feeling more troubled and uneasy than anyone. Months after the cases were closed, he still talked to visitors at length about Adeline Schwartz's death, sitting in his storefront office on Second Street, two blocks from the county courthouse.

"I could have demanded that the defendants go to jail, but I didn't," he said one morning. "Was I right? I don't know, I can't say for sure. I'm still confused. I don't even know if the sentences would have been different if we'd gone to trial. I know I'd have given up being prosecutor, being a lawyer, if I could have given Adeline back to those people, but I couldn't. Although I think I did the right thing, I am bothered and will be bothered the rest of my life. I just have an empty feeling about the whole thing. In this county, grass dealers have gotten two-year sentences. Just recently, someone got six years for dealing acid. But in this case a baby is dead, and nobody's doing any time. It sort of cheapens life, doesn't it?"

Searching for a proper and satisfactory ending, Sigler finally offered the suggestion that it would all be worth it if the harassment of the Amish now stopped. But thinking about that, he had to admit such an outcome could not be counted on. After all, the Amish hadn't changed their ways in the least—most still didn't report anything, or file complaints, or protect themselves. If the Amish have made it this far in the modern world with their ways intact, Sigler surmised, maybe they aren't ever going to change. So they'll still be vulnerable to attacks, and they still won't tell anyone if they happen.

"After all was said and done, we didn't get any answers," the prosecutor said. "This just petered out rather than being resolved. It could all happen again six months from now. I'd much rather that one hundred and fifty Amishmen had come storming up the steps to the courthouse with torches, demanding protection, demanding that something be done. But of course, that's not their way."

Sigler studied his desk, piled high with lawbooks and case files. "I don't know what my role is in this," he said finally. "You try to make things right, but you just can't always do that."

You Got to Know Your People

March 1986
Donalsonville, Georgia

Although in recent years younger and more affluent newcomers have taken to settling around nearby Lake Seminole, most of the seven thousand residents in Seminole County can still proudly say they've lived all their lives in the same rural southwestern corner of Georgia where they were born. There are not many more than two thousand households in the whole county. Greetings and conversations are traded from table to table by the families eating fried catfish and hush puppies at roadside cafés on Route 27. Folks in Seminole County resent the suggestion, advanced occasionally by some outsiders, that they are backwoods rednecks, and the resentment can be understood. People here are more likely to be found with a Bible or fishing pole in their hands than a rifle or length of rope.

That is one reason why most citizens in these parts have trouble understanding how a bunch of judges in Atlanta could possibly say their county didn't give the local Alday family's three murderers a fair trial. Yes, the six Aldays murdered were from a widely respected family in Seminole County, with roots in the region going back more than one hundred years, but still, the killers were guilty—they'd even confessed.

"If Seminole County had not been such a good Christian community," said Helen Dunlar, a local motel clerk, "those defendants would never have made it to trial."

So it is that an anguished community filled with a deep sense of right and wrong has come to challenge three judges who, in turn, are defending what they consider the highest principles of justice.

Carl Isaacs, nineteen, his half-brother Wayne Coleman, twenty-six, and George Dungee, thirty-six, were on the run when they drove into Seminole County in May 1973, escapees from a minimum-security prison in Towson, Maryland. They had picked up Carl's younger brother, Billy Isaacs, fifteen, along the way. Their police records were filled with assorted burglary, breaking-and-entering and larceny charges. They needed money for gasoline. The Alday trailer sat isolated out in the peanut and cotton fields where the family worked. The back door was unlocked.

It looked like an easy burglary, but then the Aldays starting coming home, singly and in pairs. Ned Alday, sixty-two, and his son Jerry, thirty-five, were taken to separate bedrooms and shot in the head several times. Another son, Jimmy, stopping by later, was forced to lie on the living-room couch, where he was shot through the head. Jerry's wife, Mary Alday, twenty-five, arriving home from her job at the county welfare office, was held at gunpoint in the bathroom. Ned's brother Aubrey, forty-eight, and another son, Chester, thirty-two, walking in moments later, were forced to lie on the beds beside their dead relatives, where they too were shot through the head. At least two of the killers then raped Mary Alday on the kitchen floor, drove her tied and blindfolded to a wooded area six miles away, raped her again, beat and mutilated her, then shot her in the base of the skull.

When Sheriff Dan White reached the scene at two-thirty the next morning, the first thing he saw was a beer can on the ground near the trailer. Thank God, he thought. Evidence. The Aldays don't drink. You got to know your people.

The then-governor of Georgia, Jimmy Carter, called the crime the most heinous murder spree in the history of the state. Sheriff White said it was up to the court and jury to handle the killers, but "if I had my way about it, I would have me a large oven and I'd pre-cook them several days, just keep them alive and let them punish. And I don't think that would satisfy me."

Days later, authorities found a car abandoned just short of a West Virginia roadblock. The killers were tracked down as they traveled by foot through the nearby mountains. Their fingerprints matched those in the Alday trailer, their guns matched bullets in the victims' heads, and they had Alday family jewelry in their pockets.

A week after the capture, a few townsfolk came to Bud Alday, Ned's only surviving son, and told him they would take care of these boys if he gave the word. Reporters covering the story also heard such talk. Bill Cotterell, then a UPI reporter from Tallahassee, Florida, later testified at a hearing that he heard frequent expressions along the lines of "Isn't it too bad that when they get these guys and when they're convicted it's going to take forever for justice to be done, and wouldn't it be better if we could just do it on the spot." Yet there were also some more tempered voices heard in the community. Bud Alday, in fact, told his neighbors not to do anything rash. "I talked myself blue in the face," he recalled later. "Society, the courts, had to be given a chance."

News about the case filled the pages of Bo McCleod's *Donalsonville News* and other newspapers in the region. The stories for the most part were straightforward, but not all of what they reported would be admissible at the trials. The defendants were regularly referred to as escaped convicts. Articles repeatedly reported that Coleman had confessed to an earlier killing in Pennsylvania. Journalists even tracked down the Isaacses' mother, who was quoted as saying: "They're old enough to know right from wrong and deserve what they get. They never had any respect for me or those people in Georgia and how can they expect any from us?"

More than one defense attorney balked in public at being appointed by the court to represent the killers. When he was picked, Harold Lambert, who defended Coleman at trial, said: "This is the worst thing that's ever happened to me professionally. There's just no way I can get out of it." Another appointed attorney, J. Willis Conger, said: "I'd like very much to be relieved. I don't know of any lawyer in Georgia who would want that case. I don't know of anybody who would want it. I feel the feeling in Seminole County and this part of Georgia is such that I don't want it."

The surviving Alday family, meanwhile, decided to hire a special prosecutor to augment the district attorney's efforts, something that is allowed under Georgia law. They selected Peter Zack Geer, a tall, powerfully built former Georgia lieutenant governor with a deep, resonant voice and a swept-back shock of straw-colored hair. He was a well-known figure in Seminole County, a fellow from southern Georgia who had made it in state politics. As it happens, he also was the nephew of the trial judge, Walter Geer, now deceased.

The motions for change of venue, and the voir dire of prospective jurors, were not matters that drew any special attention in the days preceding the trials. On the change of venue question, Judge Geer said no, we'll try these cases right here in Donalsonville. During voir dire, prospective jurors swore they could be impartial.

Such scenes, of course, are not unusual in courtrooms anywhere. They're not unusual, even though there are those who believe that it is a legal fiction to ask a juror whether he can set aside what he knows and be impartial. Even a good number of lawyers and judges suggest that evaluating what is inside a prospective juror's mind is ultimately a matter of intuition bordering on speculation. It's not that prospective jurors intentionally lie, they argue. They're just unknowingly conditioned toward certain responses, driven by a desire to appear fair and to be selected. That, presumably, is why the American Bar Association's Standards for Criminal Justice say that a change of venue is the more effective way to assure an unbiased jury. The ABA emphasizes that changes of venue should turn on the probability of prejudice, not a showing of actual prejudice. To determine this probability, the ABA standards say, judges need not extensively consider the testimony of persons in the community, for such testimony "is likely to be self-serving and no more reliable" than the court's own evaluation.

The ABA standards, however, are simply recommendations, not requirements. Most judges resist granting motions for change of venue, preferring instead to weed out biased jurors. Even an extensive voir dire, after all, is more manageable and less costly than shifting the trial to another locale. No one now can say for sure if that is why the late Judge Geer denied motions for a change of venue in the Alday murder trials. One local lawyer, Billy Grantham, thinks "he just wanted to show that the people here could handle something like this fairly." Whatever the reason, it was in Donalsonville that the lawyers set out to pick thirty-six jurors for the Alday murderers' three trials.

All the prospective jurors sat in the courtroom listening as a dozen at a time were questioned. Certain basic questions were presented by the prosecutors not to individual citizens, but to each twelve-person panel as a group. Please stand, the prospective jurors were told, if you are related to those involved in the case, or if you have formed any opinion or felt prejudice about the case, or if you are conscientiously opposed to capital punishment. Then each prospective juror was questioned separately, for periods ranging from five to twenty minutes. One such session, more or less typical, involved a Mrs. W. V. (Thelma) Harrington.

Do you understand that the burden is on the state to prove guilty? asked defense attorney Lowery S. Stone.

"Yes, sir," she said.

Do you know the Alday family?

"I know some of them."

Did you know any of the deceased?

"I knew Ned Alday."

Do you know of the Isaacs verdict and sentence? (Carl Isaacs's trial had preceded Dungee's.)

"Why, sure."

Do you know Dungee is accused with Isaacs and others in this matter?

"Yes, sir."

If the state should fail to prove the guilt of Dungee beyond a reasonable doubt, would you find a verdict of not guilty?

"Yeah."

With that, Harrington was sworn in as a juror.

By then, one defendant, Billy Isaacs, had pleaded guilty to armed robbery and burglary in exchange for a forty-year sentence, and had agreed to testify against the three others. Their trials lasted only days. Isaacs repeated a horrifyingly detailed account of the murders before each jury, and Superior Court Clerk Bobby Nichols, listening each time, thought it the most morbid thing he ever had heard. The defendants offered no defense at all, and a confession of sorts by Coleman was admitted into evidence.

In January 1974, Carl Isaacs, Wayne Coleman and George Dungee were convicted of murder and sentenced to die in the electric chair. Shocked and angry and bereaved, folks in Seminole County took comfort in telling themselves that at least justice had been done.

Or so it seemed to them, for a good long time.

It is fair to say the Alday murderers' cases were not the most popular to pursue on appeal. One reason law professor Donald E. Wilke, Jr., eventually withdrew as a defense attorney was the intense public pressure brought to bear against his employer, the University of Georgia. Matters did not improve when one of the convicted killers, Carl Isaacs, offered a decidedly candid confession to a television documentary team and to *Albany Herald* reporter Charles Postell. "I don't feel bad," he said. "The only thing the Aldays ever did that stood out was getting killed by me. . . . I was in hysterics [during the shootings]. I was just caught up in it and getting my kicks. I don't blame the Aldays if they want revenge. I'd feel the same way. But then again, I'd like to get out and kill more of them. They represent the type of society I don't like."

In the end, the task of defending the Alday murderers on appeal fell largely to Millard Farmer and his Team Defense Project, a foundation-funded group based in Atlanta that represents indigent defendants in capital punishment cases. Farmer understood going in that this was not an opportunity to improve his public relations. He thought these murders were as awful as anything he had ever dealt with. But it was also his feeling that a system of justice that protects everyone can never be allowed to break down. He harbored no notions that juries elsewhere could have reached anything other than a guilty verdict with these fellows. He was less willing to concede the death sentences, but even that was beside the point. To Farmer, due process was the point. It was perfectly possible that a trial could be accurate in its verdict and still be unfair, he reasoned. You can't just say we would have gotten the same result if we had stayed within the Constitution. You just can't go down that road.

Fundamental legal principles, however, were not what Farmer intended to talk about on appeal. He intended simply to lay out the facts and not advance fancy legal philosophies. "The judge lived down there, had to run for office," Farmer said later. "He didn't have the strength to do what was right—change the venue. That's what it boils down to. If the state at any point just stopped and said, let's go try this in Macon, this would be over. But they didn't."

The first judges Millard Farmer turned to, however, were not impressed with his arguments. In 1976 the Georgia Supreme Court upheld the convictions and sentences, noting that the voir dire record "establishes beyond doubt that the jurors selected stated that nothing they had seen, heard or read had caused them to form an opinion for or against the appellants and that they had no fixed opinion as to the appellants' guilt or innocence." Even if the trial should have been held elsewhere, the judges added, this was a harmless error, for given the evidence, the result would have been the same. "No other verdict could have reasonably been returned by a jury, regardless of the locale of the trial," they said. In the following years, the state supreme court denied another appeal, the U.S. Supreme Court twice declined to accept the case, and U.S. District Judge Robert Elliott, sitting in Columbus, Georgia, rejected a petition for federal habeas corpus relief. By then, Millard Farmer's efforts—and his clients—appeared doomed.

The turning point came in June 1983, when the Eleventh Circuit Court of Appeals said it wanted to hear more before ruling on Farmer's appeal of Judge Elliott's decision. The appellate panel returned the case to Elliott, saying he had to hold an evidentiary hearing on the issue of whether a change of venue should have been granted because of prejudicial pretrial publicity. If nothing else, this call for a hearing allowed the defense attorneys to subpoena and question witnesses, and thus to build a fresh record for the appellate judges to consider.

When a representative from Millard Farmer's office showed up at Dan White's doorstep, the retired sheriff glowered. Tall, broad-chested and garrulous, a straw hat covering his balding head, White as usual did not hesitate to speak his mind. "If you want me to answer your questions, you have to answer mine first," he said, slamming three Bibles onto his kitchen table. "Tell the truth. If you can put your hand on any one of these books and show me where God is against capital punishment, I'll eat it."

Other witnesses proved more helpful. During a four-day hearing in November 1984, for example, it emerged that one juror at the Coleman trial was living then with Marilyn Alday, a relative of the victims, and had since married her. It became clear that the majority of the jurors not only had known the victims, but had attended their funerals or stopped by to pay respects. Nothing that unfolded during this hearing, however, was quite as revealing as the testimony of Thelma Harrington, the seventy-seven-year-old juror in the Dungee case who during her pretrial voir dire had been asked a total of six questions.

She knew of the Aldays as "good honest Christian country people," she said at the appellate hearing. News of the murders had spread "like fire in broom sage." She had known the Geers, prosecutor and judge, for a long time. She thought perhaps they were brothers, but was unsure.

Did people talk much about the case around town? asked Steve Bright, a lawyer working with Farmer.

"My Lord. They'd have had to have lockjaw not to because that was the topic around a little town like Donalsonville and everybody was so excited and upset."

Did people indicate what they thought ought to be done about it?

"Mighty right they did."

What did they say?

"Fry 'em. Electrocute 'em."

What else?

"That's about all I heard, and that's what should be done for 'em."

That was the community sentiment, fry 'em or electrocute 'em?

"Everybody felt that, yes."

Assistant Attorney General Susan Boleyn, on cross-examination, tried vainly to limit the damage. Didn't Mrs. Harrington mean the feeling was fry them "only if they were the ones that had committed the crimes. . . . They should not be punished if they had not done the crime, should they?"

"Well, everybody knew they did it, though," Harrington said.

In March 1985, Judge Elliott, unswayed, for a second time denied the habeas corpus petition. Farmer, however, hadn't expected to change Elliott's mind. All along, he'd been thinking mostly of the federal appellate judges. Late in 1985, he filed new motions with the Eleventh Circuit Court of Appeals, attaching the record from the evidentiary hearing.

One three-judge federal appeals panel heard the arguments in Coleman's case, while a second panel considered the other two together. Two judges sat on both panels, and both, as it happens, had been appointed to the appellate bench by a Georgian—Jimmy Carter. Of the two, Frank Johnson, Jr., is the best known nationally, for his pathbreaking decisions forcing school desegregation while sitting as a U.S. district judge in Alabama. It was R. Lanier Anderson, however, who would write the panel's opinion. Anderson's profile was not nearly as dramatic as Johnson's—he was known mainly as a thorough, meticulous tax lawyer from Macon.

Unlike Georgia state supreme court justices, who must face the voters, the federal appeals judges are insulated through life appointments. So where the state judges have been criticized for bowing to political and emotional pressures in the Alday cases, the federal judges have been charged with being abstract theorists out of touch with real life. It is true that the appellate judges were inclined to focus their attention mainly on the legal issues—when Assistant Attorney General Susan Boleyn tried to recite the horrendous facts of the killings during an Eleventh Circuit oral hearing, one judge chastised her, saying they didn't want to hear about that. The appellate panel was thinking more about a landmark 1962 U.S. Supreme Court case, *Rideau v. Louisiana.*

There the high court had overturned a murder conviction because the justices "presumed" juror prejudice. They'd done so not because of anything said during voir dire but because they decided pretrial publicity had so saturated the community that selecting an impartial jury was made impossible. Since then the concept of "presumed prejudice" had been invoked only rarely, but the Eleventh Circuit panel now decided it applied to the Alday trials. In a 133-page decision delivered December 9, 1985, the appellate panel overturned the murder convictions in Seminole County.

We have no direct evidence that establishes actual prejudice among jurors, the judges said, but given the overall situation in Seminole County, we presume there had to be prejudice. We presume this even though the jurors swore they were unbiased. Such claims by the jurors were not sufficient to rebut the presumption of prejudice. "Our review of the record in the instant case leads to the inescapable conclusion that [Coleman] was denied his right to a fair trial before an impartial jury," the judges wrote. "Indeed, this case is a close case only because of the extremely high standard that must be met. If there were no constitutional right to a change of venue in the instant case, then one can conceive of virtually no case in which a change of venue would be a constitutional necessity." It does not matter that the defendants are obviously guilty, the judges said. They believed there was, in fact, "overwhelming evidence" of guilt. But that cannot affect the right to a change of venue. To uphold these convictions, the judges concluded, "would mean an obviously guilty defendant would have no right to a fair trial before an impartial jury."

In a footnote, the judges added a final thought: "No one familiar with the facts of this case and the overwhelming evidence of guilt could fail to have sympathy for the prolonged suffering of the families of these victims. The fatal error of trying this case in Seminole County was not their decision."

The firestorm of emotions this ruling spawned in Seminole County equaled that which followed the murders themselves. Most people did not so much disagree with the legal issues as plain not see them. Hundreds of furious Georgians phoned the federal court clerk in Atlanta to denounce the ruling. Local newspaper editors, with rare exception, thundered in rage. The state attorney general, Michael Bowers, vainly appealed to the U.S. Supreme Court, after the full twelve-member Eleventh Circuit on January 30 denied his request to rehear the case en banc.

"In effect, they say I lied under oath," said one juror in the Coleman trial. "It's sort of insulting. They're trying to look into my brain. You have to assume a man who swears under oath is telling the truth. The whole system is based on that."

"Not a fair trial?" said Bo McCleod, editor of the local *Donalsonville News*. "But they're guilty. They confessed. If they're guilty and are found guilty, then it's a fair trial. That's the way it is in my book."

McCleod, thin as a cornstalk, weathered in face and hand, normally mild of manner, never had seen anything like this. He'd started working at the *Donalsonville News* in the 1940s, folding editions in exchange for a free pass to the local movie house. Now as editor, in between selling classified ads in his one-room storefront office, he wrote all the news copy, and he felt particularly offended at the court's suggestion that his reporting unfairly skewed the trials. He asked himself what he could have done differently. That the accused were escaped prisoners was as much a part of the story as if they had been housewives, the way he saw it.

McCleod also had little patience for outside journalists come to town looking for signs of lynch mobs. They and the court were insulting the community, he believed. McCleod felt squeezed in the days after the ruling, reluctant to express anger because someone would use that to prove the county truly was prejudiced. Yet he was not inclined to keep quiet either. He finally poured it all into two lengthy, angry front-page editorials.

"It's a shame they don't have an innocent person to put all this effort on," he said one morning, pacing through his office in agitation. "Talk of an overworked judiciary. That's because they spent so many years on this. What does it matter if our county has ten million or ten thousand people? The courtroom's the same size. Hitler was a fool to kill himself. He should have gone to the Eleventh Circuit."

Peter Zack Geer, the special prosecutor at the Alday murder trials, now a private attorney in Albany, Georgia, also let loose eventually, after first holding his tongue. The legal issues were just a smoke screen for judges who were flatly opposed to capital punishment, he argued. The crime was reported heavily all over the state, so there's not a county in Georgia where you could get a better jury. How can the judges play God and presume what was in the jurors' minds? "Every judge that voted in favor of the new trials ought to be made to go down to Spring Creek Church, lay down on those six graves and apologize for what they have done," he thundered.

The most visible and influential response of all, however, came not from a public figure but from a soft-spoken local sandblasting contractor. Curtis Strickland, born and raised in Seminole County, traveled through three states working with farmers, and had never before been active in civic affairs. One night, troubled beyond words by the court ruling, he sat down with his wife and daughter and started reading the Constitution. He looked at the Preamble, and the First Amendment, and the Sixth Amendment, repeating the phrases over and over. In the Sixth Amendment, he read: "In all criminal prosecutions the accused shall enjoy the right to a speedy and public trial by an impartial jury of the state and district wherein the crime shall have been committed."

Those, it so happened, were the very words that the appellate judges felt duty bound to uphold, the very words that had guided them to their unpopular conclusion. But Strickland read them quite differently than did the judges. It seemed to him that the defendants had gotten everything the law required. The trials were speedy and public, after all, and right in the district where the crimes were committed. Those appeals judges had twisted the words, Strickland reasoned. They didn't care about the public and their rights because they didn't have to answer to them. Maybe folks here should not have been so willing just to sit back and be quiet and let the law do the work. Maybe folks should speak out now.

At first Strickland thought he was writing only a solitary statement, something to voice his own opinion. Only later did others, seeing his words on paper, start saying they wanted to sign it too. So it was not entirely by plan that Strickland in time found himself the organizer of a massive regionwide petition drive urging that the Eleventh Circuit panel be impeached for failing to uphold the Constitution. The petitions now can be found on front counters everywhere in southwestern Georgia—retail stores, restaurants, even motels. As Strickland travels on business from town to town, people grab as many copies as he has with him. An estimated one hundred thousand signatures so far have been forwarded to the local congressman, Democrat Charles Hatcher.

For the moment, at least, neither their congressman nor anyone else appears inclined to inform the citizens of Seminole County that it is unlikely they will be able to convince the United States Congress to impeach three federal appellate judges. Nor, for that matter, does anyone appear inclined—or rather, able—to resolve a conflict where all sides yearn for justice, but disagree so mightily over what it is. The appeals and the petitions promise to grind on for months, even years, without bringing peace in southwestern Georgia, or a resolution to this question.

For better or worse, of course, the Alday murders and the Eleventh Circuit's judgment have left another legacy besides baffled and unresolved anguish in a small rural county. Appellate rulings in one case affect later events. By establishing precedents, they shape not just the outcome of a particular case, but also the character of justice in other places and times. What is allowed at one trial is allowed at others. Likewise, what has been disallowed in Donalsonville will be disallowed in countless other towns.

In early January, amid the tumult in Seminole County, a brief and largely unnoticed news item appeared in local Georgia papers. In Gainesville, north of Atlanta, a Hall County superior court judge had granted a change of venue in the trial of a man accused of murdering a local woman more than four years before. In light of the Eleventh Circuit ruling in the Alday case, the local district attorney explained, "the judge had no other choice."

UPDATE

At a new trial in Houston County, Carl Isaacs again was convicted and received the death penalty, which he is appealing within the federal court system.

At a new trial in DeKalb County, an Atlanta suburb, Wayne Coleman again was convicted, but because all twelve jurors could not agree on the death penalty, he automatically drew a life sentence. He has been serving time since 1973 and will not be eligible for parole until the year 2003.

George Dungee was never retried. In 1988, the Georgia legislature passed a statute that barred mentally retarded persons from being executed. Because experts for both sides agreed that Dungee was retarded—he scored sixty-eight on IQ tests and was judged "significantly subaverage in general intellectual functions"—the prosecution could not ask for the death penalty. Dungee entered a guilty plea and received a life sentence. He will be eligible for parole in thirty years.

The Georgia petition drive never did persuade the United States Congress to impeach the three federal appellate judges whose reading of the Constitution had so agitated the populace of Seminole County.

If this turn of events did not settle the dispute over what constituted justice, it did reaffirm Millard Farmer's faith in the role of due process. By changing the venue, after all, the defense attorney had managed to keep at least two of the Alday killers off Death Row, just as he'd hoped.

Could This Be Murder?

September 1985
Maywood, Illinois

At the time, the words meant little to prosecutor Jay Magnuson. He was sitting at the round conference table in the second-floor branch office of the Cook County state's attorney in Maywood, a suburb just west of Chicago. Phillip Mole, director of the county Department of Environmental Control, walked in late on the morning of March 6, 1983. "We have a ticket situation," Mole told Magnuson. "There's a death involved."

The prosecutor, then supervisor of the branch office, now chief of the criminal division, knew a ticket meant a violation of the environmental code. Looking at the paper work, he saw that a worker had collapsed and died at Film Recovery Systems, Inc., a nearby plant where silver was recovered by dipping used photographic film into huge vats filled with a cyanide-water solution. Another awful industrial accident, he told himself, before turning the matter over to an assistant.

Then the initial investigative reports started rolling in, and they drew Magnuson's attention. One night, he visited Humboldt Park on Chicago's Near Northwest Side, a gang playground and shooting gallery inhabited by drug addicts, the impoverished, and about fifteen of the Mexican illegal aliens who worked at the Film Recovery plant. What he heard from the laborers made him shiver. This was no accident, he thought to himself. This could be involuntary manslaughter. He listened to more stories. My God, he thought. Could this be murder?

So began a prosecutor's—and three corporate officers'—singular march into uncharted territory.

Steven J. O'Neil, the thirty-one-year-old president of Film Recovery Systems, first learned about recovering silver from film in 1973, when he was a student majoring in commercial photography at Colorado Mountain College. One day a representative from a Denver-based silver recycling firm, RKS Future Industries, visited the college's photo club and advised O'Neil to install, beneath the club's film developing equipment, a three-gallon bucket lined with steel mesh. "What it would do would be to trap the silver before it went to the drain and we would derive the excess funds for our photo club," O'Neil later explained in a courtroom. "That was the first time that I became aware that silver was a valuable commodity to recover from film or solutions."

O'Neil left college after two years to work full time as a salesman for RKS. There, he learned how to extract silver from used film through use of a cyanide solution. It was a clever process. The film was chopped into small chips, then put into one-thousand-gallon vats that contained water and a sodium cyanide powder. The liquid would leach the silver from the film, producing a silver cyanide solution, which in turn was pumped into smaller electroplating tanks. An electric current would draw the silver from the solution to the plates like a magnet, and workers would then scrape the flakes from the plates. The flakes would be shipped to a refiner to be made into silver bullion.

When O'Neil started at RKS, the price of silver was about $3.40 a troy ounce. Two years later, it was up to $6.40, and O'Neil saw his chance. In 1978, he left RKS for a new silver recovery firm in the Chicago area, Metallic Marketing Systems, where he negotiated for part-ownership in lieu of a salary. He arrived in town with all of two thousand dollars to his name, O'Neil would recall later, so he lived at the plant for four months and used his car as a closet. The plant, in the suburb of Wheeling, consisted of four vats and four electroplate tanks that O'Neil installed himself.

All that would soon change, for O'Neil had hitched his fortune to a rocket on the rise. By late 1979, the price of silver had peaked at fifty dollars an ounce, and O'Neil's only problem was getting enough cash to buy used film and enough vats to recover the silver. "Anybody who had product in silver, from little old ladies with heirlooms to large producers of X-ray film, were calling. . . . Actual lines were forming outside of the facility," O'Neil said. To handle the rush, O'Neil made a deal with B.R. MacKay & Sons of Salt Lake City, at the time the largest private silver refiner in the country. Essentially, they formed a partnership and launched a new corporation called Film Recovery Systems, which MacKay capitalized with $275,000. O'Neil became president of both Film Recovery and Metallic Marketing, drawing a combined annual salary of $120,000. He was twenty-five years old.

In early 1980, Film Recovery moved to a leased building in an industrial park at 1855 Greenleaf Avenue, in the northwest Chicago suburb of Elk Grove Village. By the end of that year, the plant had been expanded from eight to eighty tanks and vats, and O'Neil needed help running the operation. So in early 1981, he offered Charles Kirschbaum the job of plant manager.

Kirschbaum, a thirty-three-year-old graduate of Southern Illinois University, with a degree in physical education, had spent seven years working as personnel manager at a chain of Chicago-area laundries called the Washing Well. In 1979, the Washing Well's owner, Donald Jacks, had decided to open a silver reclamation plant, and asked Kirschbaum if he wanted to get involved. Until then, Kirschbaum hadn't even known that film contained silver, but he said yes. "I was just getting married, and the dry cleaning business does not have much of a future left in it," he later explained in court. Within two years, the Washing Well plant had grown to thirty-two tanks, and Kirschbaum knew all about the cyanide-leaching process. The operation wasn't making money, though, and as a result, Kirschbaum was sitting on four bounced paychecks. In July 1981, he accepted O'Neil's offer and signed on at Film Recovery with a starting annual salary of thirty-six thousand dollars.

As the plant enlarged, so did the number of workers, from half a dozen to forty. Most were Mexican and Polish illegal aliens who earned beginning wages of about four dollars an hour. Few spoke or read English. To communicate with the Mexicans, O'Neil and Kirschbaum came to rely upon a young worker in his midtwenties named Daniel Rodriguez. Rodriguez had left school at the age of nine to work on his father's farm near Taluca in Mexico. With his wife and two children, he'd illegally entered the United States in December 1979. Soon after, through his wife's uncles, he'd found a job at Film Recovery Systems, and once there he'd quickly taught himself English by reading and listening to others. His role of translator for his bosses eventually evolved—in time, he became the one who delivered orders to other workers, and he was given the title of foreman and assistant plant manager. He earned about six dollars an hour.

In 1981, the plant expanded to 120 vats and tanks, and Film Recovery now was grossing thirteen million dollars a year. O'Neil no longer spent much time at the Elk Grove site—he instead traveled regularly throughout the country, making deals with large film brokers. He journeyed twice to Europe, where he visited Germany, Switzerland, England and France, attended a convention, solicited film and studied potential sites for an overseas plant. He also acquired a house in Florida and interests in a Chicago bar and several new corporations.

Those who did visit the plant began to notice problems. One of the physical properties of sodium cyanide is its tendency to produce potentially fatal hydrogen cyanide gas when mixed with either an acid or a weak alkali. E.I. du Pont de Nemours & Co., Inc., attaches a strongly worded warning label to every container of Cyanogran, the brand of sodium cyanide used by Film Recovery: "Poison. Danger! May be fatal if inhaled, swallowed or absorbed through skin. Contact with acid or weak alkalies liberates poisonous gases. . . . Do not breathe dust or gas. Do not get in eyes, on skin, on clothing." Water is a weak alkali. Water is what Cyanogran was mixed with at Film Recovery.

The Washing Well plant, where Kirschbaum first worked, had installed hooded side vents over the tanks to shunt the gas from the building, but Film Recovery did not use hooded vents of any sort. As a result, in July 1981, when Harvey Burns, an inspector from Film Recovery's insurer, Home Insurance, visited the plant, he was affected by an overpowering odor in the air. He noticed that the ceiling exhaust system merely moved large quantities of air about and did not necessarily remove contaminants. He noticed that the air sampling pump that Film Recovery used to test the atmosphere had an error factor of plus or minus twenty-five percent. He noticed that employees were wearing disposable respirators not approved by the National Institute of Occupational Safety and Health. He noticed that cyanide-contaminated water was splashed about the plant's floor. Burns put all this in a written report, and concluded: "I would classify this account as a fair risk. It is my personal opinion that due to the expansion of their operation they have outgrown this present facility, which has resulted in this increase of contaminants within the air."

The next year, Film Recovery did gain added space by leasing the building next door. However, only front-office personnel moved there.

The laborers stayed in the processing plant, where twenty more vats and tanks were added, bringing the total to 140.

On the morning of August 4, 1982, Kathy Arroreno, a newly hired agent for a medical supply company called Respond First Aid, visited the Film Recovery plant to service the account there. The first thing she noticed was an overpowering odor. It seemed to her as if somebody had opened a bottle of ammonia under her nose. Her nose burned, her eyes burned, the back of her throat burned. She felt nauseated and had trouble breathing. Looking around the plant, she saw row after row of huge vats, bubbling and frothing, with some sort of stuff running down their sides. A crystallike chip substance covered the floors—as she walked about, the chips crunched under her feet. The first aid cabinet, which she found outside a small office, looked filthy to her, covered with the same chip material that was on the floor. Inside, she found empty boxes of aspirin and a few other minor first aid items. "I wasn't in there more than three minutes," she later recalled. "I had to leave. . . . It took me a while to regain my composure, because I really felt weak at the knees."

Stefan Golab began working at Film Recovery on the day after Christmas in 1982. He earned $4.50 an hour. He had arrived in the United States from Poland almost one year before with a passport and a visitor's visa, having left behind his wife and son and more than twenty years of labor in steel construction. He lived in the Chicago home of his sister-in-law, Jadwiga Popek. Popek later would tell a court that she immediately noticed the job's effect on Golab. He very often came home with headaches and nausea, she testified. He would vomit.

Golab became casual friends with Roman Guzowski, another Polish worker who had overstayed his visa. They worked next to each other daily, pumping and stirring the vats. On Thursday, February 3, 1983, both Guzowski and Golab became ill at work. The next day, Guzowski stayed home, while Golab went to the plant with an interpreter, to ask Kirschbaum if he could be transferred to another section or department. Golab wanted to work, the translator explained to the man known to the laborers as "Boss Charlie," but he wanted to change to a different job. Kirschbaum said he would try to do something, so Golab and Guzowski returned to work on Monday, expecting to be transferred. Instead, they were again assigned to the vats.

Four days later, on Thursday morning, February 10, Golab rose early. His sister-in-law boiled milk for his breakfast, and he left for the plant at six o'clock. At 9:30 A.M., he and Guzowski were working over one of the vats, stirring the film chips with a rake. Golab went to disconnect the pump, then suddenly leaned back against the wall, his face chalk white. Guzowski could not leave the pump, for it would flood the plant, so he shouted at Golab, telling him to go outside. "He looked very pale," Guzowski later recalled. "And he said, 'After I rest, I will help you.' And I told him not to worry because I had taken one of the Mexicans to help me finish the work."

Golab walked unsteadily to the workers' lunchroom, where he sat on a chair. He began shaking, and foam formed at his mouth. As five fellow workers carried him outside, one of them shouted that Golab's heart had stopped beating. When Michael Lackman, a paramedic with the Elk Grove Village Fire Department, arrived at the scene at ten, he found a middle-aged man lying immobile in the parking lot, his complexion gray-blue. He was not breathing and he had no pulse. Lackman and his partner began cardiopulmonary resuscitation. Knowing that the plant contained cyanide, they asked if their patient had been exposed, but no one would confirm that, so Golab was never treated with the prescribed antidote to cyanide inhalation, amyl nitrite. Rushed soon after to Alexian Brothers Medical Center, Golab never revived.

Two officers and a detective with the Elk Grove Village Police Department had also responded to the call for an ambulance, but their investigation was limited, since they could not bear to remain in the plant. Officer Kenneth Kvidera encountered a yellowish-orange haze and an odor so foul he began gagging. "I wanted to get out of there as soon as I could," he reported later. They would not, at any rate, have been able to speak with O'Neil. The day Golab died, the company president was at LaGuardia Airport in New York, attending a business meeting in which arrangements were being made to purchase used film from sources throughout the United States.

Dr. Robert J. Stein, chief medical examiner for Cook County, performed an autopsy the next day. When he opened the body, he and his assistant smelled a pungent odor that hurt their eyes—bitter almonds, indicative of cyanide. The lungs were more than twice the size of a normal man's, and unusually red, the tissue filled with blood. When the toxicologist's report later indicated a high concentration of cyanide in the blood, Stein ruled that Golab had died of cyanide poisoning. In his opinion, he said, Golab had received the lethal dose by inhalation.

On February 18, a week after Golab's death, Phillip Mole, the director of the Cook County Department of Environmental Control, visited the Film Recovery plant. He walked through the building, drawing an engineering flow diagram and watching the silver recovery process. It was a process, he concluded, that had no type of control equipment to contain emissions of dust, vapors or hydrogen cyanide. It was also a process that had none of the required environmental and operating permits from the state and federal governments. Mole returned on February 23 with equipment to test the air in the plant. He found hydrogen cyanide levels almost twice the maximum called for in standards set by the federal Occupational Safety and Health Administration.

Michael Selway, an industrial hygienist for OSHA, visited the plant that same week and cited the company for seventeen violations. He found that employees were given unapproved respirators inappropriate for hydrogen cyanide exposure, and dust masks that had no effect against hydrogen cyanide fumes. He found there was inappropriate personal protection, including permeable cloth gloves. He found there was no safety training program for employees, or warning about the dangers of inhaling fumes, or antidote for cyanide poisoning in the first aid kit. At one point, Selway later testified, he asked O'Neil why his employees were not trained or educated. "He said he didn't want to overemphasize the hazards of the operation because that would scare employees away," Selway told the court.

The next month, at a meeting with Film Recovery officials, Mole listed the changes suggested if the plant wanted to keep operating. One was the use of plastic spheres over the tanks. Another was the use of side-drafting hooded vents. Faced with expenses of up to $250,000 to make the changes, officials at B.R. MacKay, the source of capital for Film Recovery, decided instead to shut down the plant. The price of silver in the past year had plummeted from $50 to $4.50 a troy ounce, and Metallic Marketing owed MacKay $800,000. Recovery of silver was no longer worth the effort.

Mole, however, insisted that his suggested emission controls be implemented during the shutdown period anyway, even if it was at his department's expense. He wanted to test their effectiveness. When he measured the air in the plant one more time, after the controls were installed, he found a twentyfold reduction in the amount of cyanide.

Studying the reports from Mole and Selway in March 1983, prosecutor Jay Magnuson found himself toying with the idea that Stefan Golab's death might best be described not as an awful industrial accident but as involuntary manslaughter. For that reason, during the spring and summer of 1983 he sent two Spanish-speaking investigators, normally assigned to gang-related crimes, to find and talk to Film Recovery's forty former laborers. John Ayala and Frank Hernandez came back with much to report.

"The horror stories just got worse and worse," Magnuson recalled later. "And they were all consistent."

The investigators found Roman Guzowski, Golab's friend, who told how he had only twenty percent vision in one eye because water from a vat splashed into his face one day. He told of workers vomiting regularly. He said he had complained several times to the foreman, Rodriguez, about the lack of ventilation, but was told that there was no money for changes. Never, he said, were the workers warned it was dangerous to inhale fumes from the tanks. The investigators also found Antonio Roman, twenty-eight, an unschooled illegal alien who had entered the United States from Mexico when he was seventeen. When he reported his headaches, vomiting and other illnesses to Kirschbaum and Rodriguez, he said, they told him to rest outside for a few minutes. They never told him it was dangerous to work around the tanks or explained about cyanide. Usually, he wore only a paper mask, but one day Rodriguez gave him a larger plastic mask with a filter, explaining that inspectors were coming to the plant. Rodriguez instructed him to return the mask to the office after the inspectors left, Roman said. Three days after Golab was carried in convulsions from the building, Roman said, Rodriguez told him the Pole was recovering, that he was in the hospital, that everyone should go back to work and not worry about him.

These were not isolated anecdotes—wherever they went, the investigators kept hearing the same accounts repeated, over and over. In all, a half dozen workers talked, and the details never changed. Even the women who'd worked in the plant's front office cooperated. Debra Sadzeck, a bookkeeper, said it was common knowledge that the workers in the back were sick and vomiting frequently. Kathy Erpito, a secretary and later an accountant, said they all knew cyanide was being used, although the word was never mentioned, since Kirschbaum and O'Neil had instructed them to call it simply a "chemical."

Then the investigators found Allen Drewes, a truck driver who'd carted away Film Recovery's contaminated film chips after the silver was recovered. He too had regularly experienced headaches, nausea, irritated eyes and vomiting, Drewes said. One day, he was driving northbound on the Tri-State Tollway, a load of chips in his truck, when he began gasping for breath. He felt a tingling numbness shoot up his fingers, hands, arms, chest and head. As he passed through the Deerfield Road toll plaza, he pulled to the side and asked the toll clerk to call an ambulance. After a few hours in a hospital, away from the chips, he recovered. When he complained to O'Neil about his headaches and nausea, the truck driver said, O'Neil told him not to worry, that working at the plant was not the cause of his symptoms. Drewes said Kirschbaum told him that the danger from cyanide came from eating it, not inhaling or absorbing it in the plant.

Drewes's story was revealing not just for his personal travails, but also for what it told about Film Recovery's waste disposal methods. Drewes's job, it turned out, was not an isolated one—truck drivers had regularly been getting rid of toxic loads for Film Recovery. Even as the prosecutors were talking to Drewes, other state officials were discovering that Film Recovery had stored no less than seventeen million pounds of cyanide-contaminated film chips in warehouses and trailers at nine sites throughout Cook County, presumably to avoid the cost and burden of proper disposal.

One night, Magnuson went with his investigators to visit the illegal aliens who worked at the plant, and he was appalled at what he saw. A dozen adults and children occupied a small, crumbling one-bedroom apartment. He met one sixteen-year-old who had lied about his age, so desperate to make a living that he gave Film Recovery a false name and identification. Magnuson understood, for he had grown up in Prospect Heights on Chicago's Northwest Side, one of the area's few Latino areas at the time. He'd worked the fields of a neighbor's small truck farm next to Mexicans from the time he was nine until he was fourteen, and he'd watched the evolution from open huts and migrant farm work to trailers and industrial plants. He knew the illegal aliens would do anything for steady work and a regular paycheck.

By now, the prosecutor was thinking he certainly did have a case of involuntary manslaughter. In fact, Magnuson was wondering whether he might have something more. As he reviewed the various statements and revelations, he kept going back to the warning label du Pont put on every container of Cyanogran. It was as clear as it could be, the prosecutor thought: "May be fatal if inhaled, swallowed or absorbed through skin. Contact with acids or weak alkalies liberates poisonous gases. . . . Do not breathe dust or gas." A du Pont safety data sheet spelled out the hazards in even more direct detail. Magnuson reflected. It seemed clear the people who ran Film Recovery knew of the health problems the workers were experiencing. They saw it every day. And if they knew, how could what happened be called involuntary?

Magnuson met in September 1983 with his superiors in the state's attorney's office. Without revealing his own thoughts, he laid out the details of the case. When Magnuson finished, Greg Ginex, then the chief of the criminal division, turned to Larry O'Gara, then the chief deputy state's attorney. "This is a murder," Ginex said. "We have a murder here."

The prosecutors first considered charging only the corporation. But they could not put a corporation in jail. It was then that they began thinking about charging the individual company officers with murder. The only way to deter corporate crime, Magnuson reasoned, is to get the leaders. After gaining approval from Richard M. Daley, then the Cook County state's attorney, Magnuson settled in his office and began considering how to draw up a murder indictment against three corporate officials not for actions they took—not for waving a knife, for example, or pulling a trigger—but for actions they failed to take.

He soon found himself pounding the desk in frustration, for there just were no precedents in the law. Courts almost always had rejected the idea that corporations and their executives could be charged with a crime. The reasons were several. A corporation has no mind, so it cannot be said to have intent. A corporation has no body, so it cannot be imprisoned. Fines levied against corporations usually hurt consumers and innocent shareholders the most. The complex fashion in which a corporation is usually organized and run makes it difficult to point fingers at specific individuals. Finally, corporate officers did not look like criminals and were not thought of as such.

Attitudes were changing, Magnuson realized, but even recent verdicts suggested it was still difficult to fix liability. The district attorney in the New York borough of Queens had won indictments against the Warner-Lambert Company and four executives for criminally negligent homicide after six workers died in a 1976 explosion at a Long Island chewing gum factory. The state Court of Appeals had dismissed that indictment in 1981, however, ruling that no one could have foreseen the cause of the explosion. Then in 1978, the Elkhart County, Indiana, prosecutor had obtained an indictment against Ford Motor Company, charging it with reckless homicide in the design and manufacture of the Pinto, after three teenagers died when their Pinto was struck from the rear and the gas tank exploded. But Ford was acquitted in 1980 after company documents were ruled inadmissible because they were dated before relevant state criminal statutes had gone into effect. More recently, Six Flags Corporation of Chicago and its subsidiary, Great Adventure Inc., had been charged with aggravated manslaughter after eight teenagers died in a May, 1984, fire at the company's amusement park in Jackson Township, New Jersey. After an eight-week trial, however, the jury last June 20 found the corporations not guilty.

Not good enough, Magnuson reasoned. The fact was, no corporate official had ever been charged with murder, let alone convicted.

With no case law to study, Magnuson instead began reading law journal articles. Two professors in particular had written often on the matter of corporate liability. One was William J. Maakestad, who teaches at Western Illinois University in Macomb and served as special deputy prosecuting attorney during 1980 in the famous Pinto case. The other was Christopher D. Stone, professor of law at the University of Southern California; as it happened, Stone was one of Magnuson's teachers when the Illinois prosecutor was studying law at USC from 1968 to 1971. Reading and then consulting with these scholars proved a turning point for Magnuson. He did not need pioneering precedents after all, he came to realize. He need only look to the basic criminal statutes of the state of Illinois.

Particularly, he would rely upon Section 9-1A2. Magnuson soon found himself rereading that paragraph over and over. The section says a person commits murder "if, in performing the acts which cause the death . . . he knows that such acts create a strong probability of death or great bodily harm to that individual or another." Magnuson pondered the phrase "performing the acts." What acts had the Film Recovery officials performed? It was mainly what they had failed to do that caused the harm. Looking to another article in the criminal code that defined what constituted a voluntary act, the prosecutor found what he needed. A voluntary act, the section read, "includes an omission to perform a duty which the law imposes." Finally, Magnuson turned to one more section, which addressed the matter of accountability for conduct of a corporation. Here he found his link between the murder clause and corporate behavior: "A person is legally accountable for conduct which . . . in the name or in behalf of a corporation, he performs."

The law requires knowledge and notice, Magnuson reasoned, and he had both. The du Pont warning label was the knowledge; the workers' illnesses and complaints were the notice. Firing a gun into a crowd is murder, Magnuson told himself. We have the gun—the cyanide. And we have the crowd—the workers. The prosecutor was ready to draft his indictment.

One more turning point came in late September, when county investigators entered the now-abandoned Film Recovery plant. Protected by special clothing and oxygen masks, they found thirty-four one-thousand-gallon vats full of cyanide sludge. They also found boxes of business papers—papers that enabled the prosecutor to figure out and prove the corporate structure of Film Recovery. "This is overlooked, but it's the key legally," Magnuson said later. "One of the biggest problems in prosecuting corporate crime is piercing the corporate veil. Everyone blames everyone else and says they were not responsible. Our position is, someone was in charge."

Magnuson presented his case to the grand jury on October 19, 1983. "After two and a half hours of testimony, it took them about ten seconds to return a true bill," the prosecutor reported later. "They were angry."

The grand jury indicted O'Neil, Kirschbaum, Rodriguez, and Film Recovery vice-presidents Gerald Pett and Michael T. MacKay (who was also the president of B.R. MacKay & Sons) on murder and reckless conduct charges. In addition, the grand jury indicted three corporations on involuntary manslaughter and reckless conduct charges—Film Recovery, Metallic Marketing and B.R. MacKay. The murder indictments were unprecedented—just getting the case to trial would be considered a momentous landmark.

The prosecutors' first task, though, was simply to get the defendants into the state. O'Neil was then living in Montana and fighting extradition, as was MacKay in Utah. The then-governor of Utah, Scott M. Matheson, refused Illinois's request for extradition, and MacKay's case had to be severed from the trial. In February 1984, however, a Montana judge ordered O'Neil's return to Illinois.

The next hurdle came when the defense lawyers filed a motion to dismiss the indictments. "We are unable to find any case where a murder charge has been brought against a corporate official," defense attorney Elliott Samuels argued. It was at this stage that the case against Warner-Lambert had foundered. On January 28, 1985, however, Cook County Circuit Judge Ronald J. P. Banks, who would preside at the trial, refused to dismiss the charges. "I agree with Mr. Samuels," the judge said. "I don't know of a case where corporate officials have been charged with murder. But the mere fact you don't have it before doesn't mean you can't have it today."

Before the trial began, Magnuson's superiors asked him to check the law one more time, to make one more contact that would affirm their course of action. The prosecutor called his old USC law professor,

Chris Stone, and soon after flew to Los Angeles to meet with him. Magnuson found the professor in his office, with all manner of books relating to Illinois case law piled on his desk. Stone looked up at his former student.

"Why not?" he said.

When the trial began April 15, 1985, the defense, wanting to avoid the emotional vagaries of a jury, chose instead to argue law solely before Judge Banks. Thomas Royce represented O'Neil, Rodriguez and the corporations; Elliott Samuels represented Kirschbaum; and Ronald D. Menaker represented Pett.

In the early going, the defendants and their attorneys appeared relatively unconcerned. They were convinced the charges had no basis in law—photos of O'Neil and Kirschbaum entering the courthouse regularly showed the two burly men smiling. Like the prosecutor, lead defense attorney Thomas Royce at first had looked at the case as an industrial accident. Royce in those first months thought he would be dealing with environmental and OSHA violations—at worst, there'd be a reckless conduct charge. Whatever came down, he'd assumed, would be against the corporation, not individuals. "We've defended three hundred murders," he said recently. "This certainly was not like any of the others. In all candor, this looked like an unsupported charge, unsupportable under traditional notions of criminal law. For murder, you must prove intent."

When the prosecution rested its case on May 14, midway through the trial, the defense lawyers promptly filed a motion for a directed finding of not guilty, taking dead aim at the legal foundation of the prosecution's case. "The concept that I call corporate responsibility is applicable only to the civil courts," Menaker argued. "The reason this case is unique is because the very acts the prosecution is alleging are not affirmative acts. They are not alleging [Pett] did something like shoot a gun or throw a rock or swing a bat. . . . When does a person's failure to act subject him to potential criminal responsibility?" Royce went so far as to suggest that "there is no notion in Illinois of corporate responsibility. Corporate responsibility was the creature, I think, of either *Nightline* or *60 Minutes* or *The Chicago Tribune* or *Chicago Sun-Times.* But corporate responsibility is not an established legal principle in the state of Illinois."

Judge Banks required only ten minutes of contemplation in his chambers before responding. He dismissed all the charges against Gerald Pett, ruling that the prosecution had not made its case against him, but he denied the motion for a directed finding against all the others. The trial would continue.

As the defense lawyers presented their case, several key arguments emerged as the backbone of their position. The defendants had spent much time around the vats, doing the same work and being exposed to the same dangers as Golab and the other workers, it was argued and testified to over and over. "If my client knows there is a lethal gas in the air that can kill him, do you think he would be there? Most reasonable men don't try to hurt themselves," Samuels said at one point. The credibility of former workers' testimony was attacked. Where many workers said they had no safety gear except for dust masks and cloth gloves, the defense produced others who said they had rubber gloves, boots and aprons. The defense argued that workers not only never quit because of the plant conditions, but, in fact, regularly referred relatives for jobs. The defense argued that the procedures followed at Film Recovery were similar to those at dozens of other silver recovery plants and that no workers before Golab had ever suffered serious injury. The defense presented its own medical and toxicological experts, who suggested Golab had died of a heart attack rather than cyanide poisoning. The defendants flatly denied that they knew hydrogen cyanide permeated the plant's air, or that fumes from the vats were dangerous, or that workers ever got sick at the plant. Finally, all three defendants insisted they were simply employees taking orders from other people on the day Golab died.

Rodriguez said he never was a foreman, only a worker—he issued orders many times, "but because Charles told me to tell them." Kirschbaum said that when he went to work at Film Recovery in 1981, "I never changed any process. I never changed anything in that plant from what was done before I started there. . . . I was just doing my job. I was doing what I was told to do." O'Neil testified that two months before Golab died, in December 1982, B.R. MacKay & Sons had taken over all rights and assets of the plant as payment of the eight-hundred-thousand-dollar debt owed the silver refining firm by Metallic Marketing. In February 1983, O'Neil maintained, he was simply an employee of B.R. MacKay, taking orders. "It was not my company at that time," he said.

On Monday, June 10, both sides delivered their closing arguments. Royce chose to spend much of his time citing case after case in American judicial history in which criminal prosecutions against corporations and their officers had failed; he dwelt at length on Warner-Lambert. Magnuson selected a different approach. He declined to cite any case law or precedents of any sort, still relying solely on the sections of Illinois's criminal statutes that had formed the basis of the indictments. "Your Honor, what you have heard for eight weeks may be a novel legal case, but it is an old story," Magnuson said. "It is the story of the uneducated versus the educated. It is the story of the privileged versus the underprivileged. It is a story of rich versus poor. It is a story of those who want something out of life versus those who want everything out of life at any cost."

Judge Banks, a former Cook County prosecutor, took four days to consider the eight-week-long trial. On Friday, June 14, he announced his decision: Golab's death was not accidental, but was, in fact, murder. This was so because conditions in the plant were "totally unsafe," and the workers were not told of the dangers, although the defendants were aware of them. The individuals and corporations on trial were guilty on all charges—the individuals for murder and reckless conduct, the corporations for involuntary manslaughter and reckless conduct.

The Film Recovery decision was a landmark, the first time corporate officials had been charged with and convicted of killing an employee through unsafe working conditions. The judge, accordingly, went out of his way to touch on the broader issues raised by the case: "I also find that to state that a corporation cannot be convicted of a crime because it has no mind, and it cannot therefore have a mental state . . . is totally erroneous. It is my belief that the mind and mental state of a corporation is the mind and mental state of the directors, officers and high managerial personnel, because they act on behalf of the corporation and for themselves."

The convicted men and their attorneys appeared stunned by the judge's ruling. Family members in the courtroom broke into tears, while Kirschbaum pounded his forehead with his hand. The prosecutors, meanwhile, quickly ran out a back door. En route to their office, they called their superiors on a car phone to report the news and make plans for a press conference. Then they rode in silence for several minutes. My God, Magnuson thought to himself. The court just found those guys guilty of murder. They are being led away to jail.

At the sentencing hearing July 1, defense attorney Samuels could not restrain his bitterness. His comments, uncommonly frank and hostile for a lawyer addressing a judge in court, reflected the tensions this prosecution had evoked. He felt a "grave injustice" had occurred in the courtroom, he said, and he was confident that "the errors of this court will be corrected" on the appellate level. He told the judge his decision was without foundation in fact or law and said a sentence of any length would be a deprivation of liberty without due process. He compared the proceedings to the Salem witch hunt trials. "I cannot stoop to dignify these proceedings by recommending to your Honor what I believe an appropriate sentence would be," Samuels concluded. "It's true, I suppose, that there are some narrow-minded, egotistical, publicity-seeking politicians who will rejoice in today's events. But for me, your Honor, this is a very sad day in the history of American justice."

Then it was Judge Banks's turn. His words provided strong affirmation of Magnuson's legal strategy. "What I take into effect is the law as the law is written in this state," the judge said. "It's not new law. It's old law. The mere fact that it's now being brought in a case like this, maybe it should have been done a long time ago." Turning his attention to the three defendants standing before him, Judge Banks announced his judgment. Steven J. O'Neil, Charles Kirschbaum and Daniel Rodriguez, he said, each is sentenced to twenty-five years in state prison.

In the weeks that followed, dozens of headlines across the country announced the Film Recovery decision, and more than a few commentators hailed the ruling, going on exultantly about "landmarks" and "precedents." Jay Magnuson went so far as to talk about applying criminal prosecutions to other corporate matters usually handled in the civil arena, including product liability. If officers make a conscious decision to market a flawed product because of cost considerations, he told reporters, that "gets pretty close to criminality."

There were, however, a fair share of cautionary observations as well. Norval Morris, criminal law professor at the University of Chicago and former law school dean there, noted the uniqueness of the verdict and questioned whether it would be upheld by the appellate courts. He suggested that a manslaughter conviction might have had a greater impact, since other corporations are more likely to identify with the possibility of facing that charge. Alan Dershowitz, criminal law specialist at Harvard University, worried that the verdict might dilute the impact of the conventional murder charge. The Film Recovery case, he observed, "shows a need for a new category of crime. We should have one that specifically reflects our condemnation of this sort of behavior without necessarily assimilating it into the most heinous forms of murder." In time, after the initial flush of victory, even Jay Magnuson allowed that he wasn't sure whether the appellate courts would agree that the state criminal code sections applied to this type of death.

Not everyone, in other words, could bring himself to see Stefan Golab's death as a murder, despite the evidence produced and despite the judge's ruling. The corporate officers' behavior just did not fit with any common notion of what murder meant. The Film Recovery case, some even began to argue, represented an "ominous" and "chilling" threat to American industry. The Film Recovery executives, after all, were not unlike many other men who have attempted, through their labors, to provide decently for their families. They had created jobs. They had paid taxes. They had tried to make their way in the world.

It was the defense attorney Thomas Royce who most squarely voiced this type of sentiment in public. "Mr. O'Neil's activities," Royce took to saying, "became something of the so-called American dream. . . . As a result of a substantial effort on his part, hard work, diligence, many hours, an industry was created. . . . I would argue that Mr. O'Neil's intent and conduct was not anything unlike the process that any individual goes through as he proceeds on up the ladder."

Listening from the sidelines, Jay Magnuson had to smile. The two sides shared some common ground after all, he now realized. Both the prosecutor and the defense attorney thought the Film Recovery case involved an old, familiar story.

UPDATE

On January 19, 1990, the Illinois Appellate Court reversed the convictions of the three executives and two corporations found guilty of murder, involuntary manslaughter and reckless conduct charges in the death of Stefan Golab at Film Recovery Systems, Inc. The court held that the same evidence could not be used to support both the executives' convictions on murder counts, which require proof of intent, and the companies' convictions for involuntary manslaughter, which is an unintentional crime. The convictions, the court said, were "legally inconsistent" with each other. Cook County State's Attorney Cecil A. Partee publicly expressed his displeasure with this ruling, which he said was based on "a hypertechnical reading of the law." He pledged to retry the case. In the fall of 1991 prosecutor Jay Magnuson said a new trial might begin in early 1992.

On its face, this outcome sent a blurred message, for the appellate court, sticking to fine legal issues, neither endorsed nor denounced the central notion of corporate criminal prosecutions. But whatever the eventual outcome of the Film Recovery prosecution, it may not matter as much as does the fact that it took place at all. In its aftermath, businesses, government agencies and local prosecutors began feeling more inclined to take job safety seriously. Prosecutors in New York, Los Angeles, Michigan, Illinois and Texas hauled businesses and bosses into court on criminal charges stemming from workplace hazards. OSHA reviewed its inspection procedures. Congress began considering laws to beef up federal criminal penalties for occupational-safety violations, and to clarify that local prosecutors are not preempted by existing federal labor legislation. Companies began hedging their bets in favor of safety. Stefan Golab's death, be it murder or something else, was informing the playing field. "It's easier to get improvements now," said Joseph Kinney, executive director of the National Safe Workplace Institute in Chicago. "The bosses are scared."

A Little Excitement

May 1987
Tampa, Florida

Joseph Green Brown had no criminal record when he arrived in Tampa in 1973, at the age of twenty-three, but that was only because he had never been caught. Reared in a foster home in Charleston, South Carolina, Brown knew a fair share about guns and robberies. "I was no angel," he said, "but I had never physically hurt anyone intentionally."

He crossed that line the night of July 7, 1973. Around midnight, he and a companion, Ronald Floyd, then eighteen, forced open a sliding glass door of a Holiday Inn motel room and robbed a couple. During the robbery, Brown compelled the woman to disrobe and began to molest her. When she begged him to stop, Brown looked at her, then said: "My mother was hurt once. I never wanted to hurt a lady, no matter who she was." He backed away.

The next day, a Sunday, at 1:45 P.M., Brown hailed a police car passing by on the street. He told the officer he had information about three robberies. He told the officer where he could find the gun used in the Holiday Inn robbery. He named Floyd as his accomplice.

"Remorse—I was feeling remorse," Brown recalled much later. "It was one thing to commit a robbery, but . . ."

Brown's confession, however, was destined to bring him far more trouble than absolution.

As Brown and Floyd sat in the Hillsborough County Jail during the summer and fall of 1973, police detective William Bebler took to dropping by on occasion to question them. At times he pulled one or the other from jail and drove the streets of Tampa, getting them to point out places where they had been. That was Bebler's style. Around the courthouse and in the streets he was known by his nickname, Bebop. He reminded the prosecutors of the television detective Columbo played by Peter Falk. If you knew Bebop, they would say years later when it had become an issue, you would know that he doesn't intimidate. Bebop, they would say with appreciative smiles, is a plain, downhome type of guy.

Bebler had on his mind more than a motel robbery. A thirty-four-year-old woman named Earlene Barksdale had been robbed, raped and murdered in her children's clothing store, the Just Kids Shoppe on Busch Boulevard, the same day as the Holiday Inn robbery. The timing and the sexual assaults seemed to link the two cases. Bebler was just fishing, he knew that, but why not? He was making no headway in the murder case. He told Brown and Floyd both the same thing: If you weren't the one who did the actual shooting, if you didn't actually pull the trigger in the Barksdale murder, you can help yourself. We can assist you.

Brown denied any knowledge of the Barksdale murder. Floyd, though, was steamed at Brown for fingering him on the robbery. They could have walked, he figured. So Floyd, who'd known Brown only ten days, wavered.

Later that same week, a young local attorney named Michael Shea happened to wander into a judge's chambers at the downtown Tampa courthouse. He was asked if he could take over a case from the public defender, who had a conflict with two defendants in the same case needing his services. Shea then was thirty years old, with a total of three jury trials under his belt. The court would pay him twenty-eight hundred dollars for this one. He thought it over. It was armed robbery at a Holiday Inn, and both guys had already confessed. It's a walk, he figured.

Down at the jail, though, he learned that his man's bail was big enough to choke a horse. What gives? Shea asked around the police station. Don't you know? came the answer. That Joe Brown's got a murder charge on the way. Shea began wondering what he'd got himself into. Then he met Brown. "Mr. Shea," Brown said. "I didn't do this. I'm innocent."

Bebler kept at Floyd throughout the fall. More than once, he drove Floyd past the Just Kids site. They talked about the layout inside, the setting outside. There is dispute now over who did the talking and who the listening. Bebler remembers being impressed with Floyd's detail. Floyd says the detail all came from Bebop. If you weren't the trigger-man and you tell the truth, we won't prosecute you for the murder, Bebler said. There is disagreement, but it is likely Bebler also said: You can help yourself on the Holiday Inn robbery. The prosecutor insists no such deal was made. Floyd says yes. In a deposition, Bebler, now semiretired on a piece of land just east of Tampa, first said that his memory was unclear on whether he made that offer. Then he said: "I'm sure I did."

In an interrogation room with Bebler on October 24, 1973, three and a half months after his arrest, Floyd finally turned. He told Bebler he had information on the murder. On November 1, he gave a formal statement.

Floyd's story: He had driven to the Just Kids Shoppe with Brown and a third man identified only as "Poochie." He waited in the car, parked across the street, while the other two entered the store. Floyd noticed a bulge in Brown's shirt that looked like a gun. About fifteen minutes later, Floyd went to the door of the shop, looked in, heard a shot, entered the store and saw the foot of a body lying on the floor. Brown and Poochie emerged from the shop, Brown bringing with him articles of new clothing. All three men jumped in the car and drove away. While in the car, Poochie told Brown: "Man, you didn't have to do that." The next day, Floyd, Brown and a third man, Raymond Venson, together heard a radio newscast about the Barksdale murder. Brown, Floyd said, admitted right then that he had killed the woman.

Six days after Floyd gave this statement, a grand jury indicted Brown for murder. The trial began June 24, 1974, and lasted four days. Shea faced Assistant State's Attorney Robert Bonanno, a veteran prosecutor with more than forty jury trials behind him. Brown presented an alibi defense, supported by the testimony of a girlfriend and her elderly mother, who testified that he was with them, watching television, the day of the murder. He knew the TV station, he knew the plot of the movie. Shea considered the old lady's testimony a clincher. "A Bible-totin' ol' black woman in a wheelchair," he would recall years later. "She'd go to her grave sooner than lie. She'd lie for nobody." Floyd, in turn, told his story, and Raymond Venson corroborated the part about

Brown confessing to them after hearing the radio newscast. Bonanno thought Floyd an excellent witness.

These two men's testimony, however, made up almost the whole of the prosecutor's case. Bonanno had found no fingerprints, no matching blood, no pubic hair samples. So he put on what he proudly described years later as a "negative case." He showed the jury all the police efforts to find evidence. The dusting and the aerial photos from four angles had produced nothing, but they demonstrated that the effort had been made. After watching TV courtroom shows for years, the jurors expected that, Bonanno explained.

Bonanno did have a gun, the .38-caliber Smith & Wesson that Brown had used at the Holiday Inn, the gun Brown had directed police to when he hailed their patrol car. The bullet recovered from Barksdale's body was also a .38—but it was a .38 "special" slug, which cannot fit into the chamber of a regular .38 Smith & Wesson. The state had an FBI lab report telling them just that. There simply was no question—the Holiday Inn gun could not be the murder weapon. In his opening statement to the jury, however, Bonanno said: "We also have testimony relating to a weapon which the state contends was the murder weapon in this particular case."

After that, the courtroom maneuvering grew even trickier. On his pretrial list of witnesses, Bonanno included the FBI agent who had written the ballistics report, Courtland Cunningham. Shea knew of the FBI report, and planned a dramatic physical demonstration during his cross-examination of the FBI agent. He would ask the agent to put a .38 special cartridge in the Smith & Wesson. It wouldn't fit, and that would make for a terrific jury show. But Shea made a mistake. Because the prosecutor had already listed Cunningham as a witness, Shea did not himself subpoena the FBI agent—he just waited for the prosecutor to call him to the stand. Bonanno never did, though. Instead, on the trial's last day, he released the FBI agent back to the vacation he had been summoned from, without ever notifying Shea. Frantic, Shea located Cunningham via marine radio, fishing out on the Gulf Stream. He begged Judge Robert W. Rawlins, Jr., for a continuance so he could subpoena the agent himself. The judge soundly criticized Shea for failing to subpoena Cunningham, but refused to grant a continuance. He would only allow Shea to introduce as a defense exhibit the FBI report itself. Shea to this day remembers the judge's words to him. "Mr. Shea," Rawlins said, "I assure you we are going to finish this case tomorrow."

The written report needed explaining from the witness stand, so Shea tried hard to elicit such testimony from Bebler. Bebler, though, said he just had no knowledge of the difference between a regular .38 bullet and a .38 special bullet. It wasn't until years later that Bebler allowed he always knew the Holiday Inn gun was not the murder weapon. "If it was the murder weapon," he said then, "we would never have recovered it."

In his closing argument, Bonanno emphasized to the jury that Brown carried a .38 pistol in the Holiday Inn robbery and a .38 was used in the Barksdale murder. Of the FBI gun report, he said: "They say it's a .38-caliber pistol, .38-caliber bullet. We have a .38-caliber pistol."

Shea, despairing, moved for a mistrial based on his own incompetence in failing to subpoena the FBI agent. This the judge also denied. "I was young; I had only practiced two years," Shea said later. "I don't care what a lawyer is like, the first five or six years, you're still learning. . . . My whole budget was thirty-five hundred dollars including expenses. That comes down to ten or twelve dollars an hour. There is a big difference between a poor person in this situation as opposed to a person who can afford top counsel. The best defense attorneys don't handle volume. They take a few cases and charge fees ranging from fifty thousand to three hundred thousand dollars."

Shea had but one card left to play. He tried to cast doubt on Floyd's testimony by asking him if he'd made any plea agreement with the state.

No, Floyd replied.

You pled guilty to the motel robbery in October, nine months ago, but haven't yet been sentenced, Shea pointed out. Do you have any knowledge of why you haven't been sentenced in this case?

Floyd said: "No, I haven't."

Has the state made any promises or agreements with you in the present murder case? Shea asked.

"Not to my knowledge they haven't," Floyd said.

Have you been given immunity in this crime? Shea asked.

"No, I have not, not as I know of," Floyd said.

Are you afraid that you might be charged with this crime? Shea asked.

"Yes, I am," Floyd said.

You are absolutely certain that you haven't been given any immunity, is that correct?

"I'm certain."

So you've just decided to cleanse your soul and take the chance of whether the state of Florida is going to charge you with this murder?

"Yes."

In his closing argument to the jury, Bonanno pointedly referred to all this. He said: "There was an attempt made by defense counsel to impeach Ronald Floyd. You all heard that. Impeach means to reduce his credibility somehow by showing that for some reason or another he isn't telling the truth. And I submit that there [have] been no promises made to Ronald Floyd for his testifying in this case. He testified to that from the witness stand. He has absolutely nothing to gain by testifying against this particular individual."

As Bonanno spoke, a confidential presentencing report sitting in the Holiday Inn case file contained this sentence: "Detective Bebler has requested the sentence on Ronald Floyd and Joseph Green Brown be postponed until the Barksdale murder case is developed." Shea, however, knew nothing of this document.

On June 28, 1974, Brown was convicted of murder, and on July 3, he was sentenced to death. That night, Shea went home and drank a fifth of Scotch. Five days later, the sentences for the Holiday Inn robbery were finally rendered. Brown got twenty years. Floyd got probation.

Floyd did not stay free for long, though—within a month, he was picked up in a bar carrying a gun. Probation revoked, he was sentenced to ninety-nine years in jail. One day soon after, Shea visited Floyd in the county jail, on his way to see Brown. Less than two months had passed since the trial. Shea would later claim that Floyd admitted right then that he'd lied at the trial. But that conversation, whatever it involved, forever remained a private matter. Floyd would not sign an affidavit.

Seven months later, on March 6, 1975, Shea visited Floyd again. Floyd was now in the Union Correctional Institute, near Starke in northern Florida, just a stone's throw across a small river from the Florida State Prison's maximum security facility where Brown sat on Death Row. Shea thought to himself: They're just a mile or two apart.

The prison authorities brought Floyd into a big open room.

"Floyd, Brown is still sitting on Death Row," Shea said.

"Well, I sure have felt bad," Floyd said.

Shea had brought with him a typed affidavit, summarizing what Floyd had told him back in July. Floyd's testimony against Brown was false, the affidavit said, given in exchange for "favorable consideration" in both the Barksdale and Holiday Inn cases. Floyd studied the document for a while. Then he signed it.

On June 11, 1975, by order of the Florida Supreme Court, the trial judge held a hearing to consider Shea's request for a new trial based on Floyd's affidavit. It is fair to say Judge Rawlins did not seem eager for Floyd to recant. Rawlins appointed a public defender to represent Floyd and personally advised him, from the bench, of his constitutional rights and risk of being charged with perjury. Floyd said he understood, and did not need to confer with his counsel. He identified the affidavit, admitted signing it and said its contents were true. When the prosecutor asked directly about Floyd's trial testimony, the judge again interrupted. He said:

"Let me again warn you, Mr. Floyd, you do not have to answer that question. You can claim your privilege under the Fifth Amendment . . . if it tends to incriminate you, and it's obvious to the court that an answer to that question could incriminate you. I also warn you that any statement you make . . . can be used in further prosecution for any charges . . . most specifically perjury charges."

Floyd continued to be questioned on the stand. Again, the judge interrupted, this time addressing Floyd's public defender: "Mr. Murman, for the record, being the attorney for this witness, I am going to recess now and have you counsel with him. And I wish you would explain to him the consequences of perjury in a capital case. Perjury in a capital case carries a maximum penalty, I believe, under present Florida statutes, of life imprisonment."

The court then recessed. Upon returning, Judge Rawlins corrected his misstatement—the penalty for perjury in a capital case in Florida is thirty years, not life—then called another recess.

Back on the stand, Floyd finally wavered. He still insisted that there'd been a deal struck with the prosecution, but now he retracted the portion of his affidavit that said his trial testimony against Brown was false. Judge Rawlins, satisfied, prepared to end the hearing. Bonanno rose and summarized the testimony the state would have provided if the hearing had continued. He denied the existence of a deal in the Holiday Inn case but acknowledged that the state had agreed not to prosecute Floyd in the Barksdale murder if he would testify, tell the truth and pass a polygraph. Judge Rawlins, in turn, said he would recommend that no perjury proceedings be instituted against Floyd. He also announced that he intended to deny Brown's motion for a new trial.

For years after that, Shea, still pursuing his client's appeals, regularly drove the 360-mile round trip upstate to visit Brown near Starke. He could not afford to ignore his other cases—the state was paying him only twenty-four hundred dollars for the appeals—so he usually visited Brown on weekends or nights. Shea had grown increasingly possessed by the notion that the legal system does not always convict the right man in death penalty cases. It seemed to him entirely possible that an innocent person could be sentenced to death and executed. Researching the matter, he came upon a University of Florida study that claimed 343 people in the United States have been wrongly convicted of capital offenses, and twenty-five executed. "This one got uncovered is all," Shea later would tell people. "It makes me wonder how many other cases like this there are. This case is the best example I know to show what's wrong with the death penalty."

He couldn't get any judge to agree with him, however. In all, Shea, representing Brown, lost at three posttrial hearings and three times was turned down by the Florida Supreme Court. He didn't stop trying until the prison changed its rules and restricted attorney meetings only to business hours. Barred from coming on weekends or nights, Shea's visits eventually tailed off.

Brown's string appeared to be played out until the phone rang one morning in mid-1981 at the Stamford, Connecticut, law offices of Richard Blumenthal. Blumenthal had recently resigned as Connecticut's U.S. attorney to join a private practice. Deborah Fins, attorney for death penalty litigation at the NAACP Legal Defense and Education Fund, wanted to know if he would take over Brown's appeal.

That she called Blumenthal at all was a matter of chance, the result of an offhand suggestion from a mutual acquaintance. Blumenthal was not an obvious choice, since he'd been a prosecutor, with little experience in criminal defense work and none in a capital case. Blumenthal was intrigued, though—he respected the NAACP, wanted to make a contribution, and was aware of the need for attorneys to represent Death Row inmates. Fins's summary of the case led him to question whether justice had been done. Perhaps just as important, Blumenthal was working at a law firm that was willing and able to absorb, without any compensation, the enormous cost of handling a Death Row appeal; Blumenthal later estimated his costs for Brown's defense at $400,000 in time and $50,000 in out-of-pocket expenses.

After only a little thought, Blumenthal agreed to take over the case. His first efforts, however, did not prove any more successful than Shea's. In 1982, Bob Graham, then Florida's governor, rejected a petition for clemency filed by Blumenthal. On September 23, 1983, Graham signed Brown's death warrant. On October 12, the Florida

Supreme Court denied a final appeal. The execution was scheduled for October 18.

Blumenthal, with Shea's help, now turned to the past. Ronald Floyd, after serving seven years of his ninety-nine-year sentence, had been freed in 1981. He was living in Miami, reporting to a parole officer. One day in late September 1983, the parole officer called Floyd. Some people, he reported, wanted to see him. One of them was a fellow named Shea. They wanted to talk about Joseph Green Brown. Floyd remembered Shea, remembered their meeting years before. He was two years removed from prison now, with no reason to risk a perjury charge. And yet, he would explain later, that whole thing was still burning heavily in his mind. Yeah, okay, he told the parole officer. I'll see them.

On October 4, two weeks before Brown's scheduled execution, Floyd met in Miami with Shea and an associate of Blumenthal's, J. Marion Moorman. This time, they videotaped the deposition. Yes, Floyd said, he had talked to the public defender's office and knew that there was a chance he could be prosecuted for perjury as a result of the new statement he was about to give. He was willing.

Floyd began to tell his story. It was, it turned out, much the same one he tried to tell in 1975. He'd been angry at Brown. Bebler kept coming back, taking him out of jail, driving to the murder site, showing him pictures of the store's layout. He'd never been there before Bebler took him. He was promised he would get "paper" on the Holiday Inn case—probation. He was promised that he would not be prosecuted for the Barksdale murder if he testified against Brown. He'd invented "Poochie" because the police wanted a third accomplice. He'd lied at the trial. "I went along with the program," he said. His 1975 affidavit was true, he insisted. He had retracted part of it because the judge and prosecutor were angry and threatened him. "I was given a good opportunity to back away. . . . I backed away."

What were his feelings then about Brown getting the chair? Shea asked.

"I had a conscience problem," Floyd said. "A real weight problem."

Has that continued to be a problem? Shea asked.

"As of today, it's not," Floyd said.

He knew he might now be charged with perjury. "My mind is clear," he said. "So whatever comes, I'm just going to have to accept it." One month later, Floyd in fact was arrested and charged with perjury. He eventually drew a sentence of five years' probation.

Blumenthal had exhausted all state legal remedies, so now could turn only to the federal judiciary. On October 14, with four days to go,

Blumenthal filed a petition for a writ of habeas corpus, together with an application for a stay of execution, in the Tampa division of the United States District Court.

On Death Row, officials came to measure Brown for his burial suit, an event that made him angrier than anything ever had. It seemed so cold, so full of audacity. Brown had never thought he would die in prison, but now it suddenly occurred to him: These people are trying to kill me.

Brown was moved on October 17 to the death watch cell, located some thirty feet from the electric chair. He was to be executed at seven the next morning, but could not bring himself to order a last meal. Then, at nine that evening, just as the day turned from dusk to pitch-black outside, he was called to the phone.

"You got the stay," Blumenthal said.

U.S. District Judge Terrell Hodges had granted the stay only grudgingly. This was the case's first appearance on the federal level, the judge observed, the motion having been filed just two days after state remedies were exhausted. "Of necessity, therefore, the stay was granted," he wrote.

Hodges, however, chose not to hold an oral hearing. He also chose not to read or view Floyd's videotaped deposition. After reading the court record in the case and the lawyer's briefs, he issued a ruling on March 5, 1984. He wrote: "I have concluded that none of the claims have merit and that the petition should be denied."

Blumenthal had one last avenue, an appeal of the district court's decision to the U.S. Eleventh Circuit Court of Appeals. When that appellate panel agreed to hear the case, Brown's execution once more was stayed.

Blumenthal now faced a critical task. Appellate judges usually are interested in a case for a particular constitutional issue it raises. What did the Eleventh Circuit want to hear about? After six drafts of his brief, Blumenthal finally drew his focus on a 1972 Supreme Court case, *Giglio v. United States,* where the justices ruled a conviction by the knowing use of perjured testimony must be set aside if there is "any reasonable likelihood" that the false testimony "could have affected the jury's verdict."

At the oral hearing before the Eleventh Circuit panel on September 10, 1986, Blumenthal rose with some trepidation. We intend to focus chiefly here on the *Giglio* decision, he began. The chief judge, John C. Godbold, interrupted. Good, Godbold told Blumenthal. That is what we are interested in too.

At the Florida State Prison, Brown was again summoned to the phone on March 17, 1986.

"Your conviction has been overturned," Blumenthal said.

The Eleventh Circuit in the end did not concern itself with the FBI ballistics report or the Holiday Inn case—although the judges said they thought the sentencing there quite curious. The Eleventh Circuit found the state's undisclosed agreement with Floyd in the Barksdale murder case to be sufficient grounds, by itself, for a reversal. The judges were reversing, they wrote, "because the prosecution knowingly allowed material false testimony to be introduced at trial, failed to step forward and make the falsity known, and knowingly exploited the false testimony in its closing argument to the jury, in violation of the due process clause of the Fourteenth Amendment."

Brown had already served more than the maximum on the Holiday Inn robbery conviction, so if the state wanted to keep him behind bars, it would have to retry him on the murder charge. This decision fell to the Hillsborough County state's attorney's office. There the case was assigned to Assistant State's Attorney Henry W. Lavendera. Studying the file, it seemed to Lavendera that even back in 1974, this had been a circumstantial case. Everything had hinged on Floyd. Lavendera knew that he could use Floyd's original trial testimony at a new trial, even if Floyd was now recanting. But that would not be enough without other evidence. Floyd would get roasted on the stand. There were other problems. For one thing, it did not seem to Lavendera that he had the right murder weapon. And in a new statement obtained by the prosecutor's own investigators, Raymond Venson now was backing away from his corroborating trial testimony about the radio newscast. He too had been pressured and programmed by Bebler, Venson claimed.

Lavendera was not sure whether Brown was innocent or guilty. Bonanno believed him guilty, and Lavendera had to respect that judgment. And yet, looking at the trial record, the prosecutor thought: I know a dozen lawyers in town who could have rammed this case right down the state's throat.

They would need yet another deposition from Floyd. By then he was back in prison, having again violated probation, so he now was transferred to the Hillsborough County Jail. By coincidence, Brown just then also was residing in the Hillsborough County Jail, having been transferred there after his conviction was overturned. So for the first time in a dozen years, Brown and Floyd were together in the same building.

Brown saw Floyd first. Floyd did not recognize him.

"Hey, it's me," Brown said softly.

"Hey, old man, I'm giving your lawyer a deposition," Floyd said.

On February 19, 1987, under questioning from Lavendera and Brown's newly appointed defense attorney, Tom McCoun, Floyd stuck to his recantation.

Okay, Lavendera next decided, let's put Floyd on the box. The state couldn't use the result at a trial, but still, it might answer some questions. The state's own examiner, an expert ex-FBI man, ran the polygraph. On March 5, the expert reported his conclusion—Floyd was telling the truth.

The news leaked that same day to a local Tampa television station. When Lavendera learned a story would be broadcast that very night, he and his boss, State's Attorney Bill James, agreed: Let's not appear to be reacting to the TV news. Let's do it ourselves.

At five o'clock that evening, while mopping a jailhouse floor, Brown was summoned to the phone.

"You're free," Tom McCoun said.

Brown figured that the paper work alone would take four weeks. He went back to mopping. Half an hour later, they called out his name and told him to get his stuff together. Brown walked along the second-floor catwalk to Floyd's cell. "Hey," he said. "They're letting me go. Thank you."

At seven, Brown found himself standing alone in the unadorned lobby of the Hillsborough County Jail. He had been twenty-three when he was last out from behind bars, and now he was thirty-seven. He had with him his only possessions—a large cardboard box of legal papers and seventy-five cents, the total of his personal prison account. Tom McCoun finally arrived to pick him up. "Welcome to the free world," McCoun said.

At McCoun's office that night, Brown held a beer bottle in the air, looked at it, sipped, then looked some more. McCoun left him later that night at a local motel. Friends picked up Brown the next morning and drove him north to Gainesville. Three days later, McCoun received a postcard from there. "I'm doing much better than I thought I would," Brown wrote. "My biggest problem is learning how to deal with being pampered."

There are those who insist that the system did not fail in the matter of Joseph Green Brown. They point out that the appeals process did free him. "They played it close. There was a little excitement. But the system worked," Lavendera said. Brown, though, having spent thirteen years on Death Row, sees it differently. Raised in a foster home since he was nine, he completed only the eighth grade, but a program of self-education and reading in prison has left him an articulate, if guardedly restrained man. At a friend's home and over dinner at a Gainesville restaurant one evening, Brown spoke carefully.

He said: "I have firsthand experience that the system doesn't work. Only certain people saved me—I am a real Dick Blumenthal fan. The judicial system tried, convicted and sentenced me to death. . . . How do you know a person is guilty? Are we willing to have a sentence with such finality, when that question looms? How can we tell whether a person is guilty or not? Are we that infallible? Are we that sure?"

Beyond the argument over whether the system worked remained the question of just why the system functioned as it did in Brown's case. Here, though, there was less debate—lawyers from widely varying perspectives found more common ground than differences. From all quarters, considerably more blame has been pointed at Michael Shea than at Robert Bonanno or the various judges. Bonanno, in fact, draws a number of admiring comments. Bonanno was just doing his job, it is said, an aggressively good job. What he did was just part of the system. The system might be flawed, but who knows a better one?

Even Shea said that. So did McCoun.

"The defense attorney was simply overwhelmed," McCoun maintained. "I was a prosecutor for three years. I was expected to be aggressive. The defense attorney must respond. The quality and personalities of individuals involved had a clear outcome in this case. That used to be so all the time. Now it is harder, but I can't call that an aberration. It happens."

Most likely, it is for this reason that Robert Bonanno professes to remain perplexed about the outcome of the Brown case. He is, as it happens, now a Hillsborough County circuit judge, one widely admired in the legal community. In interviews, he offers no apologies or regrets. Sitting in his chambers one morning recently, Judge Bonanno posed a question.

"They said I should have told [about the plea deal]," he said. "But where's the adversary system? I do my job, the defense attorney does his job. This is what puzzles me. That's what the adversary system is all about."

II

Matters of the Family

Shadow of Doubt

November 1989
Los Angeles, California

Last summer, returning home late one evening, I found a puzzling message on my telephone answering machine from a woman whom I will call Julie Johnson. I'd like to talk to you, the voice said.

Through a distant family connection, I'd known Julie intermittently for a long time, although not very well. Our paths had crossed for a while in the late 1970s, but I'd had no contact with her at all in the past ten years. I understood she'd married and now had two children, but I knew nothing of her husband. I couldn't imagine why she was calling me.

"There's something we need to talk to you about. Could you come over?" she asked when I returned the call. She spoke haltingly, almost whispering.

Okay, I said, but could you tell me what this is about?

Julie hesitated. "Something bad has happened," she said. "The past three weeks have been a nightmare." Now she could barely speak. "We've been accused of a child molestation."

More than a month elapsed before I was able to speak at length with Julie and her husband, whom I will call David Johnson. With them at their kitchen table were their children, a three-year-old son and a sixteen-month-old daughter, Adam and Jennifer. By then, they'd learned the case against them had been dropped. A little girl, one of Adam's playmates, had made accusations against David, but there'd been no charges filed, no prosecution. The Johnsons were more stunned than happy, though—their manner suggested survivors after an accident. They wanted to tell me their story. They wanted me to write about their experiences, as long as I didn't identify them.

Why? I asked. What's the point now? Why not let it die?

"Because I think a lot of people can be hurt and are being hurt continuously through the incompetence and lack of training of people involved all through this situation," David said.

"Because we need to vent this," said Julie. "We can't sue anyone, we can't do anything after this horrible nightmare. We want to send a warning that it could happen to anybody. After seeing the impact on an innocent family, maybe other families who hear something from their kids will think twice before making a report. . . . We want this story told."

Of course, I understood there'd be more than one story to tell. I had reported on child abuse before, and so knew well the tragic consequences that can follow when a community fails to respond to warning signs. For a book I was writing, I'd studied how such failures in the past twenty years had spurred all manner of statutes and lawsuits and public opinion that now empower and compel everyone to act decisively. Whatever had happened to the Johnsons, I expected there were understandable reasons.

All the same, over the past half dozen years, I'd increasingly heard people say the pendulum had now swung too far in the other direction, that overreaction had supplanted underreaction. In a meeting room in a small Minnesota town, I had sat in a circle with a dozen couples accused of child molestation, all insisting they'd been wronged, all with a pile of legal documents before them, all imploring me to investigate their case. Another day, I'd listened as a former director of the National Center on Child Abuse explained how he had seen the situation change in a handful of years from people ignoring even the most grievous cases to people phoning in with what he called "a lot of junk," much of it related to divorce and custody fights. I'd heard lawyers say that authorities, in their well-intentioned drive to stop child abuse, were trampling on the rights of parents and entangling innocent people in tortuous investigations.

In these exchanges, the respective voices always sounded so certain—

either we'd gone way too far or not nearly far enough in addressing child abuse. Where was the truth? The Johnsons' situation roused my curiosity. If my various connections to the topic created conflicts, they also provided a sense of context.

Okay, I told the Johnsons. But I'll need to hear from other people involved in this case, people who might have viewpoints different from yours.

"That's fine," Julie replied. "We want you to do that. We've sat here in a nightmare for three weeks, hearing nothing, being told nothing, wondering what was in their minds. We want to know what was in their minds."

They offered names and phone numbers of everyone they'd encountered during their experience—caseworkers, detectives, prosecutors, neighbors, clergymen, educators, the little girl's parents. They gave me the private journal they'd started keeping on the day the police and the Department of Children's Services caseworker had arrived at their door. They signed a release, saying anyone could speak about them and provide me with reports and files.

In this fashion, I began hearing in detail about how a community and a government system responded to one report of child molestation, and by extension, to all such reports. In time, I learned a good deal—more people than I expected were willing to talk as long as I didn't identify them by name, and their recollections of events did not differ greatly. All the same, I ended up anything but enlightened.

Although some people were certain the Johnsons had been wrongly accused, I gradually came to realize others thought them guilty, even though they never were charged. This unsettled me—ambiguity is intriguing, but just then clarity seemed much more desirable. For a time, I tried to puzzle out the question for myself, until I realized doing so was impossible.

Only this much seemed certain: A little girl had said she was molested. The molestation was reported to authorities. A system responded. As a result, a family was investigated and maligned and ostracized but never charged or cleared, while a child molester—whoever he is—went unstopped and unpunished. No resolution was ever reached.

"The problem is this," explained the police detective who investigated the Johnsons. "Once the accusation is made, there is no way to prove guilt, and no way to prove innocence."

· · ·

By all accounts, the investigation of the Johnsons began when a little girl's mother—like the Johnsons, an educated professional—noticed her three-year-old was acting oddly. When she questioned her, the little girl talked of being molested. She described the abuse in detail and identified her playmate Adam's daddy—David Johnson—as the molester.

I cannot report precisely how the identification was made—whether, for example, the little girl volunteered the name or was offered a choice—partly because the little girl's parents were among the few who would not speak with me. The question is not at all a minor one, of course. Was the little girl led by her questioners, was she directed away from identifying someone else, was she unable to name someone closer to her? Or did she speak without guidance? Was it important that the little girl's mother worked with children in her job? These are the sorts of issues that would be examined for days in a courtroom, and have been—in cases ranging from the protracted Virginia McMartin Preschool prosecution in southern California to the ill-fated proceedings in Jordan, Minnesota, where charges against twenty-three families eventually were dropped long after their children had been removed from their homes.

I can report only that the mother took her daughter to a medical center, where a physical exam yielded evidence of molestation. Even this much might be contested, though—a deputy district attorney later explained to me that a defense lawyer in such cases might argue the bruised labia were the result of other causes.

Ten years ago, the matter most likely would have stopped here, but now the process was just beginning. The medical center called the police, as required under state law. The police cross-reported to the Los Angeles County Department of Children's Services. Because the DCS was contacted on a Saturday, the report went to a DCS emergency command post, an after-hours response desk created three years before. The details of this particular case, a DCS supervisor decided, fit the category that required immediate action. The command post contacted a caseworker whom I will call Sam Rowan, and read him the report.

Rowan, in his early forties, had been a DCS caseworker for four years. He'd brought with him to the job a master's degree in family and marriage counseling, and the DCS had added three weeks of training before sending him into the field. Rowan's first task now was to assess the safety and credibility of the little girl. He visited her family, questioning both the parents and the young victim. He found the experience difficult. The mother was crying, the father appeared to be in shock. Rowan considered: Is it a functional family or not? What are the patterns of behavior? What are the intelligence and verbal skills of the child? Does her statement have details and logic? Is it specific or vague? Is this age-appropriate information she's providing? Is this family screwed up?

Making such judgments is difficult and the pressures are considerable. Caseworkers and their departments in recent years have faced civil suits and criminal prosecutions when they have failed to identify abuse or protect a child. In an effort to eliminate mistakes and precisely control responses, lawmakers and administrators have tried to quantify and standardize the decision-making process. Caseworkers like Rowan now carry with them multipage charts and questionnaires aimed at defining what constitutes abuse and high-risk conditions.

Despite such attempts to codify good judgment, human beings still have to make decisions. Rowan finds judging the credibility of small children in molestation cases the toughest of all. He calls the experience a nightmare.

"Sexual molestation cases are very, very difficult," Rowan told me when we met for dinner one night. "My job is to believe the allegation unless proved otherwise. . . . I am biased. My job is to be the advocate for the children. . . . I have to justify every act I take. There are checkpoints, laws, regulations, guidelines. If I make a bad judgment, it comes back to haunt me. I face lawsuits all the time. This thought is constantly on my mind. I'm a good worker. I carefully document what and why I do, every step of the way. I'd rather err on the side of the children. There are checkpoints and oversights beyond me. I can be overturned and reversed."

To Rowan, the statement of the little girl who accused the Johnsons was detailed and consistent—he heard some of it directly from her, a good deal more as relayed by the mother. It contained descriptions Rowan felt no three-year-old could imagine or fantasize, but was told in the language of a little child—"peepee," for example, not penis—and Rowan thought this particularly telling. He saw no apparent troubles in her own home. Rowan decided she was credible.

He steeled himself, for now he had to visit the perpetrator. That's what he called David Johnson—"the perpetrator." Johnson had two children of his own, and these kids might be in danger, too. A "companion case," the DCS labels it, when the accused has access to other children.

"Visiting the perpetrator is a very nasty, difficult business," Rowan said. "You go to the police station, get a unit to go with you. We drive over in two cars. Once there, I ask the cops, how do you want to do this? Eighty percent of the time, they say, you're the expert, you handle it. It's hard to believe that in two years of doing this, only one family has said no when I appeared at their door. Most are so shocked, they let me in. We go into the home, we explain the allegations."

That Sunday was such a nonday, the Johnsons would say later. There's little else to remember about it.

They'd spent the afternoon by the pool at David's sister's home. Adam and Jennifer played with their three cousins, and the grandparents took all the kids to McDonald's for lunch. The Johnsons returned to their own home around four o'clock. They ate dinner with their children, maybe a pizza but they weren't sure. They sat in the den, watching the news on television. The kids were tired and cranky, and so were they.

It was shortly before seven in the evening, midway through a long holiday weekend. The Johnsons were trying to think through chores they needed to do later that night, in preparation for a barbecue they were hosting the next afternoon for sixteen people. A tuna dip still needed to be made, and a Jell-O mold. Julie lay stretched on the couch, Jennifer on top of her, clutching a blanket. David sat in the big corner chair with Adam. Because his position gave him a clear view through the window by the front door, David was the one who first noticed the police car cruise slowly by the house. He rose and walked to the window. Police cars were an uncommon sight on their quiet, secluded residential street. By the time he reached the glass, the road was empty.

Two minutes later, David saw two uniformed policemen walking up his driveway, accompanied by a man dressed in slacks and a short-sleeved cotton shirt. They rang the bell. "I'm with the Department of Children's Services," the man in the cotton shirt said when David opened the door. "There have been accusations of child abuse in your home. . . . Can we come in and talk about this?"

Julie was standing in the front hallway, Jennifer in her arms and Adam at her side. The policemen, she said later, looked so big to her. David took Rowan outside to the backyard to talk out of earshot of his family, but their golden retriever started barking so crazily that Rowan finally asked if they could go back inside. They ended up at the dining-room table.

Rowan began reading the allegations from a sheet of paper. David, he said, had been accused of sexually molesting a little girl, a playmate of his son's, while she was visiting their home. The little girl said Adam's daddy placed ice and a hairbrush handle in her vagina while he masturbated into a bottle. The little girl said this happened in Adam's room. The little girl said Adam was there with them.

David stared across the table as Rowan recited the precise charges. He was in his midthirties, a professional who'd done well enough to own a house in the hills with a view. Out his back window, mountains rose against a moonlit sky. In his kitchen, photos of his family and their friends covered the refrigerator, stuck there with magnetic smiling faces.

"Julie," David called to his wife. "Julie, you're not going to believe this."

Johnson by nature is an assertive man accustomed to controlling his world. His only experience with the police until Rowan's arrival involved speeding tickets. Once, years before, when he was working as a lifeguard, he'd given a cop lip while being written up for having his motorcycle on the sidewalk. The cop had thrown him in the backseat of his patrol car and slammed the door on his legs, and David had almost lunged at the guy. That was the closest he'd ever come to serious trouble. Now, listening to Rowan, David did not feel in control. He began to defend himself, to deny the allegations, to reclaim his territory.

"Could I speak alone to your son?" Rowan finally asked.

"Fine," David said. "Ask him anything you want."

Julie was uncomfortable watching the caseworker lead Adam into the den and close the door, but she didn't know what to say. She felt this man could do anything he wanted in her house just then.

While they waited, one of the police officers turned to the Johnsons. "You know, I got accused of this by our pediatrician once," he said. The second officer added another comment: "We've been in houses where by now we've already taken the kids out."

Only then did David and Julie realize the DCS worker might be there to take their own children from them.

Everyone stared at the closed den door. Jennifer started crying and whining. Julie tried to put her in a high chair, give her something to eat, but that didn't help. Please not now, Julie told her. The last thing she wanted was these people to see her child uncomfortable.

When Rowan and Adam finally emerged from the den, Adam rushed to his room and reemerged in a second with an inflatable dinosaur to show the visitor. The DCS caseworker approached the Johnsons.

"At this point," he said, "I don't see there is a threat to your kids. We're just collecting information. We'll be in touch."

The Johnsons thought Rowan looked more relaxed now, less on edge, less certain David was the guilty party.

"We thought it was over," Julie said.

They were wrong.

Adam had told Rowan nothing at all that sounded suspicious. But the little girl's detailed description was, to the caseworker, conclusive. He absolutely thought Johnson was guilty. He discounted Adam's denials.

"Interviewing a kid that age in their own home is very difficult," Rowan told me. "It usually produces negative results. The prosecutor won't let me use anatomical dolls. It's their house. I have only a few minutes. All I can do is try, and write it up. I ask, 'Did you ever play with Daddy without clothes on?' But they're scared, don't understand why I'm there. In that setting, I'm not likely to get anything. . . . If I leave, it's not always because I think they're innocent. It's because I have no statement or evidence."

The Johnsons' visitors had been in their house just twenty minutes. It was now 7:20 P.M. David and Julie settled at their kitchen table with a cordless telephone.

"They walk out and we're just sitting here shocked," David said. "Absolutely shocked, not knowing who to call, what to do. The first phone call I made to anybody was to our minister."

The clergyman was more than their spiritual leader; he was their connection to the little girl's family. Adam and the little girl were in the same class at the church preschool. The parents knew each other, had visited in each other's homes, but only while picking up their children—the little girl had played at the Johnson home some half dozen afternoons.

When the minister didn't answer, David left a message on his answering machine. Then he called his best friend. You're not going to believe this, he began. Can you recommend a lawyer?

"Between these phone conversations," Julie said, "we're thinking this has got to turn around because we're the people we are. We're innocent, we're good people, things like this don't happen to people like us."

While David was talking to his friend for a second time at about 9:30, the operator interrupted with an emergency call from Sam Rowan.

"New evidence has been brought to our attention," the DCS worker said. "Evidence that you may possibly be a threat to your children. I can't tell you the evidence. But we feel there is a threat in your household to your children, and we're required to remove your children from your house."

"No!" David was shouting. "You're not taking my kids out of this house. You cannot do this."

Rowan was taken aback by what he considered Johnson's bombastic manner. "If you don't quiet down, we'll take your children out of your house," the caseworker responded. "We do have alternatives, though. If you will calm down, we will tell you what the alternatives are."

The kids could remain if David left the house immediately, went to a motel, Rowan said. Or if a third party, a responsible relative, came over to stay with them.

The Johnsons demanded to speak to Rowan's supervisor.

"Do you have any children?" Julie asked this woman when she came to the phone.

"What's that have to do with it?" she replied.

"It has a lot to do with it," Julie said. "You have no idea what this means to us. We're innocent people, and you're telling us you have to take our children. Who are you? Who's going to protect our children from you?"

"It's the law," the supervisor told them. "No matter who you are, or how innocent you are, if there has been an accusation, this is what we have to do."

The Johnsons agreed to get David's father over to the house immediately. While waiting for him to arrive, the phone rang again. It was the minister, returning their call.

I've been accused of this molestation, David began.

Yes, I know, the clergyman said.

David later offered his recollection of their conversation: "The next thing the minister said was, 'Before you say anything else, I want you to know that I am waiving clergy privilege.' I said, 'What?' He said, 'Well, the seriousness of the matter is so much . . . that if anybody asks me a question about it, I have to tell them what I know.' And at that point, he really caught us between the eyes. I said, 'What? You're assuming we're guilty.' He said: 'Oh, no, no, it has nothing to do with guilt, I am not assuming you're guilty, but whatever you say, if somebody asks me,

I'll have to tell them.' I said, 'What are you telling me? . . . Can you tell me what you know?' 'I can't tell you,' he answered. I said, 'Well, can you talk to [the little girl's parents] and find out what they know and what they think, and tell me?' 'I can't tell you that,' he said."

Julie continued their account: "And I said 'This is a nightmare.' And the minister said: 'Yes. You're right. That's exactly what it is.' And I said: 'What are we going to do?' And he said, his one spiritual advice to me, was: 'Life is long.' "

The phone rang yet again minutes later, just as David's father was walking through the Johnsons' front door. "You have to take your kids down to the hospital for a scan team exam," Sam Rowan said. "Tomorrow morning at nine A.M. It's the law. Children of the accused must be examined for sexual abuse."

David and Julie sat in their darkened living room talking until two o'clock, then went to bed but could not sleep. "We tossed and turned," Julie said. "And I think we went to look at the children."

"If I call back later," Rowan told me, offering a hypothetical answer to a hypothetical question, "it's perhaps because I've spoken to someone . . . who has suggested something that gives me further motive to separate the kids."

What new evidence had come up in this case? I asked, this time more directly.

"I think I just reevaluated the case later that Sunday night. . . . In retrospect, leaving two kids with a grandparent there is not that effective."

When the Johnsons, their two children and David's father arrived at the hospital emergency room at precisely nine o'clock the next morning, they found Rowan waiting for them. David thought he was acting a little more empathetic now. "You won't be charged for the examination," Rowan said.

David asked that Rowan repeat the allegations to his father. "You tell him what you told me last night," he said.

As the three men retreated to a private room, Julie held both children on her lap while a nurse took their temperature and vital statistics. "Is this going to hurt?" Julie asked. "On a scale of one to ten, how painful is this going to be for these children?"

It's not going to be bad, the nurse replied. They'll just take a few cultures. Mainly they talk with the social worker.

Julie had been imagining two hours of poking and probing. Relieved, she felt the impulse to cry but held back because Adam was sitting on her lap.

Time passed—a half hour, then an hour, then two. No one came for the children. Down the hallway, the Johnsons could see Rowan and hospital personnel sitting in a circle in a room with glass windows. David thought they were looking at them, trying to decide whether they were molesters.

As it happened, the people in the glass-windowed room were arguing. The doctor in charge of the emergency room didn't want to do the examinations.

"I wasn't trying to not cooperate," she told me later. "I was trying to make sure this was the right thing, not just something convenient for the social worker or us. It seemed to me like they were going from A to D, instead of A to B. I was not convinced enough history had been taken, enough interviews with this family and kids. I started asking, have the children admitted anything happened, disclosed anything? No, they said. I asked, are you convinced there is something? They said they didn't have enough time to make that determination. So it was my judgment. It seemed to me these children were safe. The interviewing process had not occurred. I wasn't so sure what sort of message we'd be giving to the kids. What we do in a physical exam is very close to what is done in the supposed molestation. What we do is very much close to rape. We can't judge guilt or innocence. But there were missing pieces of information. People were trying to hurry things along."

The emergency room doctor remembered this case particularly well because she felt threatened.

"The DCS guy [Rowan] was saying, 'If anything happens to these children, it's your responsibility, you're taking the responsibility.' . . . I finally said, 'Okay, I will take the responsibility.' There are complexities here, folks. We need to view every situation separately. You can't develop a routine for every case. It's easy to just do everything that protects. It's much harder to be sensitive, to make judgments. For the moment, I felt intimidated by the system, but I resisted. I've done it before, I do it all the time, but each time you put yourself on the line."

At eleven-thirty, Rowan and a social worker emerged from the room. "I have good news for you," the social worker told the Johnsons. "Your kids won't have to be examined today because the scan team's not here."

David erupted. He pointed his finger at Rowan. He hollered: "We came down here today specifically to get this over with. You're not giving me good news. You brought us down here for nothing? You people are no longer going to be coming into our lives. You will not disrupt our children again. You talk to us through an attorney."

After Julie quieted David down, he walked off. "I realized I was getting completely out of control," he said. "I was going to hit the guy if I stayed much longer."

The social worker turned to Julie. "This is not good that your husband is showing such aggressive behavior," she said. "This is going to impact negatively. You'd better control your husband."

Later that week, Sam Rowan asked his supervisor to remove him from the Johnson case. He also decided he no longer wanted to work for the emergency response command post.

"This case was going to be horrific," he explained to me later. "I saw that anyone touching this case was going to get burned. It was much more emotional than most cases. Mainly because of the behavior of the perpetrator. I was threatened with lawsuits. Then the emergency room doctor . . . And the little girl's mother crying. Seeing the victim. Going out to the perpetrator's house with the cops. All the pieces were there. I don't always have all the pieces. This time I saw it all. The nastiness of the allegations. I hated reading the allegations to the couple. . . . The only thing I can liken this work to is when I was an Air Force intelligence briefer in Korea. I was pointing out routes and danger spots for pilots. Lives depended on me spotting the dangers."

Monday evening, after their hospital visit and after their barbecue for sixteen guests, the Johnsons received a phone call at seven o'clock. It was their minister.

They'd been friends. The Johnsons had been considering inviting the clergyman and his wife for dinner. But the conversation now was strained.

According to the Johnsons, the minister said he did not think it would be a good idea for David or Julie to bring Adam to their preschool the next morning. Was there a third person they could get to bring Adam to school?

Julie later offered her recollection of what followed: "I said, 'No, there's not a third person that can take Adam to school.' I'm thinking, why shouldn't I bring him to school? I don't want anybody else to bring him to school. Then he said: 'Okay, okay. Why don't you keep him home tomorrow and do something really fun. Go take him to

Disneyland. Do something really fun with [Adam].' I said: 'Okay, I'll keep him home tomorrow, I'll bring him to school Wednesday.' "

Although authorities had never told the Johnsons precisely what day the molestation was said to have occurred, Julie later that night suddenly recalled when the little girl had last played at their house. They'd had an out-of-town friend staying with them that day about three weeks ago, because one of Julie's girlfriends was getting married. David had come home late that afternoon from work and settled in the den to visit with the friend. Julie was sure the little girl's father had arrived half an hour later to pick her up. Julie was sure David had never been alone with the children.

The next morning, the minister called again. According to the Johnsons, he'd changed his mind—Julie could bring Adam to school the next day. But Adam should be in another classroom for the rest of the year. Since the little girl had been through such trauma and associated Adam with it, he should be the one to move.

The minister called once more late that night, just before midnight, waking the Johnsons. Adam definitely was going to be moved to another classroom, he said. They'd met with a psychologist, the little girl's psychologist. She advised doing this.

That's not acceptable, the Johnsons said. What are you going to tell parents when they ask why Adam's not in the class? What are we going to tell Adam? "David was just screaming on the phone," Julie recalled. "We were yelling and screaming."

They discussed a compromise. Maybe Adam would go to the connected classroom next door, since he spent half the day there anyway.

The next morning at eight-thirty, Julie drove Adam to school. The school director was standing at the door of Adam's regular classroom, pointing the little boy not to the connecting classroom but to another one at the far end of the hallway, one full of younger children. Adam objected, and asked why.

"What are you going to tell Adam?" Julie asked the school director. Then she looked at her son, who was starting to whine. "Adam, you don't look like you're feeling really good," Julie said. "Let's go home."

Back in her house, Julie called the church to say she was withdrawing Adam from school and the family from the congregation. Then she took both Adam and Jennifer to their family pediatrician, who examined them and agreed to verify that they showed no signs of molestation. Then she took Adam to the La Brea Tar Pits, his favorite place of all.

At ten that same morning, a Los Angeles police detective, whom I will call Sullivan, visited David at his place of business. David had called him the day before, urging the meeting—he'd gotten his name from the officers Sunday night. The detective and Johnson sat on a bus bench on the sidewalk outside David's office.

"I am asking you to investigate me," David said. "Do whatever it takes to find out whatever information you need. I have nothing to hide. . . . What can I do to prove that I'm innocent? I will stand in front of a lineup, you can have my picture. I'll take a lie detector test. Our pediatrician will tell you what kind of parents we've been. What can I do?"

Sullivan listened, his expression blank.

"Do you know of any reason why this family would implicate you?" he asked.

No, David did not. He offered instead the name and phone number of the out-of-town friend who'd been staying with them the afternoon the little girl last visited.

Well, maybe we'll get that later, the detective said.

The officer had new information for David: The little girl had implicated Julie in her statement, too. She said Adam's mommy had walked in and seen them and gotten angry. She said Adam's mommy had told her she better not tell anybody, because no one would believe her and she'd get in trouble.

David repeated his offer to take a lie detector test.

We don't put much credence in those, the detective explained. And we can't use them in court.

"There is nothing you can do," the officer added just before leaving. "Don't expect this to blow over. This can drag on for the statute of limitations, six years. I've seen cases that have gone that long."

It was after this encounter that David first began thinking his family might lose everything they had—his profession made him dependent on people in the community coming to him out of trust and paying for his services. He started considering the necessity of selling his home and moving away.

The next day, David wrote in his log:

"In my 45 min. discussion with the detective yesterday, I told him my strength and ability as a fixer. I fix broken cars, toys, office equipment. . . . How do I fix this! A broken reputation, a damaged position in the community. He didn't have an answer. . . . I'm roaming around the twilight zone with no way to switch the channel. . . . I have absolutely no explanation for how or why I have been implicated. . . . How has this happened? I don't have an answer."

The detective who sat on the bus bench with David was a twelve-year veteran, the last six devoted full time to sexual assault cases. He'd heard plenty of stories like David's, plenty of equally ardent denials, enough not to be greatly impressed.

"This man [David] wanted to be proven innocent," the detective told me. "How can he prove himself innocent, he asks. He can't. The only way is if he could prove he wasn't there. . . . Child molestation reports are the most difficult to handle. The only source is usually the victim, a small child. The judicial system is not equipped to handle this."

In his own mind, though, there were no doubts.

"I don't think there's any question he did it," the detective said. "This little girl's story has not changed from day one. The same person is identified all the time. Lots of people in this guy's position can't prove themselves innocent when accused, but only a small number are truly innocent. We can weed a lot out. This guy kept saying to me, 'Why would I do this? I have too much to lose.' Well, in my years I've handled plenty of successful established community leaders. Position and status mean nothing to me. I'm not impressed."

Why, I asked, did he reject David's offer to take a polygraph examination?

"It wouldn't stop our investigation if he tested truthful. Some people can pass even if they're lying. And this guy was not going to confess if we got negative results, so what was the point? I made that judgment."

Why, I asked, wasn't he interested in the Johnsons' out-of-town guest?

That was a question much on my mind just then, for I'd placed a long-distance call to this visitor that very morning, before driving to the police station.

She remembered the day clearly, she told me. She and her husband were in town for their friend's wedding. She remembered the little girl visiting the Johnsons that day. She'd talked to Adam and his playmate about school, and thought the little girl really cute.

"Then [Julie] sent them to play in [Adam's] room, and started frying fish for the kids. [Julie] and I were going out to a bachelorette party that night with our girlfriend who was getting married. I'm trying to decide what to wear for the wedding. Then [David] came home, around five-ish, somewhere around that time. [David] went into the den. I remember having to walk around him for the next hour, because all our luggage, six bags, were there in the den. [David] was half asleep, talking to me, watching the TV news. I was in and out, dressing in the bathroom just off the hallway right next to [Adam's] room. When you step out of the bathroom, [Adam's] room is right there. The door was always open. The kids were both sitting on the floor playing with stuff. I was going back and forth into the den. [David] was stretched out in there. I had to crawl around him to get to the phone at one point, then to get to my luggage. Then the little girl's daddy drove up. I remember his car, even the color. I could see it on the driveway. I told [the little girl], 'Your daddy's here.' She came out from the bedroom. [David] was still sitting with me in the den. It was now around five forty-five, six P.M. The little girl left with her dad. Fifteen minutes later, [Julie] and I left. . . . All I know is what I saw that day. There is nothing that could have happened that day. No way on earth he could have done it the day I was there. Just wasn't a chance. Absolutely no way."

Have you told anyone else this story? I asked.

"No one has called me," she said. "I was expecting a call. I was very disappointed that no one called me. It really amazes me that no one has asked me what happened."

The woman's recollection was precise, but which day the little girl said she was molested remained an unresolved issue. This was a problem common with abuse cases involving small children, who often can't pinpoint exact dates.

The detective shrugged when I asked about this visitor and recounted my conversation with her. "It's their friend," he said. "And this little girl never said exactly which day the molestation happened."

Other mothers, noticing that Adam no longer was in school, soon started asking questions, and Julie tried to deflect them, but then one woman ventured to ask a teacher at the school what had happened. The teacher shook her head. "I can't say, but it's unbelievable," she answered.

Julie exploded when she heard about this comment—"now we knew it was going through the grapevine"—and demanded of the church that such talk stop. Soon after, the Johnsons decided they'd better tell their friends before they heard it from others. On Friday afternoon, five days after the DCS first appeared at their door, Julie and her good friend, a woman I will call Diane, took their children bumper bowling. When they returned to the Johnson house, David appeared at the door and asked Diane to come inside. The two of them walked into the backyard alone. Diane's little daughter was Adam's best friend.

"Diane, I've got to tell you something," he began.

The next day, David wrote in his log:

"My discussion with [Diane] unloaded quite a bit of dread about friends knowing our situation. She responded as I would have hoped but deep down I still feel pangs of suspicion. Everyone keeps asking the same question. Why us, why has this kid so arbitrarily and steadfastly picked us as her molesters?! The question itself implicates us. What on earth can be going through the minds of other people?"

It was Tuesday of the next week when the Johnsons learned from Diane that DCS caseworkers were contacting several of their acquaintances—parents whose children had played over at the Johnson house. There's been an allegation of child molesting, a DCS worker would say. Your child has played at the house of the accused person. Has your child showed any signs of abuse? Can we come over and talk to you and your child?

One mother soon realized the caseworker must be talking about the Johnsons. To another who wasn't sure, the caseworker identified the Johnsons by name. Soon these women called Julie, frantic and perplexed. One rushed to the Johnsons' house that night to hear the story. Julie met another in the park two days later and explained everything as they watched their children scramble through the sandbox and playground. Late one night at a dinner party with Julie's three closest friends and their husbands, she and David turned down the stereo. "We have something to tell you," Julie began. "A terrible thing has happened to us. We want to tell you because this could happen to you and we want to protect you." Then she started crying openly, for the first time since their experience began.

David, instead, grew angrier. He took to the phone, hollering at those whom he felt were maligning his good name. He called the DCS caseworker who'd contacted their acquaintances. He called the detective. He called the deputy district attorney who had his case.

In his log he wrote: "I refuse to go down without making as much noise as possible. . . . I've been starting to get real bizarre and violent thoughts about DCS possibly showing at my front door to take my kids. Hopefully, I could maintain a level of rationality, but I'm not sure. No one will take my kids, no one! . . . Every time the phone rings or a car pulls up to our house we are on pins and needles. That is no way to live! Not when you are good people!"

He learned about the nonprofit advocacy and support organization called Victims of Child Abuse Legislation (VOCAL) and visited its representatives. He contemplated filing lawsuits, but when he consulted a lawyer, he discovered that virtually everyone in the system was immune from such litigation. Then, on a Monday morning two weeks after the charges against him were revealed, David drove to the office of a nationally recognized private polygraph expert recommended by a VOCAL lawyer. There, he took a polygraph exam and passed.

The DCS caseworker who received David's bellicose phone call felt more conflicted than offended. I will call her Leslie Kirkland. In her early forties, with a master's degree in social work, she has been a social worker for more than twenty years, most of them in children's services.

"His call was part of a day," she told me when we met. "It's the nature of the system. I get lots of calls from upset people. I don't blame them, but I don't know the answer. How to protect the child and adult at the same time? I think sex abuse is a very hazardous issue. I don't want to see anyone charged falsely. But how do you ever disprove? How do you find out the truth? You have very little evidence. Children don't lie, but they can't separate fantasy from reality; fantasy is part of their lives. My own daughter, seeing another child misbehaving, once turned to me and said, 'You used to spank me when I did that.' Well, I have never spanked her in my life. On the other hand, you want to protect children. I have to err on the side of the child. . . . As long as I'm acting in the interest of the kid, I'm protected in what I do."

The calls she made to other parents concerning the Johnsons, she said, were standard procedure.

"Once someone calls and says a perpetrator molested one person but has access to others, we must do something. I have to go out and question people. How do you do it without identifying the accused? The law doesn't say I have to protect him. The law says I have to see the potential victims face to face. I have to tell them, 'this might have happened.' "

Kirkland expressed no more satisfaction with the system than did David.

"It seems you can never have a middle balance," she said. "I wish you could. It's great that it's opened up, that sexual abuse is dealt with now, but the balance always swings so sharply. Right now it's against the accused. There must be a better way. Now everyone looks for sexual molestation everywhere. The pendulum has swung too far the other way."

Kirkland mentioned that last point more than once during our lunch, so just before leaving, I asked her why she had done so. She hesitated, then answered:

"I got referred to DCS myself once, two years ago. My ten-year-old daughter was playing 'having a baby' with a four-year-old neighbor girl. This was once considered natural kid sex play, but now it got reported. The DCS showed up, wondering whether my daughter was being molested. The caseworker took her into another room and questioned her. . . . It was dropped, but still. It's like a Kafka novel. . . . I do not trust anyone saying absolutes. I cannot tell the truth, how can they?"

By the third week of the Johnsons' experience, though, absolute attitudes were abundant. The certainty of their opinions was driving people to act.

Some started rising to argue in defense of the Johnsons. One was Julie's friend and neighbor Diane, who protested to the DCS and without hesitation regularly continued to bring her daughter to play at Adam's house. Diane in time grew so bothered, she felt compelled to call the mother of the molested girl. She knew and liked this woman—their daughters regularly played at each other's homes. She lay awake one night, rehearsing what she'd say, then picked up the phone the next morning.

"DCS has called me," Diane began. "I want you to know you absolutely have the wrong people. I'd put everything I have out there on that. What's happened to your daughter, I feel really badly, I wish it never to happen. But she must be protecting someone close to her. When you find out, I hope you can deal with it."

Others responded quite differently. Although no accusations involved events at the church preschool, the Johnsons' minister nevertheless felt it necessary to send a certified letter to all families enrolled there, advising them that an allegation of child molestation had been made against the parent of a child attending the preschool. Some of those so informed apparently managed to connect the report to the

Johnsons after learning that the accused couple had left the preschool. This, at least, is what the Johnsons' pediatrician later heard from one of his other patients who belonged to the congregation.

The minister and others from the church also began calling the DCS and the police station. "This case got more attention than normal because we were being contacted regularly," Detective Sullivan said. "The church, the minister and their lawyer called me often. The minister was asking what they should do. He wanted to consult me. I avoided doing that. They were worrying about liability. One call, the minister expressed the wish we'd prosecute, so we would solve their problem."

When I phoned the minister one Sunday night at his home, he said he was "shocked" to learn the Johnsons had approached a journalist.

"This just won't die," he said. "I wish we could put this behind us. . . . We did not point the finger at them. We did not make the accusation. We were just concerned for our children. Our main concern was the ethics of the situation. We were concerned with protecting the children and with maintaining privacy. We consulted counsel and followed their advice. . . . The [Johnsons] do not understand our situation. They have dumped all their rage on us. In hindsight, I feel the congregation and leadership handled this as best as they could. . . . There is a difference of opinion about whether they are guilty or not. I don't know. I'm not a professional in that area. I tried to stay clear of that judgment. I've had no training, no preparation in this. It's an imperfect situation."

The minister agreed to meet for an interview, but insisted that neither he nor his church be named in any article. "I don't want the church involved," he said, more than once and with considerable feeling. I agreed, since I wasn't identifying anyone else by name, but when I called him a week later, the clergyman had changed his mind.

"I've said all there is to say," he explained. "Our concern was with protecting the children and maintaining privacy. That was our concern."

In our first conversation, the minister had given me the name of the psychologist who'd been meeting regularly with the little girl, and had urged that I call her. I now did so.

The therapist turned out to be a middle-aged woman with a master's degree in social work and some dozen years of clinical experience in the field of child abuse. She spoke with deliberation.

She'd started out assuming kids never lie, she told me, but over the years she'd learned that wasn't so. Kids don't always tell the truth. She's had four- and five-year-olds make things up. She's had one parent lead a child into saying things against the other parent. She's had to poke holes in more than one kid's story.

All the same, there was absolutely no question in her mind about the Johnson case.

"This little girl was molested, and by the man she accuses," she said. "The story does not change—not the precise details, not the effect. I ask what she saw, she says, 'I didn't see, I felt.' I raise topics for the third time, she says, 'I already told you.' She is articulate and bright."

I asked whether the little girl might be transferring the charges to David from someone else.

"I never see kids transfer in that way," she said. "Noncredible kids are few and far between, and it's usually a situation where they are angry at a parent. Rarely do we get a kid saying something false about someone outside the family. They have no investment in accusing such a person. They would have to be truly psychotic."

The therapist's words unsettled me greatly, more so than any I'd heard in all my interviews, for she appeared assured and certain, but not at all given to quick, absolute judgments. Unlike the others, she'd had the opportunity to talk regularly with the little girl. In the face of her comments, echoing so closely those of the caseworker and detective, I had to wonder what exactly my story was really about. This late in my inquiry, the truth seemed to be receding, not getting closer. Or rather, it seemed to shift from interview to interview, like a chameleon.

The Johnsons had brought their story to me and had imagined my article would be an account of the experiences of a wrongly accused couple. But I was gradually realizing I couldn't tell exactly that story.

When I so informed them, the Johnsons hesitated only briefly before saying they still wanted the article written, whatever contrary opinions it contained. At least people then would know what they'd been through, they explained, and how the system worked.

Perplexed, I found myself rereading the pages of the Johnsons' deeply anguished thirty-five-page journal, wondering whether it could conceivably be a masterful literary con job, thinking that prospect so hard to fathom. I spoke to a DCS caseworker not connected to this case, who said perpetrators often kept such logs, and warned that it was impossible for a normal mind to understand one controlled by a monstrous pathology. I considered David's nature. By now it was apparent he did not strike everyone as a particularly gentle man—he'd offended people in the system with his insistent temper. Did that prove he was a molester, though? During my visits to the Johnsons' home for interviews, I watched their interactions with their children, and I spent time alone with their son Adam, never sensing anything remotely out of the ordinary. What did that prove?

What didn't I know? What was in case files not available to me? What hadn't I been told in interviews that, by wavering between the hypothetical and the particular, unavoidably left some matters murky?

One morning I called the specialist who'd administered David Johnson's polygraph test. He is a former U.S. Defense Department and Los Angeles Police Department instructor and examiner who has operated his own private testing firm for sixteen years. In the past five years, he told me, his business has greatly changed because of the rising volume of molestation accusations. Where he once mainly tested people accused of murder or assault, he now sees a flood of accused molesters, three to four hundred annually, seventy-five percent of his total workload. He felt he'd come to know well, over time, the differing patterns between the guilty and the innocent. He was willing to be named, and I don't here only to protect other people's identities. "[Johnson] absolutely without a doubt is telling the truth," he said. "His test is not borderline or equivocal. . . . There is no question. . . . The victims in these cases not infrequently point elsewhere. . . . I absolutely do not hesitate to say this man is telling the truth."

The sense of confusion I by now felt was mirrored in the words I heard soon after from the Johnsons' pediatrician. He warmly endorsed them and talked of David's being made a "scapegoat," but then nervously balked at unequivocally declaring their innocence. "You can't say that," he said. "You don't know what's inside me, I don't know what's inside you. . . . Even after all your research, I doubt you'll ever be able to decide."

Investigating a report of a child molestation seemed a daunting task indeed. All sorts of dangers were apparent. Nationwide, some sixty percent of all molestation reports end up being labeled unfounded, although no one can say how many are false and how many just unprovable. In Los Angeles County, the DCS doesn't separately track the outcome of its sexual abuse reports—19,121 in the year ended in June 1989—but the department says half of all its abuse and neglect reports end up being labeled unfounded or not a cause for intervention, while another thirty to forty percent get handled only briefly. How many molestations and how many false accusations went uncorrected amid these numbers?

Neither the therapist's judgment nor the polygrapher's comments, both so certain, were the sort the law allows to be offered as fact. The therapist couldn't get up in court and testify that the little girl was telling the truth any more than the polygraph expert could proclaim Johnson's innocence. The polygraph exam was not admissible at all, and the therapist could testify only about general patterns of behavior in such young children.

Not long ago, therapists were more readily accepted as expert, but then came a string of problematic prosecutions in which the truth proved elusive. Lawyers found that various therapists held differing opinions. So had I. In 1984, I talked with several therapists who'd questioned the children involved in a reported sexual abuse ring in Jordan, Minnesota. Some of the therapists flatly told me that such young children could never make up specific sexual stories or lie about who molested them, some explained at length why and how the children could be led into saying anything, and a good number said they just didn't know.

The accusations against the Johnsons didn't involve the type of custody dispute that often generates false reports. All the specialists who talked to the little girl believed her, without qualification. So did others, though, who'd done nothing more than read the case file. "You develop where you don't trust anyone in this business," the therapist had told me as I was leaving her office. Had their constant exposure to abhorrent behavior sharpened these people's instincts or left them overly inclined to make their case?

Why would this little girl single out Adam's daddy if she wasn't telling the truth? Why would the Johnsons be urging an unrestricted examination of their now-closed case if their statement wasn't true?

These were the two unimaginable possibilities in the Johnson case. But one had to be true.

Three weeks and one day after Sam Rowan first arrived on their doorstep, another caseworker called the Johnsons, their first contact with the DCS since that indelible Sunday.

"Is your father-in-law still staying there with you?" the caseworker asked Julie.

"What?" Julie said. She was incredulous. David's father had left after the first two nights.

Following the initial contacts, it turned out the DCS file had gone to a regional office whose jurisdiction includes the Johnsons' home. From what I was later told, it seems likely the Johnson report went to the bottom of one caseworker's pile there, since it had already been acted upon, and didn't reach the top for three weeks.

"No, my father-in-law is no longer at our house," Julie said.

"Didn't you have a deal with the police that he was to stay until your children got scanned?" the caseworker asked.

"Let me tell you about that scanning . . ." Julie began.

When she'd heard all of Julie's story, the caseworker proposed that they start over: She wanted to come visit them. She wanted the Johnsons to take their children for the scan team exam they'd never received. If their pediatrician and the scan team said they were okay, the caseworker suggested, then we'd close the case.

David, bristling when he heard of this proposal, called the new caseworker's supervisor and protested: "My kids are safe. Our pediatrician will tell you the same thing. I am not going to allow you people to do any more harm to my family."

Five days later, on Friday, having heard nothing more, David called both the detective and the DCS. Later that day, he wrote in his log: "I asked the detective straight out whether there were plans to charge me or not. In a disappointed tone he said as far as he was concerned the case was closed and after our last discussion he never wanted to talk with me again. . . . I then called the DCS supervisor and asked what was happening with them. She then rifled through her papers trying to remember my case and who I was. After a few minutes she found it and informed me that the caseworker had called our pediatrician and they also had closed the case. I didn't bother asking her why she hadn't called to tell me that."

In time, I learned there never had been much likelihood of the Johnsons being charged or prosecuted. In fact, not much of anything had been happening during the three long weeks their case hung in limbo.

The police detective had interviewed the little girl and her family, the girl's psychologist and physician, and the Johnsons. That was all. There'd been no deeper look at the Johnsons, no additional questioning of their son Adam after Sam Rowan's few minutes with him that first Sunday night. Nor had anyone further assessed the little girl's family, or looked there for a possible molester. The district attorney's office had not asked for more. There was no point.

"In a sense, the case was doomed from the start," Detective Sullivan explained. "I knew it wasn't going anywhere. You tend to categorize cases when you get them. This one, soon as I picked it up, I saw that there were no witnesses and the victim was a very young age. Everyone who talks to her could be said to have asked leading questions. At that age, she has to be led. To not prosecute was an agonizing decision, but it wasn't a close one. It was inevitable. It's just that no one wanted to make it."

"I'm not going to tell you this guy did it or did not do it, because I don't know," said the deputy district attorney in charge of the case. "There's a very good chance this happened as the little girl said. But 'probably' is the threshold in civil cases, not criminal prosecutions. I have rules as a prosecutor. In this situation, the ball is in the [accuser's] court, and it's difficult for a little girl like that to get on the stand. What you need is an older child, or an adult eyewitness, or corroboration. It's an imperfect system. You have to balance between the needs of a small child and the whole panoply of constitutional rights. That balance causes the imperfection."

After the case was dropped, David and Julie—angrier at the minister than at the DCS caseworkers, whom they believed simply were doing their jobs to the best of their abilities and training—demanded and got a meeting with church leaders. There, accompanied by David's parents, they expressed their grievances, while the minister disputed their perception of his role. The Johnsons requested a written apology. None was offered.

Back home later that night, David wrote in his log: "I really feel they're ignorant of what is the right thing and need the advice of counsel to tell them. That is quite sad since counsel really is not concerned with doing the right thing. They are only concerned with not doing the wrong thing."

When they met with me, the Johnsons talked at length about their feelings of frustration and shame and isolation. They were avoiding involvement with the children or the parents at the new school where they'd placed Adam. "Kids can come over, but their parents have to be here with them," Julie said. "Or we go to the park."

Of course, the little girl's family also was feeling great pain. I repeatedly called their house, but heard only the little girl herself, speaking sweetly on a phone answering machine. If I could have visited them, I very well might have found another anguished journal in their home, and certainly feelings of grief and anger. Weeks after first reporting the molestation, they sent to the DCS's Sam Rowan a single-spaced five-page letter recounting in fine detail everything their daughter had told them about the molestation. They had their own frustrating meeting, this one with the deputy district attorney and detective, who explained why they couldn't prosecute the case. Then the family learned I was working on this story and through a lawyer asked that it not be published, or at least not identify them. Later, they wrote their own letter to my editors, strongly protesting what they understood to be this article's fundamental themes.

They objected to any story that equated the plights of victims and accused molesters, or cast doubt on disclosures of sexual abuse. They feared that the story I was preparing would "make it sound like a gray fog in which all questions are open, in which guilt or innocence has no clear meaning, and therefore in which children's reports may, or may not, be true." They believed that the "implicit message" of such an article would provide a "green or amber light to molesters and will allow horrors, such as that inflicted on our daughter, to continue." Objecting to my connection with Julie Johnson, they suspected that this article's intent might be to "plant a public relations piece in a local newspaper as part of an accused, but not cleared, child molester's strategy to reclaim apparently lost honor." In urging that this article be "jettisoned," they said "we want to be buffered from the outside world as time and treatment help us."

The last person I spoke with happened to be Detective Sullivan, only because he was on vacation when I'd visited the others. He knew which case I was calling about before I gave him any names. It was still fresh in his mind.

"It was a horrible case," he said. "There are no winners. All losers. I lost sleep over this one. I know the DA did. It's one of those cases where it eats at you. One of the things I told [Johnson] was, 'We'd really like evidence to prove you innocent or guilty, because if you're guilty, you should be tried, and if you're innocent, we want to find out who is out there, victimizing others. . . . But unless someone shows us a better way, this is it. Soon as someone gives us a better way, we'd be more than happy to use it.' "

We were sitting in the cramped cubbyhole office he shares with two other officers. He'd been talking for an hour now, and was finding it difficult to let go of the topic. He lifted a thick pile of pink report forms from the in-basket on his desk and waved them before my eyes.

"Thing is, I have to live with cases like this day in and day out," he said. "This case stands out only because of how vocal the suspect was. Otherwise, it's not unusual. The fact is, more go this way than don't."

I stood to leave soon after, and as I did the detective asked me a question that made me chuckle, because I thought he was kidding. But then he repeated himself, and I saw not humor but yearning in his eyes.

"I mean it," he said. "If you turn up any new evidence, will you let me know? If you learn anything new, will you call me?"

Although the events in this story are factual, all names and certain identifying details have been changed to protect the privacy of the families involved.

A Time to Die

January 1983
Los Angeles, California

John was not the type of person who normally would have wanted to die. He embraced life more than most and he journeyed through it bellowing and roaring. He was large and flamboyant—six feet two inches tall, well over two hundred pounds—and his appetites and interests were powerful and varied. He managed to combine a coarse vulgarity of manner with a refined sensibility. Single conversations with him often included detailed observations about everything from family relationships and sex to automobile carburetors, Cole Porter, Menachem Begin, football and the precise manner in which allergies affect the movement of cilia inside the nose. He was an engineer and could repair everything from cars and water heaters to air-conditioning systems and tape recorders. In his basement workshop he made jewelry, built cabinets, devised electronic gadgets. He liked food. He stocked his kitchen with mustard, salmon, sauerkraut, white pistachio nuts and twenty-pound boxes of hot dogs, all specially ordered from a delicatessen in New York. He bought sides of beef and carved them himself, after asking family members how thick they wanted their steaks. He had definite thoughts about how sharp knives should be, found all restaurant cutlery wanting, and carried a six-inch pocketknife with him for cutting his meat when dining out. "Now this is a knife," he would inform the alarmed waiters, waving it in the air.

Until John was forty, he roared about on a motorcycle, dressed in a black leather jacket and boots, one or the other of his two daughters on occasion riding behind him. He owned a retail shop, among other enterprises, and was not unwilling to accept football bets on the side. Some of his pals were the kind who kept money in ten-thousand-dollar bundles, wrapped in tinfoil in their freezers. Others played golf at local country clubs. He earned enough to provide his wife with a Cadillac, diamonds and a home in an upper-middle-class neighborhood, but he favored trucks and Sears worksuits for himself. He was as likely to enlighten as to embarrass his family. His daughters, Leslie and Cindy, marveled at what they called his "wisdom," but as children they were so ashamed of the rattling van he drove that they'd insist he drop them off a block from school. Then they'd yell, " 'Bye, uncle," as they walked away.

John loved music—jazz, blues, show tunes—and prided himself on a large record collection that included everyone from Cole Porter and George Gershwin to Duke Ellington, Billie Holliday and George Shearing. He had sat in with ad hoc bands ever since he was fifteen, after teaching himself to play the piano, trumpet and guitar. He vainly tried to train his daughters to harmonize on such songs as "You Are My Sunshine," but they did so poorly, he would laugh and give up. "Family is everything," he always reminded them.

It was sixteen years ago, when he was in his late thirties, that John first became sick. He had neck pains. Vision in his right eye sometimes blurred. He became impotent. After a battery of tests, doctors decided he had multiple sclerosis, a degenerative nerve disease with no known cure.

"When he was first diagnosed as having MS," Leslie recalled, "we understood, but it didn't mean much. He was still vital. He still rode his motorcycle around and everything else. We never thought he'd be crippled."

One hot afternoon, as John walked up his driveway after mowing the lawn, his legs, unable to support his weight, quivered and buckled under him. He poked fun at himself, and his family laughed. For the first time, though, John realized his illness was serious. After that, slowly, gradually, symptoms appeared and intensified. He tired easily, he limped, his fingertips became so numb he no longer could make jewelry. About eight years ago, he had to start using a walker to get around. He first needed a wheelchair five years ago. He resisted each stage passionately and insisted on continuing his normal way of living. He also retained his singular character. When he saw someone else in a wheelchair, he usually would nudge a companion and snarl, "Look at that cripple." When the other patient was a woman, he'd sometimes vary the line: "Hey, I think I found a girlfriend."

Many nights, as midnight approached, he would convince exhausted friends and family that the evening was not yet over, then would preside, from his wheelchair, over ribald talk sessions that lasted until four o'clock. Marijuana, inhaled through a giant waterpipe, often fueled these gatherings, for John had discovered it eased his pain.

He remained able to drive for a long time because he outfitted his car with a hand device so he would not have to lift his left leg to operate the clutch. When Leslie was attending college away from home, years after he'd become sick, he could still drive hours to her campus to fix her car.

When his daughters would rail against the unfairness of his suffering, he'd insist that he still believed in God. "He never accepted his disease," Leslie said, "but he saw it simply as a part of life. He never had believed life was fair. No one was to blame."

One week in early 1979, he flew to another city and checked into a hospital for major experimental spinal surgery. Once installed there, he refused to observe the no smoking rule. When the nurses tried to explain that smoking was dangerous because of the oxygen equipment at his bedside, he delivered a learned engineering lecture about why the oxygen equipment could not blow up. The nurses retreated. After his operation, his first act upon waking in his private room was to reach for a long list of every football game being played that day across the country. A moment later, he groggily demanded that his visitor monitor TV news broadcasts for all the scores. When the unfortunate man could not record them fast enough, John growled his displeasure.

Within days, he was ready for dinner at one of the most elegant restaurants in town. In his hotel room, Leslie, eyeing his flowery sport shirt and wrinkled slacks, reminded him that this restaurant required coats and ties. John grinned. "What can they do to a cripple?" he said. He was right—the maître d' even helped carry his wheelchair up the stairs. Once seated at a table (albeit one not too far from the kitchen door), John beamed with appreciation at the background music—Cole Porter's "Begin the Beguine," his favorite song. He ordered duck.

When it arrived, he pulled out his pocketknife and happily tackled his meal.

But John kept getting sicker. When he moved about, he winced in pain and tears came to his eyes. Four years ago, he had to stop driving a car. He tired easily at work and gradually started going to his shop for just half a day, then a quarter of a day. Longtime customers were shocked at how lifeless he seemed. Leslie, who had moved to another city to start her career, was dismayed at his decline each time she returned home to visit.

A year and a half ago, he stopped going to the shop altogether. He became incontinent and largely immobile, but refused to use a catheter or have a full-time nurse, and he would not consider a nursing home. There were accidental bowel movements to clean up. The daughters and their mother had to visit repeatedly during the night to turn him over. "He was disgusted, so disgusted with what was happening," Leslie said. "Once Mom and I were trying to hold him up so we could put a bucket under him to urinate. We were all struggling, and he started crying. 'I'm not human, no human should have to go through this,' he said."

From then on, tears came more often. "He would cry not over his difficulty, which he could handle, but at what he looked like in the mirror," Leslie said. "He saw a totally helpless man who couldn't do the basic functions without help. This was a man who had mastered and shaped his own life, who now couldn't control anything. Before he became sick, he never watched TV. I never remember him sitting around. He was never bored. He was always doing something, building an addition to the house or whatever. Now he was watching *The Brady Bunch* on TV."

Leslie and Cindy acknowledge that the years of accumulated anguish took a toll on their parents' relationship. Their mother had grown heavily depressed and brittle, and physically depleted, from the unremitting misery. She rose at six every morning to open and run the family shop by herself, then retreated, exhausted, to her bedroom by seven every evening. Her weight dropped to ninety-five pounds and Leslie thought she had aged ten years in eighteen months; the family doctor worried as much about her health as her husband's. Meanwhile, their father, who'd always been bossy, now was sometimes petty or abusively demanding. He would force his daughters to drive miles for the particular barbecued ribs he favored. He would insist that only he could eat the bacon or smoked salmon bought for Sunday morning breakfast. He'd berate Leslie when, late at night, after hours of visiting with him, she needed to sleep. Under these conditions, John's wife at times could not hide from him her feelings of resentment and hostility. The daughters also wearied of the unending anguish and pressures, but they were better at masking their feelings.

About a year ago, John finally gave in and accepted the aid of full-time nurses—three shifts, around the clock. He took to his bed, grudgingly and out of necessity. "That's when the whole situation really declined," Leslie said. "His health got worse, because it was linked to his mental state." Within three months, he lost control of all functions. Nurses had to feed him. He urinated through a catheter. For hours on end, John would sit on the edge of his bed, hunched over, deeply depressed, thinking to himself. He started telling his family that he was not serving any function and should be dead. A psychiatrist visited him twice. "We'd say, 'No, no,' and dismiss his talk of dying," Leslie said. "We just denied it all. But he'd continue. And we'd keep saying, 'No, we need you.' Still, he just grew worse. He was in so much mental anguish, so miserable. It was so bad."

John began asking various friends for help in killing himself. "If I were a sick horse, they'd have shot me," he would tell them. "If I were a sick dog, they'd have given me a shot." But his friends refused, and John never asked his daughters directly.

Then, one year ago, Leslie and Cindy on their own began thinking about helping their father die. "I started to think, maybe if this is what he wants, I want it for him," Leslie said. "When I came home to visit then, I could see he had lost something—a fight. When I saw him, I could see this wasn't him anymore. Because he'd been so vital and adventurous, I really needed to know he wanted to die. It was difficult. When I visited, he'd be so lively and fun. We'd stay up late, talking and laughing. It was so great. But he'd remind me that I'm only home two weeks a year. I'd point out that other people come over. I would see how much he added to their lives. They looked up to him. He'd tell me that was only one hour a day, and what about the rest of the time. I was so ambivalent."

What followed was a litany of horror stories, spiced with John's particular brand of macabre humor. He attempted repeatedly, but vainly, to kill himself.

In April of 1982 he tried to starve to death, drinking only juice and eating a cracker when he felt nauseated. He had already lost considerable weight because of his illness, so by May, his once husky body had shriveled to 130 pounds. Leslie hurriedly flew home that month after her mother called to say she thought he was dying. When she entered his bedroom, Leslie thought her father looked like a survivor from a concentration camp. She rarely left his room that day—they spent hours talking. Later, in bed, across the hall from his bedroom, she listened to him all night long, moaning and groaning. "It was so painful," Leslie said. "He had bedsores through to the bone. I can't even imagine what he was experiencing, both physically and emotionally."

One morning that month, while Leslie and Cindy sat with him in his bedroom—he had taken to sardonically calling it his "cell"—Cindy finally spoke the words: "Dad, if you want to die so bad, we'll help you. We'll get you pills." His response was one of overwhelming joy. "A big wave of relief swept over him," Leslie said. " 'You don't know what this means to me, that you'd be there and help,' he said. His emotion was so genuine. It was enormous. It gave me comfort, it made me feel it was right, to see this great relief in him. He started being happy, acting like his same old self. We went on after that, joking and talking about all kinds of things, just as in the past."

Leslie, though, soon had second thoughts. "Telling your dad, 'Okay, take your life'—that's a very hard thing. I didn't worry whether it was right or wrong to help him. I had no problem with that. But it was difficult to think that Dad, who had more lust for life even in his condition than anyone I've known, wanted to kill himself. I was puzzled."

Cindy was more certain: "He was such a vital man that there wasn't a doubt in my mind that he couldn't live like that, that death was so much more preferable. I didn't need assurance. I knew that whenever he made a decision it was made rationally, fully thought out, pros and cons examined. I believed in him. . . . Suicide suggests someone who gave up, who is cowardly, but I looked at it as Dad being able to exert control over his life again. It was in keeping with his personality, the way he's always been. I felt very proud."

Leslie and Cindy continued talking to and questioning their father for the next several days, hours at a time. "He kept trying to assure us that this is what he wanted," Leslie said. Finally, the daughters agreed to get the pills. Over several days, they managed to collect twenty-three tablets of fifty-milligram Demerol, a morphine-type pain killer.

Still, though, they hesitated, unable to shake an unsettling thought. Leslie and Cindy were worrying that their father wanted to die only to end his family's suffering. Their concerns, in truth, could not be easily dismissed. John had become a burden. His wife by now was virtually barricading herself in her bedroom most nights, unable to face the life beyond that door. Leslie and Cindy, watching this retreat, knew they were witnessing the loss of a mother as well as a father. They couldn't help but long for a single stroke that would at least bring her back, that would make their home normal again.

Visiting their house regularly, one of John's friends, a younger man named Brian, could sense this mood, and it made him feel greatly conflicted. On the one hand, he told others he was outraged that his friend was "forced by society and laws to just linger, with no cure, when he was so really miserable. . . . He should be able to check himself into a hospital and ask to be deceased, as long as he can pass tests as to his mental capacity." All the same, Brian himself refused to help John die, and he held this position partly because of the strained, grim moods he'd sensed in his friend's family. "He feels he's a burden to his family and friends," Brian explained to an acquaintance. "He might be more willing to bear his situation if he felt wanted and needed."

It was a thin line, Brian sensed, between giving someone permission to die and giving a message that he's expected to fold up his tent because he's a burden. There was the potential for abuse. It was quite possible that a person would choose death—that was no more unreasonable than other decisions such as whom to marry or whether to have a child—but there was something about what Brian knew of human nature that made him wary. It was just so normal to wish for escape from sick people, and so easy, as a result, to encourage their surrender. Whatever he thought of John's particular case, Brian was sure, at least, that legal killings should never be made public policy.

John's daughters flat out disagreed. When such issues arose, Cindy would erupt, talking bitterly about convicted murderers who were executed by lethal injection. One day when the newspapers were filled with reports of just such an event in Texas, she pointed to the headlines and snarled: "That guy got to die peacefully, while my dad goes through all this horror. When I hear about stuff like this, it turns my stomach. Last wishes, meals he wants, friends around. All my dad has to do is murder someone and he can go that way too."

One evening, the whole family met in John's bedroom. His wife said she loved him. She said she needed to know he didn't want to die because of her own sometimes bleak feelings. Then the husband and wife held hands, hugged, kissed. Cindy cried. Leslie was comforted by her parents' warm display—an uncommon scene in recent years.

Soon after, at three o'clock one afternoon in early summer, the daughters were sitting with their father in his bedroom, watching

Barnaby Jones on television. "Okay, give it to me," he said, suddenly. Cindy took the bottle and poured the pills down his throat. John told his daughters to leave. They hesitated. "Leave now. Get out of here," he insisted. He smiled. "I guess I won't find out if Barnaby Jones gets his man."

The daughters, crying, drove to Cindy's apartment. They called two friends and their mother. At six-thirty, they drove back to their parents' house. Their father was sleeping deeply—something he hadn't done for months. They prepared for his death. At ten, the night nurse looked in his bedroom, then came out to the living room. "Leslie and Cindy," she said, "he wants to see you. He asked to see you."

Stunned, they entered his bedroom. Their father was awake. "If these are the pearly gates of heaven," he growled, "it sure looks like my cell." The daughters started laughing hysterically. They celebrated. "I was so relieved," Leslie said. "I was sad in a way, knowing what was ahead in terms of his pain, but I was so happy he was alive. It was almost supernatural. I thought he was God, immortal. He'd taken twenty-three Demerols and slept just six hours."

John, dazed and shocked, remained awake all night. In the morning, he began hemorrhaging, and his blood pressure plummeted. His family and the morning nurse insisted he be taken to a hospital, but he refused. "I'll die this way," he said. He bled all day, growing weak and ashen. At eleven, overwhelmed by pain, he finally relented and told the night nurse to call an ambulance.

Back at home, in July, he tried to die again, this time with a combination of fifty pills. Again, he slipped into a deep sleep, and again he woke up. He and his family by now were numb, but John and his daughters still found reason to laugh. They joked together about John being an indestructible god. "I sure can't die," he would say.

A friend from out of town came to visit John late one evening in July and found him almost completely paralyzed, in constant pain, unable to shift his body into a comfortable position. During a three-hour conversation, John repeatedly had to ask his friend to lift him and shift his position, to light his cigarette, to raise a glass of water to his lips. Their conversation ranged over many topics—John's daughters, his wife, Las Vegas, car engines, local politics. John said he was grateful for the chance to "talk to someone with a mind." At one point, he switched on the television to watch ABC's *Nightline*. The show that night featured Israel; John still had enough energy and interest to deliver an elaborate lecture on Middle East politics.

Then he brought up his failed suicide attempts. Talking with neither bravado nor pity, in a matter-of-fact tone, he described his constant pain—by now impervious to even the most powerful medications—and the frustration of not being able to move his body. "There's nothing left for me to do," he said simply. He insisted he was in no way happy that his suicide attempts had failed. He was going to try again, he said, this time with a gun. He'd always loved guns, and that was the way to go. He was having a friend—not a family member—rig a rifle so he could pull the trigger with what little movement he had left in one hand. He raised his hand and squeezed slightly. "I'm practicing," he said. "I'm in training." He grinned with pleasure and anticipation.

Soon after, John demanded a brass urn for his room and started asking everyone to bring him canes of all sorts. He sent Brian for one. His wife had to buy three. "The whole time, everyone thought he was going mad, asking for all those canes," Cindy said. "But his mind was working. He was always one step ahead of everyone. He needed a place in his bedroom to hide his rifle."

One day near the end of the summer, John called Cindy to his bedroom and told her to look in the brass urn filled with canes. She saw the rifle.

"I can't help with a gun," she told him. "Anything but a gun. I'm afraid of them."

"Please help me," he implored.

Cindy weighed the legal implications—"what would happen to me after he was gone?"—but in time she agreed.

Leslie, at home in another city, warned by Cindy, called her father. "We talked for half an hour. I told him he was the most important thing in my life, that I loved him. He told me he was sure of what he was doing. He really sounded good, up. He was still joking."

John's wife knew what was happening but kept her distance. She called Cindy at one point during the day and talked casually about dinner plans. Did Cindy think Dad would want chicken? she asked. "Mom, what are you talking about?" Cindy snapped. "Dad's not going to be here by dinnertime." Her mother hung up.

In midafternoon, John called Cindy into his bedroom and told her exactly how to position the rifle between his legs. She needed two hands to lift the heavy firearm. She was afraid it would go off. She used Kleenex to avoid fingerprints. "I didn't think he would die. I really didn't want him to die, for my own selfish reasons," Cindy said later. "I thought he was immortal. I thought it's not going to happen, even though the gun was there. I thought I'd see him again. I'd visit him in the hospital tomorrow."

Her dad smiled, lying there with the gun across his body. "Let's talk," he said. Cindy could not talk. "Maybe you'd better go then," he said. She said she loved him, turned on the cassette tape recorder by his side, and left. It was 3:45 P.M.

"There's a time to be born and a time to die," John said into his tape recorder. His voice was quavering and he was crying softly. "And my time to die is now." He explained that he had been severely depressed for several months and that this was no way to live. He thanked his lawyer, wife and friends. He said good-bye to his daughters, leaving each a personal message.

"I think I'll smoke another cigarette and sit here and think awhile," he said finally.

To Leslie, what followed was in some way appropriate to her father's nature. Pulling the trigger on the rigged rifle was not as easy as John had imagined. The last ten minutes of the tape are a tortured record of him struggling with the string, breathing heavily and cursing vividly. "This goddamn thing is harder than I thought," he grunts at one point. Then comes the explosive noise of a rifle being fired.

The police knew this was not a simple suicide, because the rifle was modified. There were questions. Soon after John's death, two detectives appeared at the family's store. Carl, the shop manager, wouldn't let them talk to anyone in the family. The detectives asked who had modified the gun. "I don't know," Carl said. "But John had a thousand friends. Any one of them would have done it for him."

Time has not softened the daughters' feelings. They deeply miss their father, and they cannot stop thinking about the manner of his death.

"I have trouble with the violence of the whole thing," Leslie said. "When I think of him sitting there, struggling with the gun, when I listen to the tape of what he was going through those last ten minutes, it's hard."

"I find it difficult to think that a man who gave so much to so many had to die alone," Cindy said.

However, the daughters do not for a moment believe they did wrong by helping their father die. Leslie allows that her family might indeed have conveyed certain unhappy signals to him, and she acknowledges that her father felt himself to be a burden. Okay, she agrees, his desire for death came partly from that feeling—"among a combination of things." But in the end, she says, "being the type of man he was, he would have felt he was a burden no matter what we did. When he lost total control of all his functions, that's when he started feeling he was a burden. . . . I can think of no greater pain for him than just to be nonfunctional. Any kind of torture would have been better. His lust for life could only take him so far. When you have that lust, and you're so confined, what is there to live for?"

Talk of fine lines and potential abuse and all that just does not move Leslie anymore.

"All the people who say this is wrong, he shouldn't kill himself, we shouldn't have helped—how many of them have such an awful disabling disease, or have someone close who is suffering?" she asks. "Those who debate ethics, they don't know. I assure you, if they had to go through what we did, their attitudes would change."

As she speaks, Leslie's expression is unreadable, her eyes flat brown stones. This demeanor remains no matter what direction the conversation takes. These days, Leslie does not appear easily affected by anything.

The Pendulum Swings

February 1989
Des Moines, Iowa

There was a time not that long ago when few would have listened to Michael Hall's outburst at the Broadlawns Medical Center in Des Moines. Hall, after all, was a patient in Broadlawns's psychiatric ward, involuntarily committed, and he seemed obsessed. Here was a short, loud man of thirty-one years, with long brown hair reaching to his shoulders, telling everyone that his wife Joan had yanked their infant son by the arms.

He'd been brought to the ward the previous evening by a Polk County sheriff's deputy, after an eventful afternoon that included drinking a case of beer, fighting with his wife, waving a knife, cutting his own chest, and hurling the blade into the floor. His wife Joan and a neighbor had signed the emergency commitment papers. While being led away, Hall had told his wife: "If I can't have the baby you're not going to have him." Now, talking to psychiatric caseworker Toni Brown the next morning, July 6, 1988, he sounded determined to keep the conversation focused on his wife's treatment of their son. He did not feel he or Joan could care for their baby. The infant, he said, should be placed in a foster home.

In the following days, investigators and doctors could find no evidence of abuse or physical harm. The baby appeared healthy and happy, and a judge concluded the arm-yanking had never happened. All the same, Polk County authorities' interest in the Hall family did not entirely abate. If just a handful of years ago the Halls' unfortunate lives would have remained a matter for them to endure in private, this no longer was the case.

By the middle of the 1980s, Iowa and many other states were seeing unprecedented numbers of abuse cases and a huge increase in demand for treatment services. Fueled by public outrage over several horrifying, much-publicized reports of battered children's deaths, governments responded with all sorts of programs—child protective investigative units, focus committees, task forces. State legislatures began drafting laws that encouraged social workers to intervene before harm was inflicted, whenever they perceived a potential risk. Agencies that didn't intervene quickly enough were finding themselves on the receiving end of million-dollar lawsuits and, occasionally, criminal prosecutions. "If this same case came up five years before," observed William Ketch, an Iowa Department of Human Services (DHS) district administrator, "the baby might have been removed, but if so, it would have been the work of one lonely social worker fighting a bunch of lawyers." It being 1988, the Halls instead encountered a multidisciplinary government team exceptional for its speed and depth.

At 9:02 P.M. on July 5, a DHS oncall worker logged Broadlawns Medical Center's referral of Mike Hall's abuse report. By 10:30 the next morning, child protective investigator Phyliss Franklin had the case. By 10:45 A.M. she had checked the state's central registry, seeking any past allegations against Joan Hall, and had found none. By eleven, she was at the Halls' front door.

No one was home. Franklin left a card, asking the Halls to contact her.

At nine-thirty the next morning, Franklin found Joan Hall in her apartment with the baby. Here was a plain-looking woman of twenty-eight, five feet six inches and 135 pounds, with round glasses and a muted demeanor. She spoke quietly, with little expression. Methodically, she told Franklin her story.

Both Halls came from small Midwest towns and broken homes. He finished the seventh grade, she completed high school. Mike Hall spent some months in a mental health institute as a teenager. Neither had held a job for longer than six months. She'd worked as a cook and waitress, he washing cars and dishes.

In 1979, Joan said, when she was eighteen and unmarried, she had given birth to a daughter, Christina. There were "pressures and problems." A string of abuse reports soon accumulated—Franklin hadn't found them in the central registry because they were listed under Joan's maiden name. Authorities finally placed Chrissy in a foster home when she was seven months old, but two years later they gave her back to Joan, who by then was married and had another daughter, Jessica. That first husband drank, abused her and resented Chrissy, Joan said. She also boozed and did drugs in those days. In fact, she was speeding on uppers the night Chrissy died. Chrissy had thrown up and wet her pants, Joan explained, so she'd gotten angry, lost control, pushed Chrissy against a wall. Chrissy had fallen. She was just lying on the floor, her body moving funny. Joan had called her name but she hadn't answered.

After Joan pled guilty to voluntary manslaughter, a juvenile judge had terminated her parental rights to Jessica, her other child, and sent Joan to prison, where she took parenting classes and visited a counselor weekly. Three and a half years later, in January 1987, the corrections department had paroled her, releasing her to a drug and alcohol treatment facility in Des Moines called IAUP.

That's where she met Mike Hall. He arrived at IAUP the same month, also through a court order, which had been issued because of a drunken suicide attempt. There was a wife and child somewhere in his past, Joan said, but he'd been living for several years in his parents' basement, unemployed, selling blood at a plasma center twice a week for money to buy alcohol and drugs. It was in that basement that he'd tried to hang himself with an electrical cord.

Joan and Mike had married in April and left the IAUP program against their counselors' wishes, Joan explained. Mike had an explosive temper and a taste for alcohol and drugs. The couple separated four times in their first months together. He sometimes bruised her and once bit her. They were separated when Joan learned in early August she was pregnant. She called Hall and talked about the idea of getting an abortion. After weighing alternatives, Hall moved back into the apartment.

"We had wanted to have a baby but not quite that soon," Joan Hall observed. "But we were happy about it."

Michael Lee Hall was born May 18, 1988. Two weeks later, the proud parents visited their alma mater, the IAUP center, to show the counselors their newborn. Since then, Mike Hall has continued to fight with her, Joan said. That's why she committed him to Broadlawns. But he has never physically harmed the baby.

Phyliss Franklin looked about her when Joan finished her troubled story. She was a hard-nosed veteran who'd stuck it out in what is regarded as a burnout position, and her experiences had seasoned her attitudes. She saw what she considered to be a spotless apartment, adequately furnished. The baby Michael Lee was clean and appeared very healthy. The interaction between the mother and child appeared most appropriate. Joan Hall was tender and comforting to the baby when he fussed.

All the same, Franklin felt concern, so in the following days, she made a number of calls. When she phoned the Halls' pediatrician, he too reported that the baby always seemed clean and healthy, the mother appropriate and caring. Recent X rays of the baby, he said, showed no hidden fractures or broken bones. When Franklin interviewed the neighbors, they also described Joan as loving and attentive. They regularly saw the baby nestled happily in her arms. They sometimes left their own children with Joan.

The neighbors, however, could not be as encouraging about Mike Hall. They said he drank and smoked dope. He would rant and rave at Joan while she cradled their baby in her arms. He would just "go off," staring into space and losing control. Sometimes Joan would retreat to a neighbor's apartment, the baby in her arms. Sometimes neighbors would come out and intervene. Sometimes neighbors would take the baby to their apartments. The police showed up often.

Franklin could take some comfort in noting that at least Mike Hall was no longer residing in the home. That circumstance, however, soon changed. Three days after being committed to Broadlawns, Hall faced a hospital hearing. His chief examiner, Dr. Karl Northwall, decided he carried diagnoses of alcohol abuse, marijuana abuse and antisocial personality disorder—but no psychotic mental disorders. Hall presented a danger to others when drunk, but so did many others, the doctor reasoned. Hall got drunk a lot, but so did many others. Northwall figured he couldn't lock them all up. Broadlawns released Hall on July 8.

Eight days after the Broadlawns commitment, the Halls were back together. What's more, now Hall was saying he'd made up the arm-yanking story. Accordingly, when Franklin made an unannounced visit one day, Hall seemed less than pleased with her involvement in their lives. His body and hands started shaking. His eyes appeared to Franklin to change color and focus. He would do the talking, he yelled. He would tell them what he would allow and not allow. He had no problem with someone coming to check on his baby, as long as it didn't get to be too much. He did not want anyone telling him what he had to do or how to live in his own home. If it got to be too much, he would take his wife and child and leave the state and they would never find him.

Franklin, retreating in alarm, had much to consider. The Halls' lives were a sorry mess, but in this they were far from alone. If government agencies removed babies from every house where angry parents fought and abused alcohol and drugs, they would need millions of foster homes. On the other hand, all the ingredients involved in the death of Joan's daughter Chrissy seemed to be in place again: an abusive, addictive husband; violent fights between the parents; alcohol and drugs; money problems; isolation from family or community support; an infant going through the stages of soiling his pants and spitting up.

Which kind of gamble, Franklin wondered, should the state take? Put another way, what type of mistake would she, herself, rather make?

The impulse to protect children brings with it various uncertainties. Bruises and broken bones can be seen, but potential risk must be divined. Parents come in all sorts of stripes, many not so attractive. When should authorities intervene and how to decide? What is the threshold of risk? Is it to be judged by gut instinct or statistics or cultural sensibilities? Are the alternative foster homes any better? Public officials traditionally have balanced their obligation to protect children against the rights of families to be left alone. The balancing act shifts regularly, in tune to public opinion, the law and a host of less visible considerations.

The civil rights of parents, a sense of fairness and the drive to keep families together create pressure of one sort. Removing a child is a traumatic experience for all concerned, especially with infants at a critical stage of bonding. Finding a better alternative is highly problematic, given an acute national shortage of adequate foster homes. Parents' rights groups do not hesitate to speak out. Many complain that cultural biases often guide state agencies, leading them to move most frequently against the poor, uneducated or unconventional. Arguments offered by mothers deprived of their children also can be affecting. "It's pretty discriminating to act before even giving a human being a chance," said Joan Hall, defending her own cause. "We never abused our baby. He is our child. He needs to grow up in our family. I feel like I'm on trial again for what happened to Chrissy in 1982. I've served time for that. The sentence didn't say I couldn't have other children. . . . Nobody said I could never have kids again."

The prospect of a child's being harmed, on the other hand, creates a different type of pressure. Caseworkers and judicial officers have seen enough brain-dead children and cocaine-addicted infants to shake even the most deeply felt liberal political tenets. The benefit of the doubt, they often end up thinking, should go to the child. "You lie awake at night and say, 'Oh, I hope I did the right thing,' " said John Fairweather, a DHS bureau chief. "If we take a kid out because of imminent danger, we're accused of busting up a family. If we leave a kid home, everybody thinks we don't care. . . . The public doesn't want authorities busting in on families, but the public also doesn't want kids hurt. The pendulum swings on this."

In the Hall case, as it happened, another more particular pressure eventually emerged to complicate the usual concerns about public opinion and pendulums. During her investigation, Franklin learned that a million-dollar lawsuit was pending against the Iowa DHS, filed years ago by Chrissy's paternal grandparents, who'd charged the Iowa DHS with negligence in Chrissy's death. The lawsuit, it turned out, was due to come to trial within weeks. What's more, because of the lawsuit, the local *Des Moines Register* was planning to publish a three-part anatomy of Chrissy's death.

Perhaps Iowa authorities were correct in their later insistence that lawsuits and news articles played no role in their Hall case decisions, even though by then they'd found it wise to settle the lawsuit filed by Chrissy's grandparents for seventy thousand dollars. There were, after all, plenty of other elements to consider. Whatever the mix of reasons, the Polk County system in mid-July 1988 began to move decisively against the Halls. DHS supervisors were briefed, meetings held, prosecutors and juvenile court officials consulted. On July 26, a special Polk County multidisciplinary team of experts unanimously recommended immediate removal of the baby. They did not believe the baby had been abused, but they feared he would be harmed in the future. At 3:30 P.M. the DHS obtained a court order.

Joan was sitting in her living-room rocking chair, feeding Michael Lee, when the Halls heard a knock. It was five o'clock. Hall opened the door to four people—two uniformed police officers, another in plainclothes, and a woman named Candace Bennett from the juvenile court. The one in plainclothes handed Mike the documents.

"We have an order for the removal of your son," he said.

Joan started crying. She clutched hard at her baby. Candy Bennett reached down to take the infant.

At noon two days later, the Hall case file came before yet another Polk County advisory body, a group of doctors called the pediatric consultation team. Their task normally is to judge whether a child has been abused, and in what manner. The Hall case represented the first time they were being asked to consider the risk to a child who had not yet been abused.

"We needed some way to show the risk," said Dr. Rizwan Shah. "We needed a scientific way to make the judgment."

The doctors found what they needed in a recent edition of the journal *Child Abuse and Neglect*. A team of doctors had studied forty-five abusive parents at a large urban medical center's child abuse program, matching them against twenty-two different variable factors bearing on reabuse. Joan and Mike Hall's profiles were full of those factors. According to the report, the range of risk for families such as the Halls ranged from sixteen to sixty-six percent. The Polk County pediatric consultants fixed the Halls' risk factor at precisely forty percent.

"Once the government gets into the business of protecting, there is no alternative but to get involved in the prediction game, whether you like it or not," observed Randall Wilson, an Iowa Civil Liberties Union attorney who represented the Halls' baby. "In the old days, they might take away a child on instinct. Now we must prove it, have due process, base it on something, even if it is our myth. Statistics and risk calculations are what we use. I don't think they are a myth, unless science is a myth. It's what we rely on."

To arrive at answers in the Hall case, Juvenile Court Judge Larry Eisenhauer presided over three hearings—one in August on whether to continue the emergency removal, a second in October to determine if Michael Lee was a child in need of assistance, and a third on December 8 to decide where to place the baby. The hearings unfolded in a small room on the fourth floor of the Polk County courthouse. Four lawyers ringed the conference table, one each representing the county attorney, the baby, Mike Hall and Joan Hall. Rob Garver and Tom McCann, the Halls' attorneys, were both court-appointed.

They had spent the past weekend painting the baby's bedroom, the Halls told the court at the October hearing. They had bought a dog. They had jobs now. They liked their jobs. They were renovating an upstairs apartment for the landlord to get a free month's rent.

What about baby expenses? Hall was asked. After all, their combined annual incomes totaled just $6,700, with both working part time at a minimum wage job sorting mail for a private firm. Sitting on the witness stand, Hall dutifully produced the family budget, scribbled on a wrinkled piece of paper. He stared at his budget. "I can just stop drinking pop. I spend thirty, forty dollars a week on pop. I don't need that."

Joan Hall took the stand. She too studied the budget. She spotted an item from the previous week's expenses. "We can get by without ordering that Domino's pizza," she said. "One pizza costs the same as a pack of sixty diapers. We don't need pizza."

The Halls' lawyers, meanwhile, labored mightily to unravel the meaning of the risk factors attached to their clients. They grilled the doctors. "No, I cannot pick out who will abuse and who will not," allowed Dr. Fred Aldrich from the pediatric consultation team. "I can say you have a high or higher likelihood of abusing. I cannot say this person will reabuse. If I could, I would not be here. I would be saying sooths." Garver and McCann were beside themselves. Risk factor analysis seemed quite an ephemeral tool to use against their clients. How did they get those figures? Above all, how could the figures be reduced so the Halls could get their baby back?

The Halls have modified their behavior since the baby was removed, the lawyers pointed out. They were living in a new, clean apartment with an extra room for the baby. They were attending Alcoholics Anonymous meetings and hadn't had a drink in three months. They weren't fighting. Wouldn't all that change the risk factor?

"No . . . I can't change my opinion," Aldrich said. "That's still the way I would see it."

How could they reduce the risk? The lawyers pawed through their notes, as if looking there for answers. "But that forty percent risk factor," Garver sputtered, "it's based on elements in the Halls' past, elements that are not true today."

"Do you have a question?" the judge interrupted.

"I'm working on it," Garver said.

He paced around the table, then sat down, staring at his notes.

"No further questions."

Garver's difficulty was understandable. He was, after all, fighting an invisible opponent. At the core of the Hall case sat an unspoken notion, an unacknowledged implication: If government agencies are going to remove children from people such as the Halls on the basis of potential risk, are not they bound to seize newborns from all parents who are innately, chronically at high risk? And if so, given that the parents' conditions are innate and chronic, how could the babies ever be returned?

A fair share of child protection officials, weighed down by what they see daily, flirt with such uncomfortable questions privately, but most hesitate to face them publicly. Instead, authorities talk of "due process" and handling matters "case by case." On the witness stand at the Halls' hearing, for example, the doctors said the Halls' risk could be reduced but not eliminated by "longterm multipart therapy."

The Halls, however, are regarded as high risks simply for who they are. Longterm multipart therapy seems unlikely, since Joan Hall carries a ten-year history of refusing and remaining impervious to all manner of counseling services. She rejected three assistance programs and canceled half a dozen appointments with social workers in the weeks before Chrissy died, and she has done much the same since Michael's birth. In truth, the Halls are not considered likely ever to alter their basic natures—doctors and caseworkers say both of them have basically untreatable antisocial personality disorders. DHS investigator Franklin wrote in her report's conclusion: "It should be noted that this child, Michael Lee Hall, is at risk by the mere fact of his existence. Joan Hall places any child at risk by merely bringing them into the world."

In the end, the Hall case raised, but then did not address, a hard question indeed: Should some people, a good number of people, just not be allowed to have children?

Judge Eisenhauer summoned all the lawyers to his chambers midway through the October proceeding. Unless you've got something to show me, he said, don't drag this out.

Eisenhauer, a limited jurisdiction judge handling only juvenile cases for the past four years, had only once before removed an unabused child. He'd ordered a newborn removed at birth from a woman who had sexually abused her other child. You're saying my client can't have kids, that woman's lawyer had argued. Eisenhauer couldn't refute that. It was true. She was not going to molest another child. She was not going to have a baby in Polk County. "The longer I've been doing this, the easier it is to do," Eisenhauer said in his chambers just before his ruling. "I came from a viewpoint of looking out for everyone's rights. But the nature and severity of the abuses I've seen make it easier to rule on behalf of the child. . . . If the parent has injured children in the past, I'm not bothered much with the thought of removing them as soon as they spit them out."

On November 2, Eisenhauer found Michael Lee to be a child in need of assistance. On December 8, he ruled the baby would remain in foster care while the Halls once more underwent extensive counseling. If the counseling efforts again failed, the court could at a later date terminate parental rights.

That, at least for now, would seem to be the end of the Hall affair. It may not be, however. The Halls are thinking about having another baby.

Mike Hall says he wants one. Joan is not sure. She has had two hard deliveries so far, and worries that authorities will just take away a new baby.

Authorities say if the conditions remain the same, they would do just that. They'd go back to square one and start the whole process over again.

"No they won't," Hall responds, "because they won't know where we are."

Given all their problems, the Halls were asked one recent afternoon, why do they want children?

Mike Hall answered without hesitation. "Because we're not complete," he said.

UPDATE

After the infant Michael was taken away from the Halls, the couple signed a "parent contract" with the county that, if followed, would have eventually reunited them with their child. The Halls continued to have problems, however, and Joan Hall became lax in meeting the contract's terms, which included psychiatric and substance abuse treatment and parenting classes. Eventually, the Halls formally relinquished their rights to their baby, and left the state. Their whereabouts are now unknown—just as Michael Hall predicted.

III

Matters of Science, Matters of Medicine

Unborn Patients

November 1986
Los Angeles, California

I. NOW THERE ARE OPTIONS

Over the last five years, Dr. Greggory R. DeVore has looked at thousands of human hearts, each the size of a thumbnail, and he has learned much from them. He can measure, in a fifteen-week-old fetus, the thickness of the heart wall, the size of the aortic valve, the dimensions of the four heart chambers, the number and nature of the heart's contractions. Drawing on what he has seen, DeVore usually can recognize when something is wrong. That makes him proud. He describes himself as a "fetal advocate."

There are days, though, when his skill leads to a fetus's demise.

One morning in his office at the Genetics Institute in Alhambra, aiming his ultrasound machine at a pregnant woman's abdomen, DeVore saw on the sonar screen one slightly dilated fetal kidney, a small, incidental malformation that could be easily treated. The woman was reassured. Eager to refine his knowledge of fetal hearts, DeVore then chose to look also at the cardiovascular system. He found another malformation, a small hole in the heart, a sort that often closes on its own. He felt pleased with his ability to spot such a subtle defect.

This added news, however, frightened the woman. Soon after, she decided to terminate her pregnancy. When she told him, DeVore winced, fighting a vague apprehension.

If I had not done that, if I hadn't been so thorough, that fetus would be fine, he thought. A lot of folks are born with holes in their hearts and they close after birth. I wish I hadn't turned on the machine.

This is the conflicted world of the newly evolved, highly specialized fetal doctors. Their ability to see and diagnose defects has far outpaced their ability to cure them, or even to describe accurately how they will affect the babies. The chief therapy for most problems remains selective abortion. The doctors' science, transforming the amorphous embryo into an unborn patient, has far outstripped society's concepts about the nature of the fetus, and advancing technology already on the horizon promises even greater complexities. Above all, the doctors deal with uncertainty. Most cases present several choices, none clearly better than the others.

Many diagnoses and prognoses are ambiguous. Doctors can see a microscopic nick on the tip of a chromosome, but they cannot always say what it will mean. They can tell a mother her baby will have spina bifida or Down's syndrome, but they cannot tell her whether it will walk or talk.

Doctors can keep fetuses alive that would not have survived in the past, draining dangerous fluids from heads and kidneys, but when born these babies sometimes are badly retarded or need constant dialysis for chronic kidney failure.

At times mistaken diagnoses lead to termination of healthy fetuses. Overlooked defects lead to the birth of badly damaged babies.

Defects found late in pregnancies, past the time for a legal abortion, force hard decisions about the risks and benefits of intervening aggressively at birth with such procedures as a cesarean section.

Some defects can easily be treated after birth, so raise questions about whether they should be diagnosed at all prenatally, since the chief purpose of such early diagnoses would be to terminate.

Some couples use prenatal diagnosis to learn the sex of their fetus, and abort if it is not what they want.

Knowing these difficulties, more and more couples are nevertheless turning to prenatal diagnosis, three times as many as just a decade ago. Where the doctors once saw only older women, who are at higher risk, they now also see many younger women, under thirty-five. Some seek reassurance, some seek a perfect baby. Some come because a cautious family physician, worrying about lawsuits, wanted a specialist's opinion.

So doctors and patients alike wrestle with an overwhelming wealth of information not available five years ago. Once, babies were either born or they were not. Now there are options.

DeVore, forty, an associate professor of obstetrics and gynecology at the University of Southern California, is among a small but growing group of fetal-maternal experts who face these issues every week. The short list includes two under whom DeVore studied at the Yale University Medical School—obstetrician John C. Hobbins and pediatrician/medical geneticist Maurice J. Mahoney—as well as DeVore's colleagues at the Los Angeles County–USC Medical Center and the private Genetics Institute: Lawrence D. Platt, USC professor of obstetrics and gynecology; Janet Horenstein, USC assistant professor of obstetrics and gynecology; and Robert Wassman, a pediatrician and medical geneticist. They all offer much the same comment about their work. They have little time for philosophy, they say. They are willing to steel their minds and live with complexity and gray areas. They accept their perpetual uncertainty.

The doctors' use of language colors the world of fetal medicine in a manner that is at once obvious and unexamined by those in the field. Termination is the word heard regularly, abortion almost never. The blurred images that fill screen after screen, day after day, get called all manner of names. Dr. Michael R. Harrison at the University of California–San Francisco Medical Center refers to them as "the kids" and sometimes "that guy." Dr. Angela Scioscia, 32, who works with Hobbins and Mahoney at Yale, calls them "the babies," unless she decides they are "little turkeys." Hobbins usually stays with "the embryo." Platt tends toward "the fetus."

The doctors talk without disguise about their limitations, but they also point to triumphant moments when lives are helped and saved. If all our cases ended with abortion or badly malformed babies, they say, we would not do what we do. Couples with known genetic risks or a previous malformed child, who never would have considered having more children, now go forward with pregnancies. Fetuses that would not have survived now are born healthy because doctors can judge when and how to deliver, and arrange for pediatric surgeons to be present in the delivery room, ready to perform immediate procedures.

So there are stories with happy outcomes.

A pregnant woman came to DeVore, already diagnosed through amniocentesis as carrying a fetus with Down's syndrome, a chromosomal defect resulting in retardation of widely varying severity. Many Down's children can live full and happy lives. Sometimes, though, the retardation is accompanied by severe heart malformations, which create greater problems. If the heart is normal, patients often tell DeVore, we will keep this Down's baby, but only if it is normal.

That was what this woman was saying, sitting across from DeVore.

He is a soft-spoken, religious man, a Mormon bishop and the father of seven. He studied his ultrasound screen.

The use of ultrasound waves for medical evaluations is not new, having been first used experimentally in the 1950s, but the techniques and machinery DeVore employs are the products of refinements made only in the last three years. An ultrasound machine, an adaptation of the sonar method used by the U.S. Navy in World War II to detect enemy submarines, works much like the guidance system for a whale or a bat. It sends inaudible high-frequency sound waves through a transducer, a small hand-held device that the doctor moves slowly across the pregnant woman's abdomen. The sound waves reflect off fetal tissue and organs in varying patterns, which are translated by computer and projected on a video screen, creating a blurred, translucent image of the fetus. The most advanced machines now provide images good enough that pregnant women often stare in amazed delight at the screen, waving and talking to their fetuses as they roll and kick before their eyes. The machine, however, requires an educated, practiced eye to sort out the blurred gray shapes and understand what they mean.

It was just such a skill that DeVore now summoned. On the screen, he watched the contractions of the heart wall. By placing and measuring electronic markers on the screen, he gauged whether the heart wall was unusually thick, a condition that results when the heart has been pumping too hard, trying to overcome a problem. He looked for malformations in the chambers. He searched for the ominous black pockets that are evidence of fluid buildup. He studied the shape of the skull and searched for excess fat around the neck, linked by some to Down's babies.

He considered. What he was doing had only been put into clinical use with patients during the last two years. He knew some other doctors did not believe or trust his work, but he believed that was because they did not know enough about his field, echocardiography. He knew his burden. To conclude whether a thumbnail-sized heart was normal probably would decide the fetus's fate and affect the parents in unknown ways. If someone is going to terminate a pregnancy based on my diagnosis, he told himself, I'm going to be sure. But then he thought: We're not perfect. We're not God.

"The heart looks fine," he told the woman.

She decided to continue the pregnancy. The baby was born without a heart defect.

"I asked her after she had the baby, how much did it really make a difference what I had diagnosed," DeVore said later. "She said it made a tremendous difference. 'When you told me my baby's heart was normal, I could then have the courage to continue the pregnancy.' That's the other side of the coin. If we don't do what we do, people would terminate. Parents tell us that. That's how we approach this and that's how we justify it. We're not close to being right-to-lifers, but we are trying to help and prevent. We take the good with the bad. That's why I can keep doing this work."

Much of the time, however, the doctors face situations where they simply cannot provide clear, certain answers, even though they know couples are going to make life-and-death decisions based on what they say.

As Maurice Mahoney sat at his desk in the Yale–New Haven Medical Center one morning, staring at test results, he looked troubled, for he knew he had just such a case before him. His patient, a forty-year-old woman, had undergone a still risky, experimental test called chorionic villi sampling, in which a tissue sample is taken from the outer membrane enveloping the fetus early in its development. CVS detects most of the same abnormalities that amniocentesis does but much earlier, by the ninth week; results of amniocentesis, in which a small amount of amniotic fluid is withdrawn from the uterus by means of a needle inserted through the mother's abdomen, are not available until about the eighteenth week. Now Mahoney had before him what the CVS said about his patient's fetus. What the CVS said was puzzling.

A normal person's cells have twenty-three matched pairs of chromosomes, ordered by number from the largest to the smallest. One of the most common types of chromosomal abnormality is trisomy, an extra chromosome, three rather than a pair of a particular number. An extra twenty-first chromosome, trisomy 21, means Down's syndrome. Trisomies 13 and 18 cause even more severe retardation. Doctors rarely see fetuses with most other trisomies, because they spontaneously abort soon after conception. But the test results on Mahoney's patient indicated trisomy 7, which in its pure form always results in spontaneous abortion.

If the results were accurate, the fetus was doomed. But were they? Mahoney knew the experimental CVS test could have gathered irregular cells not representative of the fetus. Or the trisomy might be present in only a few of the fetus's cells, something the scientists call mosaicism.

Mahoney sighed. Tall, lanky, sometimes darkly contemplative, in his customary running shoes he devours the medical center's hallways with such outsized strides that those walking with him must break into a jog. The father of six, he'd entered pediatrics because he loved children. In a few hours, he knew, he would have to call a couple and present them with not only bad news, but uncertain news. He would urge them to wait a few weeks until they could do an amniocentesis. He hoped that what he said would not frighten them into premature termination.

That night on the phone, the couple listened carefully to Mahoney's words. When he finished, they said only that they would think things over.

The next morning, Mahoney saw further results that showed some cells in the sample to be normal. This fetus was not a pure trisomy 7; this one was either perfectly fine or mosaic, in which case it could survive but have some problems. Mahoney calculated that there now was no more than a twenty-five percent chance trisomy 7 was involved in some way. If an amniocentesis at fifteen weeks and a fetal blood test at nineteen weeks yielded normal results, the chance of any trisomy 7 cells in the baby would be down to one or two percent.

If the couple waited that long, though, the fetus would be approaching twenty weeks. They very much did not want to have a late abortion, after they felt the fetus moving and the pregnancy was physically apparent. That, Mahoney knew, was why they had agreed to the CVS.

Midway through the afternoon, the couple called Mahoney. They had decided, they said, to terminate the pregnancy.

This baby was normal, Mahoney thought. That's the probability.

After the phone call, he sat silently, cupping his hands together, his eyes fixed at a distant spot on the far wall. "I feel uncomfortable to a degree," he said slowly, choosing each word with care. "But not so uncomfortable as to change what I do here. . . . There is a recognition that we aren't perfect, that our attempts to improve people's lives do a fair amount of good and also cause problems."

That same week, Mahoney's colleague John Hobbins also watched an uncertain prognosis lead to a termination. The fetus looked fine, until Hobbins started measuring. He gauged the circumference of the head, the length of the leg, the width of the chest. They were all too small, way too small. Growth was a full month behind schedule. Hobbins considered. When they had gotten the mother off her feet, growth had started, fluid had built up. Maybe the fetus was okay, maybe it would catch up. Still, when the couple asked if the baby was damaged, what could he say? Perhaps its lungs were underdeveloped, or it had suffered neurologic damage from a virus.

Over the next few days, during many phone conversations, Hobbins talked to the prospective parents for a total of four hours. In the end, the couple decided to terminate the pregnancy.

Hobbins by nature is a cheerful man with boundless enthusiasm. The newly evolved technology has transformed what he does, opening new avenues of treatment, making work for him fun, something very exciting. But he was troubled by this couple's decision. "What bothers me," he said later, "is I think we scared the hell out of them. With our inadvertent meddling, maybe we gave them more information than they could handle."

The range of severity in certain maladies makes giving precise prognoses all the more difficult. Doctors, for example, can see fluid on the brain, and they can call it hydrocephalus, but they cannot say how greatly the baby will be retarded. My machine doesn't measure IQ, Larry Platt always tells his patients.

Platt, thirty-eight, talks like that to pregnant mothers, patiently but bluntly. An internationally recognized ultrasound specialist, he is a man of unceasing energy who runs his office at Women's Hospital in Los Angeles like a master of ceremonies, ushering visitors in and out, taking phone calls, making introductions, playing matchmaker.

Neural tube defects such as spina bifida, where the spinal column does not close, are among the toughest for him to judge. Spina bifida is associated with mental and physical defects that vary in degree from mild to severe. Often it involves retardation, lower limb paralysis and lack of bowel and bladder control. Sometimes the defect can be surgically corrected after birth. Sometimes the child does okay on his own. Sometimes the child walks.

Platt, searching for the words as he tries to explain this to patients, thinks to himself: We walk on fine lines all the time. The couples, meanwhile, listen to him, then stare back, expressionless, with no idea of what to do.

Hobbins sees much the same at Yale. "In the past, we used to just diagnose spina bifida," he said. "Now with our more sophisticated stuff, we can tell how big and high on the spine the deformity is. The higher and bigger, the worse the spina bifida is. So that gets us into deciding quality of life. It puts pressure on us to be accurate."

How does he deal with that burden?

"Through a lot of waffling," Hobbins said.

Most of the doctors harbor even greater worries than incorrectly diagnosing a defect. Their greatest fear is that they might intervene to save a doomed fetus, only to have it born severely damaged.

There was, for example, the first blocked bladder Larry Platt ever treated. The pregnant woman had flown in from Las Vegas, her fetus's urinary tract obstructed, the bladder looking on the ultrasound screen the size of a watermelon. They discussed risks and choices, and finally Platt, watching all the time on his sonar screen, guided his needle through her abdomen right to the fetus's bladder. Gently, he pushed the point in, and the fluid drained out. It was a memorable experience, one that placed Platt and the mother on local television when a station did a series on fetal medicine. The fetus survived in the womb to thirty-six weeks, longer than it probably would have otherwise, and then they delivered.

Once the baby was out, though, they found that the enlarged bladder had put pressure on the kidneys and damaged them before Platt ever operated. The child has had chronic kidney failure since birth and has been on constant dialysis.

Platt and his colleagues still have mixed feelings about that one. What they did was logical, they told themselves, but did they do these people a favor or not? The mother, a religious woman, happily embraced her infant, although such babies tend to deteriorate physically and mentally over time. Some pediatric specialists thought Platt was crazy, thought he should have left the fetus alone. One would not talk to him.

"Who knows who's right?" Platt said. "If this baby gets a kidney transplant, it does well maybe. He's three years old now and alive. The next lady who came through the door with the same thing, the kidneys looking even worse, we offered her all the same options and she elected to do nothing but pray. We watched that kid get better in utero without us doing anything. A third time, we had the same type thing, we put one needle in, once, and after that one needle the fetus got better, was fine."

Platt was pacing up and down his small examination room as he spoke.

"What this tells me is that I don't know the rules of the game yet.

Are we tampering with nature? people ask. Oh, sure. But we're tampering by doing cesarean sections all the time. Everything begins with, should we do nothing? In other words, is it 'God's creature,' God's will? I believe God's will is for us to be educated. God's will is for us to learn and study and to improve life."

Like his colleague DeVore, Platt is religious, an Orthodox Jew whose faith allows abortion only if the mother's life is endangered. Neither doctor will himself do abortions. Sometimes, though, Platt finds himself cast as an abortionist.

One morning, a young woman, twenty weeks pregnant, decided to terminate after Platt saw that her fetus had hydrops, its belly and chest a huge black blob, full of fluid. It was Platt's task to call the woman's treating obstetrician with the news. That doctor responded icily. She did not want to see her patient again until after the abortion. You know I'm an ardent right-to-lifer, she told Platt. I won't do any good in this case. Platt drew a breath before responding. "I want you to understand that abortion doesn't come easy to us either," he finally said. "I'm an Orthodox Jew and my partner is a Mormon bishop. We don't do the procedure ourselves. But we don't want to abandon patients. Where would your patient turn to?"

The exchange left him feeling uncomfortable. The other doctor's tone suggested that Platt's job was mainly a search-and-destroy mission. He tried to ignore his discomfort, hoped it would just go away. Then he told himself: I am willing to be uncomfortable.

Doctors sometimes see problems where there are none, creating at the very least unwarranted anxiety.

One day, DeVore saw a pregnant woman, thirty-five weeks along, who had been scanned in the doctor's office by a traveling ultrasound technician. She had been told her baby was a dwarf. For confirmation, her doctor had sent her to a local maternal-fetal specialist at a nearby hospital. The specialist had said the baby's not a dwarf but it has bad kidneys, polycystic kidneys. One doctor had told her that's lethal, another that it could be treated. By the time she reached DeVore, the woman was nearly hysterical. He scanned her and couldn't understand what was going on. This was not a dwarf, the kidneys were normal, the bladder present, the fluid normal. This fetus was absolutely fine. "Go home, don't worry, there is nothing wrong with this baby," he told the mother. "You will have a nice, normal baby."

Sometimes, such misguided diagnoses lead to unwarranted terminations.

Mahoney remembers one such case. A couple's firstborn suffered from a particular type of mental retardation and organ malformation that was marked physically by small dysplastic fingernails. During the second pregnancy, Mahoney and his colleagues were asked to examine the fetus. This was not the type of problem that would show up on amniocentesis, and the sonar screen could not provide a fine enough image. They used instead a fetoscope, essentially a tiny spaghetti-thin periscope, inserting it through the abdomen so they could look directly at the fetus's fingers in the womb.

It was, as always, a judgment call. They had limited experience then, and the few other cases they had seen had been during varying points of gestation. Still, Hobbins and Mahoney both agreed it seemed as though the fingernails were malformed—the fetus looked afflicted. Hearing this news, the family decided to terminate.

Afterward, Mahoney studied the tiny abortus. Try as he might, he could not convince himself that the fingernails were abnormal. Nor could Hobbins or the pathologist. Mahoney was more bothered than the family. On the one hand, he felt unwilling to do such a diagnosis again, given his limited ability. On the other hand, not to try again was to obstruct the learning process. Mahoney also wondered about something else. Would he feel worse if he had told the family the baby was okay and it was not?

Mahoney still does not have the answers, but he has learned to live without them. The troubling cases just do not stay in his mind.

"I let them go," he said late one Friday afternoon. "There are too many new ones next week. If I were a philosopher, I might dwell on them. But I and most physicians are empiric tradesmen. That's what we really are—empiric tradesmen."

II. WRESTLING WITH NATURE

The doctors' diagnoses are not only used to decide whether to abort. Just as frequently they influence how a baby will be delivered. In fact, in fetal medicine, the timing and mode of delivery can itself be a major form of therapy—or an unspoken decision to let a baby die.

For example, when problems are detected late in pregnancies, past the time for a legal abortion, doctors and their patients must decide whether they will opt for a cesarean section delivery if there is fetal distress at birth. Sometimes, the mother flatly says no. Dr. Larry Platt often senses that those women are hoping the fetus will just expire naturally, on its own. He knows that, in a handful of cases, doctors have taken women to court to force them to undergo cesarean sections. He occasionally feels frustrated, feels he should be doing something, but he would never consider such coercive steps. It's the women's choice, he reminds himself. They have a right over their bodies. Decisions are individual. He doesn't have a cookbook on how to do this.

Other times, the doctors themselves are not sure they should try a cesarean section. The procedure involves more risk to a woman than a vaginal delivery, so before cutting open a woman, they want to know what kind of fetus they are trying to save. They often suggest checking, by amniocentesis or a fetal blood sample, to see if the defect is isolated or related to more widespread chromosomal abnormalities.

Making the final decision to intervene is not easy, for each option involves a different mix of risks and benefits. Sometimes they fight, and win. Greg DeVore did that once.

They were twin fetuses, thirty-three weeks along. One developed fluid in the chest and abdomen late in the pregnancy. When doctors deliver a baby in that condition, they must immediately give it oxygen. Fluid-filled lungs, though, won't expand and take the oxygen. Usually, the doctors stick needles in the baby's chest right at birth, try to withdraw the fluid, then quickly pump in the oxygen. This involves tense, tricky timing, though, for they have precious few minutes without oxygen before the baby suffers brain damage. What is more, because ultrasound doesn't work with air, doctors find it hard to see the needle on their ultrasound screen once oxygen enters the infant's lungs. So DeVore and the parents talked over their other options. What they fixed on, DeVore had to admit later, was rather neat. Immediately before the cesarean section, while the fetuses were still in the womb, DeVore studied them on his ultrasound screen, then pushed a needle through the mother's abdomen and into the sick fetus's chest. On his screen, he could see the dangerous fluid spilling out.

"Cut, deliver the baby, ventilate the baby now," he told the obstetrician.

Minutes later, the second healthy infant followed her sister into the world. Just the other week, DeVore received a very nice letter from the mother, thanking him and reporting that both were home and doing fine.

Sometimes the doctors gamble with time, balancing risks and benefits as they judge when to intervene. Janet Horenstein, Platt and

DeVore's colleague, faced just such a task when confronted with a case similar to DeVore's.

Horenstein has performed abortions. Terminating a malformed, nonviable twenty-one-week-old fetus with an extra eighteenth chromosome is easier for her than aborting a relatively healthy fetus visible on a screen, but she handles both, for she's seen plenty of abused, unwanted children, too many. She has also seen her fill of confused, anguished pregnant women. What will my baby be like, they always ask, and what would you do? She tells them: We don't know, we really just provide information.

A fetus, thirty weeks old, had fluid in the abdomen and lungs and a probable heart defect. Horenstein knew that if she tried what DeVore had done, they then would have to deliver immediately. Otherwise the fluid would regather. But this fetus was dangerously premature, more so than the other case. If she left the fetus alone, it would die. There was a ninety percent chance it would die anyway. The mother was willing to undergo a cesarean section, but was the risk to her of that procedure worth it, given the slim chances her fetus had anyway? Horenstein knew amniotic fluid had already been drawn and the results of chromosomal studies were due shortly. Wait for the genetics results to show how much other damage there is, she told herself. Wait and buy time.

Nature would not wait, however. Nor, in this case, would it be mastered. Two days later, the fetus died in utero.

Not everyone chooses to terminate when the doctors find major problems. The doctors at LAC–USC, particularly, see many such couples, for the patients there include a high proportion of Spanish-speaking Catholics. Many end up in Platt's office because they have had a simple blood test taken in their doctor's office.

When the spine fails to close, a fetal substance called alpha fetoprotein leaks out of the opening into the amniotic fluid. So one of the tests regularly conducted on amniotic fluid is for high levels of alpha fetoprotein. Because AFP can also be measured in the mother's blood, the state of California in 1986 became the first in the nation to require doctors to offer all pregnant patients such a blood test. The test, though, is merely a screen. Those with abnormal AFP levels still need an ultrasound examination and often an amniocentesis. So suddenly women who know nothing of prenatal diagnosis and advanced fetal medicine find themselves before Platt, facing unmanageable questions about needles and abortion.

I am a Catholic, the mothers say, many speaking in Spanish. I would not do anything anyway even if the test is bad, so what is the point? If that's what my baby has, then that's what my baby has. I will take what is given to me.

As the mothers talk, Platt sometimes looks at the screen and sees fetuses without skulls or chest walls.

John Hobbins faces the same situation at times, and those cases trouble him as much as the couples who needlessly terminate. He has seen how a severely retarded fifteen-year-old can destroy an entire family. He has seen a mother sitting in the hospital nursery with a bedridden baby while three healthy children at home clamor for her. "The flip side pisses me off, too, those who are against anyone aborting horrible fetuses that will survive with major abnormalities of the brain and neural tubes, that won't die," he said. "What bugs me is not that some are against prenatal diagnosis and termination, but that they seek to impose [their views] on all others."

So he worries about the Supreme Court. "If they get one other justice on there and the [*Roe v. Wade*] decision goes the other way, I'm sure there wouldn't be an exception for abnormal babies. People who come to us now have a choice. God, that would be awful, to have no choice. I'd have to tell them, 'You got it, and there's nothing we can do.' It would greatly limit our ability to treat. We'd dry up. That's something to think about."

Just as abortion is a constant theme in the doctors' world, so too is the concept of the fetus as a patient. As the unborn moves ever more within their sight and reach, the doctors cannot avoid feeling conflict, for the distinction between a fetus and a newborn infant begins to blur. Horenstein walks through the neonatal intensive-care ward at LAC–USC, looking at tiny 750-gram, one-day-old spremature babies wrapped in tubes and oxygen tents, and they are little different in size or shape from the fetuses kicking on her ultrasound screen. Dr. Angela Scioscia monitors some of those fetuses on a screen and aborts others. She tells herself they are forming but are not as real as someone you talk to or relate to. Dr. Robert Wassman, associate director of the Genetics Institute in Alhambra, cannot forget the first time he saw a human fetus, a miscarriage, lying in a bedpan in the back room of the ward. A junior in medical school at the time, he stared at it for an hour. This looks less like a baby than a bizarrely proportioned adult, he thought. This would have been a human being.

The families often straddle this blurred line along with the doctors.

One day, an amniocentesis at Yale on a nineteen-week-old fetus disclosed Pompe's disease, a malady in which the body accumulates glycogen in the heart muscle, leading to certain death by the time the baby is six months old. The family had already lost one baby to this disease. It was just a matter of when to say good-bye, the doctors told the parents. The couple decided not to wait. After the termination, the couple held their aborted fetus in their arms.

This is not so unusual. Jodi Rucquoi, a Yale family therapist and genetics counselor, has watched similar scenes often. "They feel like murderers. It's that simple," she said. "In their heads, they know why this was done. That's why they had the test. But inside, they feel like murderers anyway. I encourage them to see and hold the fetus. Most do. They say hello and good-bye. They'll handle fingers, say things like, 'Oh look, she's got your shape fingers, Daddy's long legs.' " Rucquoi paused and stared down at her hands. "I'm just thankful that when I had my kids we didn't have any of this," she said softly. "I would have been so scared."

The reality of the unborn patient is new to us, Dr. Maurice Mahoney observed later that afternoon. It is a true and good concept, he said, as long as it is based in fact and is not distorted by the type of images evoked in *Silent Scream.* That film, produced by those opposed to abortion, had suggested tiny embryos were screaming in pain at the touch of a needle. To Mahoney, that simply misses the point. When life begins, and whether the fetus is a person, "are political, not biological, questions. In this country right now, it comes down to when it can exist on its own. In a theocracy, there would be different issues, matters of revealed truth rather than discovered truth. For me as a doctor, the fetus is a patient right from the beginning. . . . But I have a commitment to pluralism as a mainstay of this society."

Abortion, Mahoney reasons, is the less bad choice of the options available today. It is hoped there will be better choices tomorrow. In a sense, selective termination is euthanasia allowed at a stage that is not available later. "As in other areas, technological advances leap past other concepts. If I planned the world, maybe I would keep things together, but I don't see how it could ever work like that. I don't see the world ever slowing down, not competing, not advancing. We create tension if it doesn't exist. Maybe we have gone too far too fast, but that is the nature of human beings."

It is only when they manage to help a family that the doctors' doubts and confusion dissolve. Then their success seems to serve as justification for all the uneasiness. In these moments, the doctors are transformed—in their patients' eyes at least—from uncertain tradesmen into brave pioneers in uncharted territory. Their hands appear steady, their eyes knowing and kind.

It seemed that way the morning that Hobbins met a pregnant mother who had traveled alone from Michigan to New Haven. She was carrying twins, one dead in the womb since early in the pregnancy. Her doctors weren't worried about the dead fetus, for it remained harmless in the uterus, but over time they had become concerned about the possible cause for its demise. Did the mother have a type of blood that might be reacting against her own fetuses, forming antibodies to fight and break down their red blood cells? Had the fetus died from the blood problem, or from something else? Most important, was the live fetus's blood now under attack?

To judge, Hobbins needed to take a blood sample from the living fetus. He studied his ultrasound screen for twenty minutes, searching for the right spot, a spot that would be safe for his needle. Finally he found it. "Okay, let's go," he said. Holding a twenty-five-gauge needle over the woman's abdomen, he watched the screen, then pushed it through her skin. On the screen, he could see the fluorescent point enter the uterus. He guided it toward the fetus's umbilical cord. His target, the large blood vessels where the cord joins the placenta, was all of three millimeters long. The fetus, a foot long and a pound in weight, suspended in amniotic fluid, floated away as the needle approached. "It's like bobbing for apples," Hobbins said. On his screen, he could see that his first insertion had slanted in between two veins. He had to remove the needle and start again.

"You're not going to believe this, but I have to cough," said the pregnant woman lying on the table.

"I don't want to believe it," Hobbins said. "Hold on."

Finally, he reached the spot he wanted on the umbilical cord and drew blood. Hobbins carried the sample down the hallway to the lab for testing. Ten minutes later, he bounded back into the room.

"All right, good news. The baby's blood is normal. Whatever's going on in the amniotic fluid, it's not a problem with this fetus. We can send this lady back to Michigan."

The mother was grinning broadly. So was Hobbins.

There are other moments, though, that achingly remind that the newly risen world of fetal medicine is nascent and complicated, a wondrous but anguished mix. There is, for example, the case of Barbara.

She was thirty years old, a warm, soft-spoken woman with a husband and healthy four-year-old boy at home. Now she was pregnant for the second time, lying on an examination table in her doctor's office as he studied her fetus on an ultrasound screen. This doctor seemed to be taking a long time, and he wasn't saying anything.

"Is it all right?" she asked.

"Oh yeah," the obstetrician answered.

So Barbara rose and went back to work. It was not until later in that day that her doctor called to say one of the fetus's kidneys seemed enlarged, way too big.

He referred Barbara to the Genetics Institute in Alhambra. Arriving there the next morning, she was ushered into an examination room. In a corner stood an ultrasound machine that looked much bigger and fancier than the one in her own physician's office. A doctor walked in, a man of about forty, sandy-haired and gentle-looking. "Hi," he said. "I'm Dr. DeVore."

He studied his screen and confirmed that the right kidney looked inflated. He could not say why, or what it meant. Barbara felt scared. She was not sure she wanted to go on with the pregnancy. Her boy had been born normal. She hadn't realized all that this fetal medicine involved, the problems doctors now could detect. DeVore recommended an amniocentesis, so they could tell whether the kidney problem was connected to larger chromosomal problems. She agreed. Barbara would be twenty-three weeks pregnant when the results came back in two weeks, just at the outer limit for legal abortion. She would have to decide immediately.

Those two weeks were a difficult time for Barbara. "It's hard to make a decision to take a life, or to take the chance of having a severely retarded baby," she said. "No one can be absolutely sure. I couldn't talk to anybody. My husband doesn't say much, he keeps to himself. I just could think to myself."

It didn't help that Barbara could feel the fetus moving inside her. She could also see it rolling and waving on the ultrasound screen. Barbara and her husband finally decided they weren't going to continue the pregnancy if the amniocentesis came back bad. They just couldn't handle that.

On her second visit to the Genetics Institute, DeVore told her the kidney was getting larger. He believed there was a cyst, a sort of pseudo-tumor, growing inside the organ. He also told her the amniocentesis test had come back normal. The chromosomes were okay.

So Barbara was left with mixed signals—and time, still, to stop the pregnancy. She talked to DeVore and the nurses and the counselors. She knew she couldn't get a guarantee, but the more she heard that the left kidney was good, the more she started thinking, it's really not worth it to take a life.

When she returned to the Genetics Institute for a third visit, however, DeVore seemed more concerned than ever. There definitely was a cyst, he said. The kidney had grown still bigger, so big it was pressing up against the fetus's diaphragm, compressing the chest wall, stunting the lung's development, causing the heart to start failing. On his screen, DeVore could see the ominous black patches around the heart that indicated fluid accumulation.

DeVore sent her to his colleague's office at the Women's Hospital in the LAC–USC Medical Center. Barbara walked down drab winding hallways to a small crowded office on the fifth floor. A stocky man with dark hair, brimming over with energy, sat barking into a telephone. "I'm Larry Platt, I'll be right with you," he said.

Platt stared at the image on his ultrasound screen and considered. He was well aware of the baby he once saved, only to have it born with chronic kidney failure. He recalled also the fetus that got better on its own, and the one where he drained the fluid and the baby was born in fine condition. Who knows what would happen this time? Platt thought. The baby might end up with all kinds of complications and problems. It might end up with chronic dialysis. It could die when he put a needle through the mother and started poking. Maybe it's better to let it go into heart failure and die in utero.

Platt chewed on the matter, but not all that much. It was not in his nature to let the baby die. Platt explained what he could to Barbara and her husband. He and his colleagues spelled out the risks and options. They called in a pediatric urologist to explain what the baby most likely would be like, with one functioning kidney.

Barbara and her husband asked questions. Would their baby be retarded? What kind of physical limitations would they have to place on the child? Barbara's husband, taciturn by nature, spoke up. Could my son play football?

The doctors and counselors knew they were walking along a fine line. They knew that with their tests and diagnoses they were disrupting a desired pregnancy. This was not a couple who started out wanting an abortion. Words were chosen carefully. It was possible that growth could be stunted. It would not be a good idea to play football, because there was only one kidney to risk getting kicked or kneed. But there are many people walking around with just one kidney who survive and live normal lives.

Barbara would have liked some precise figures and percentages. She knew she was not getting really definite answers. But, listening to Platt, her fear began swinging over to optimism. "I knew my baby wouldn't make it if we left him alone," Barbara said. "I knew that was not a common cold. I was very scared, but Larry was great. He made me feel confident. I trusted him. He is incredible."

Platt went after the bad kidney late one spring morning. Barbara, awake, stared up at nine doctors and assistants. The technique he used to drain the kidney did not seem much different from amniocentesis. Platt guided a needle through her abdomen to the fetus, watching on his ultrasound monitor. She followed the fluorescent tip of the needle. She could not believe how Platt just went right to the kidney with no problem at all.

The baby was in perfect position, Platt would say later. I would have to have been blind to miss something so big. Anyone could do that. Don't make me into a hero.

One week later, Barbara returned to Platt's office. Together, they looked at the ultrasound machine. The bad kidney had shrunk to a third of its inflated size, from six to two centimeters. But chemical tests, Platt advised Barbara, showed a high sodium level, which indicated it was not functioning well.

"That's fine, as long as the other kidney is okay," Barbara said.

Platt spoke precisely, choosing his words carefully. "There is nothing to indicate a problem with the other kidney," he said.

Barbara stared at the screen. A veteran by now of ultrasound, she knew how to look at the blurred images. The fetus was twenty-six weeks old. She could see the heart beating. She could recognize the eyes, the nose, the mouth. Barbara laughed out loud, and waved to her baby.

The story should end there, but it does not. In early September, Barbara gave birth to a full-term, seven-pound boy. Although he looked perfectly healthy, he was, in fact, unwell.

The inflated right kidney, as previously diagnosed, was essentially nonfunctional—but there was also something wrong with the left kidney. It looked structurally normal on the ultrasound screen, but tests showed an elevated level of waste products. The baby's chemistry was askew. Perhaps there was something functionally wrong with the left kidney, something the ultrasound could not see. Maybe it had been damaged by the growing cyst, before Platt operated months before. Or it might have developed abnormally. Perhaps the problem was reversible, and nature would heal its own mistake. Perhaps the baby was destined for kidney failure, dialysis and a possible transplantation.

Barbara's emotions swung from fear to confusion. Platt felt surprised and depressed, but he told himself this outcome would not make him gun-shy. This baby would likely not have survived without his intervention. He would not hesitate to give patients information in the future. This experience would just add to the knowledge he could share.

Then, as the days passed, the infant's chemistry seemed to improve. A biopsy of tissue from the left kidney, however, indicated an inflammation, an infection. The baby went home, still ill but possibly on the mend. The doctors simply did not know. Final answers would not come for weeks or months. Barbara, confused but hopeful, still thought the fetal doctors were wonderful. If she had known about the left kidney's problems, she would not have had the baby, but now she was glad he was born.

"We don't know how this will end up," Platt said recently. "We did what we had to do. It's frontiers. When you cross frontiers, you don't always know what's in front of you."

III. WHY NOT GET A LITTLE CLOSER?

Michael R. Harrison, a pediatric surgeon at the University of California, San Francisco, used to look with frustration at babies emerging from the womb with lesions and malformations. Draining blocked bladders and injecting medicine was helpful but limited, and conducted at a distance, through the mother's abdomen. If we could just get a little closer, Harrison would tell himself, if we could just operate more directly, we could fix some of these babies.

The notion was staggering but unavoidable: Why not lay hands directly on the patient? That is the question Harrison began to ask himself. And that is what he finally began to do. Harrison is part of a team at UCSF that has, in the past five years, several times opened a pregnant woman's abdomen and uterus, partly removed a fetus from the womb, unblocked a urinary tract, returned the fetus to the womb, and sewed up the mother.

The Unborn Patient is the title Harrison and his colleagues, perinatologist-geneticist Mitchell S. Golbus and ultrasonographer Roy A.

Filly, gave their textbook on prenatal diagnosis and treatment. Harrison and Golbus are professors at the UCSF medical school and codirectors of the university's vaunted Fetal Treatment Program. When Harrison, forty-three, talks of his field, he is visibly excited about the future, even while candidly cautious about the present. "When we first started doing this work I would go and talk about it to all kinds of people, but often to pediatric surgeons and people who deal with kids only after birth," he said. "They'd say, 'That's really stupid, you don't want to do that. You'll have to make all these hard choices.' I feel that is absolutely wrong. That's just being afraid of knowledge. I think you ought to have a choice. It's never better not to know."

It was in early 1981 that Harrison's team first began its march into the uncharted territory where others, including Platt and DeVore, would later follow. They began with bladder and kidney problems not because they were the most common in fetuses, but because they were particularly accessible, visible and treatable. Their initial step was a careful preamble—they touched the fetus only with a needle, not their hands.

The mother, Rosa Skinner, was seventeen weeks pregnant and carrying twins, an apparently healthy girl and a boy with a blocked urinary tract. The doctors knew the condition could be deadly to both. A blockage in the urethra, which passes urine from the bladder, causes a backup and swelling into the fetus's abdomen. The kidneys can balloon and suffer permanent damage, or the amniotic fluid—consisting mainly of fetal urine—can disappear, causing severe abnormalities of the face, limbs and lungs. To reduce the risk to the healthy twin, the doctors waited until her lungs were mature enough to survive a premature birth, knowing surgery might trigger just such an event. When the fetuses were thirty weeks old, Harrison passed a needle through the mother's abdomen and uterus and into the male fetus's bladder. The doctors watched on the ultrasound screen as fluid drained into the amniotic sac. Attached to the end of the needle was a spaghetti-thin, hollow plastic tube, with a one-way valve that allowed fluid to flow from but not into the fetus's bladder. The doctors pushed the tube off the needle, leaving it implanted halfway into the bladder. This shunt would keep the bladder drained until birth.

Fifteen days later, labor began and the twins were born by normal vaginal delivery, six weeks prematurely. The shunt was removed from young Michael Skinner, a healthy newborn boy.

Not everyone applauded, though. Because the procedure came only two weeks before delivery, some doctors wondered why the risky procedure was done at all. If the fetus had survived to thirty weeks with an obstruction, they suggested, it could have made it to thirty-two weeks.

A good point, Harrison agreed—in retrospect. But they couldn't know the baby would be born so early. The rationale, the hope, was for a later delivery, a full-term delivery. Besides, the procedure had worked, and to Harrison that was the key.

In time, he and Golbus repeated the procedure on a number of other fetuses, becoming known as specialists in the field. Teams at medical centers throughout the world have followed after them. Worldwide, doctors have unblocked urinary tracts seventy-nine times. Among those cases, thirty-four infants survived the neonatal period, all but two without long-term problems. Among the forty-five deaths most came after birth because of lung problems, and eleven were aborted therapeutically before delivery because of chromosomal abnormalities or lack of kidney function. Three deaths were linked to the attempts at fetal therapy.

Some doctors also began using much the same shunt technique to drain fluid in fetal brains. Results with these hydrocephalus cases were much more discouraging. Doctors found they could not pick the right fetuses to operate on. They could not tell which had fluid on the brain because of an obstruction that would benefit by decompression, and which simply had a massive fluid buildup that would not be helped by a shunt. Doctors also found that draining fluid did not always mean the fetal brain would rebound unharmed and resume development. Fetuses often were operated on and then born severely retarded. Doctors have tried the brain shunt forty-five times. Although thirty-eight fetuses survived, two-thirds of them have serious brain damage.

Harrison and Golbus decided against pursuing operations for hydrocephalus. Harrison had something even more ambitious in mind anyway. Even as he was experimenting with shunts inserted through the abdomen, he felt dissatisfied with the limits of the procedure. "Little tubes stuck in by needle were clearly not going to work over the long run," he said. "It's going to fall out, it's going to fall in, it's going to get plugged up with something. The kids are going to grab them and yank them out. These things are all going to happen. Little tubes don't work very well long-term."

What would work, Harrison decided, was to open up the abdomen and uterus and operate directly on the fetus.

The mother was eighteen years old, and her twenty-one-week-old fetus had an enlarged bladder and kidneys, indicating a severe urinary tract blockage. Because of the position of the fetus and the mother's unusually small uterus, Harrison decided that implanting a shunt was impossible. He felt scared, really scared—there was a genuine risk to the mother. Harrison had experimented with sheep, but nobody had done this with a human patient. They were groping in the dark.

The doctors explained the risks to the mother. She or her baby could die from the surgery. The fetus could spontaneously abort. A hysterectomy might be necessary, or she could be rendered sterile. The fetus could have other undetected defects. The surgery just might not work, and even if it did, the kidneys and lungs might be too damaged or undeveloped for the baby to survive.

Save my baby, the mother said.

On the morning of April 20, 1981, the UCSF team administered a general anesthetic to the mother. They also gave her crucial drugs, not available until recently, to relax the uterus and prevent premature labor—the most immediate danger in such open-womb surgery. Then the doctors made an incision in her uterus and, with the fetus still attached to the umbilical cord, lifted its bottom half out by the legs. They made two small incisions on its flank. The ureters, which carry urine from the kidneys to the bladder, were brought out, opened, and sutured to the skin so urine could drain directly out the lower back into the amniotic fluid. Then the fetus was returned to the uterus, and the doctors sewed up the uterus and abdomen. The operation took less than half an hour.

Monitors offered encouraging signs. Ultrasound showed the urinary tract had completely decompressed and fluid was draining. The fetal heartbeat was normal. The amniotic fluid, however—low to begin with because of the blockage—was not reaccumulating, and this indicated the kidneys weren't functioning well. Too much damage had been done in the weeks before surgery.

The baby was born at the thirty-fifth week. Because of the diminished amniotic fluid, his lungs had not matured enough to support life. He died after nine hours.

In an article in *The New England Journal of Medicine* reporting this case, Harrison and his colleagues wrote: "The ability to treat a few fetal disorders gives new importance to prenatal diagnosis and raises complex ethical questions about risks and benefits. . . . Although surgery offers new hope for the fetus with a correctable defect, the risks are high and there is considerable potential for doing harm." Such surgery must be undertaken "only with great trepidation."

Still, the operation had worked. Harrison marveled at the technical accomplishment even as he felt sad about the outcome. The mother went on to have two normal pregnancies, allaying his fears about the damage he might have done to her. The real challenge was to select a suitable fetus, Harrison decided—the first one had been too sick to begin with.

So the UCSF team members began work on greatly refining their ability to select fetuses. Without fanfare, they have now performed similar open-womb procedures several times. Until they publish their accounts in scientific journals, they will talk about only two of them. The results indicate both the increasing refinement of the science and the remaining potential for harm.

A family had traveled to San Francisco from the Midwest, seeking help for a fetus with a badly obstructed urinary tract. Harrison's associates knew they were improving but had not yet mastered the art of evaluating each case. The family accepted the not inconsiderable risks and agreed to the surgery. Harrison opened the mother's abdomen and uterus and operated directly on the fetus. Thinking about it even now, when he is well aware of the final outcome, Harrison cannot help but remember that the procedure went beautifully. The technical accomplishment was all they could have hoped for. Not until the family returned home and the baby girl was born three months later did doctors discover that the urinary tract blockage had been only part of bigger, multiple anomalies. The kidneys, the intestines, most of her organs were defective. The doctors had missed it all.

"This nice young family then went through a lot of agony with this kid over months and months, and then finally she died," Harrison said. "If we had done nothing, it's awfully hard to know. Probably it would have died in the womb or at birth. Then they would have saved all the months and months of agony."

Yet there might have been an even worse result, Harrison believes. The baby might have survived, in a severely damaged state. "That's probably the scariest part, particularly with kids with central nervous system problems like hydrocephalus. Really the worst tragedy might not be that you intervened and screwed up and killed a kid. You could argue that it might be a worse tragedy to take a kid who would have died and then you convert him into a kid who is terribly damaged. That is the one thing I would fear the most. No, that's the second. The worst fear would be to hurt the mom."

The next fetus, a boy operated on in July 1985 at twenty-two weeks gestation, yielded the best results to date. He recently celebrated his first birthday in relatively good health, although he has only fifty percent function in one kidney and none in the other. So Harrison plans to move on—next he will treat a fetus with a diaphragmatic hernia, where a hole in the diaphragm (which separates the abdomen from the chest) allows the growing intestines to spill into the chest cavity and stunt the growth of the lungs. For the surgeon, it is a bigger challenge, a more difficult procedure. It is also a more pressing malady, for these fetuses all die needlessly.

"The anatomical problem is a hole in the diaphragm and through it goes the intestines and various things that live down there," Harrison explained. "That's easy to fix after birth. We operate, put it back, close the hole. But the problem is, the lungs' growth have been stunted by the intestines and are too small, haven't developed. You need your lungs at birth, so the babies die."

The only solution, Harrison knows, is to open the uterus and correct the defect before birth. He has experimented over and over on lambs and other animals, successfully. He has been looking for the right human patient. In fact, he almost had one recently.

When he counsels families, Harrison notices most seem to have reached decisions, one way or another, from the start. Some are going to do everything they can, and some, given the slightest hint of bad news, are going to get out. Neither type is nearly as anguished as the ones who cannot decide. Such a couple came to Harrison from out of state. The woman was carrying a fetus with a diaphragmatic hernia. Harrison thought it was a good candidate for surgery and told them so, his words positive and encouraging. Yet in such situations, the UCSF team provides counseling from several people, and these other counselors were not nearly as supportive. As a result, the couple decided to terminate.

Harrison understood. The matter was full of ambivalence, after all, and he, being a surgeon, always wants to operate. Still, it was troubling —particularly since the couple still calls Harrison, long distance, to talk about options they no longer have.

"I am not a psychologist," Harrison said, "but I think even if they had elected to try this operation, and it was a total failure and the kid just died right in the operation, they would have been happier." He reflected in silence for a moment. "Whether that is worth the risk, I don't know."

There are other types of risks. Harrison could diagnose a problem where there wasn't one, leading to a healthy fetus's abortion. One recent morning, for example, a woman came to him carrying a fetus with gastroschisis—its intestines were hanging outside the body. Harrison knew he could handle this easily after birth. Just stuff the guts back in and sew him up. "But this woman came in very early, the earliest one I've ever seen, and we thought since the thing was already out, the guts were already out at fourteen weeks or some god-awful early time, the kid would almost certainly be on the very severe end of bowel damage. It seemed like it just had to be a disaster because the survival with gastroschisis depends on the extent of bowel damage. If it's a good bowel they do great."

This was not the type of defect that allows for treatment before birth. The doctors' task was to provide an accurate prognosis, so the mother could decide whether to continue the pregnancy.

What will my baby be like? she asked, just as they all do. What should I do?

Harrison considered. He didn't know if the baby was going to be born with an unfixable situation. They might operate ten times and then it would die anyway. That would be devastating, a heavy number. In the end, he was negative, openly so, in what he told the couple. So were the other doctors. But the couple refused to listen.

"The family were extremely good people," Harrison said. "They were at the age where this was probably their last chance for a child. They had been childhood sweethearts who had married other people; each had two children by different mates, then they split up and got together and were very happy and this was their first child together. This family had their mind set that they were going to keep this child. I think we really sort of tried to talk them out of it."

The doctors, surprised at the couple's decision, continued to monitor the fetus, checking to see if the bowel was deteriorating. They figured the family might still have a chance to terminate before twenty-two or twenty-four weeks if things got worse. The bowel did not get worse, though. Instead, it got better and better.

"It was an absolute total surprise to us," Harrison said. "Her bowel was just great. Delivered her at thirty-seven weeks. Stuffed it all back in with one shot—it was the easiest thing. It was just wonderful. The kid is perfect. I saw her last week and she's absolutely adorable. It was just a good example of how sometimes there is some sort of unspoken wisdom that sort of defies everything else."

Harrison grinned at the memory. Clearly, he was not at all alarmed by the implications of his story.

"I just told them what I thought at the time. That's all you can do," he said. "You just have to be as honest as you can and know that you're going to look back on a lot of these things and say I was flat out wrong. . . . People who actually deal with problems like this don't have a philosophic bent. We just say, we're not very good at this. We're really pretty stupid at this. I'm sorry but you'll have to decide."

Harrison's team has had to wrestle with the problem of twins in the womb, where a monstrously defective and doomed fetus is threatening the life of a healthy one. Normally, doctors who abort sick fetuses stick needles in, shoot air into the heart, inject medication into the blood. But they can't do that with identical twins who are sharing circulation —inject something in that situation, and it goes to the healthy fetus too. Some time ago, facing this, Harrison told his colleague Mitchell Golbus what they should do. "Well, Mickey," he said, "don't screw around. Just take the kid out."

At first, though, the team members felt they could not dare intervene in this manner. The doctors preferred to wait long enough during the pregnancy for the healthy one to be viable outside the womb, then do an early cesarean section. The least invasive approach is always the first choice. They tried that with several cases. They would get far enough into the pregnancy for viability, then wait to see if the healthy twin turned bad. If it did, they would go in promptly, but they did not want to do anything until then. The problem was, the healthy fetuses never turned bad—they just died. "The mother would come in one day, you'd look at the kid, he'd be perfectly happy and his heart would be beating," Harrison said. "They'd come back the next day and he'd be dead. They died just like that. It was incredible, and it happened several times while we were following and planning to intervene as soon as he looked bad."

So the doctors decided they should take more direct action. First they thought they might just open the uterus and put a clip across the umbilical cord of the damaged fetus. "But if you're going to do that, you might as well take him out," Harrison said. "And that's in fact what we did a couple of times recently."

Harrison will talk philosophy, even though he does not feel it counts for much in his field. The father of three, he is a practicing Catholic. Sitting in his office one afternoon, he pointed to the picture of a fetus on the cover of his textbook. "Our science makes this guy a patient, that's all," he said. "This enterprise can be viewed in a lot of different ways. For example, we could be the darling of the right-to-lifers. You know, prenatal diagnosis before was aimed at search and destroy and killing all these kids. Now we come along, we can treat them, so, oh my God, we're in there and they're patients; therefore, they're people. And there is truth in that. That's sort of my own slant. . . . In practice, though, the thing is, prenatal diagnosis more often than not turns up bad kids. The problem is, we don't have answers for them. I mean, in the big picture these little things we do are for diseases that are exceedingly rare. The vast majority we don't have answers to. Many of the things we see, the families choose to abort the pregnancy and that seems to me to be the right decision. So, you know, you could argue where that's on the other side of the coin. . . . We're not going to save all these little babies. Some of them were not meant to be saved at the present time. The fact that families can abort and start all over again and avoid five months of hopeless pregnancy seems to me to be the right thing to do."

Harrison looked mildly pained. "Don't tell my church," he said.

In truth, if he thought out and defined all the issues his work kicks up, Harrison suspects he would be out of the Catholic Church. He says he would rather just admit there are conflicts, unsolvable ones, and exist in a state of ignorance.

Still, he has thought about it all a good deal.

"I look at those guys hopping 'round on the sonogram, having a good time, and I think, they're just the same as we are," he said one afternoon. "But that's just the point. I don't think that being in the womb or out has anything to do with it. There are some sick fetuses and there are some not sick ones, some that live and some that don't. . . . Or one has this terrible problem and one has a pretty good problem, so this one we refuse to operate on and that one we are happy to try to fix. The thing is, fetuses are not any different than we are."

IV. YOU HAVE TO INDIVIDUALIZE THESE CASES

The new fetal doctors toil in a world devoid of signposts and boundaries. Faced with decisions, they have no guidelines to draw from, neither the officially legislated sort nor the complex codes produced by hospital committee. Choices are made case by case, shaped by the individual details they bring with them. Diseases and defects quickly take on an unofficial but clearly delineated pecking order.

The most severe abnormalities are definite candidates for abortion. Anencephaly, failure of the brain to develop, tops the list. Small-brain development and extensive fluid on the brain—microcephaly and giant hydrocephaly—rank high. So do major kidney failure and the disastrous, inherited metabolic and chromosomal diseases such as Tay-Sachs disease and trisomies 13 and 18, in which an extra chromosome produces severe retardation.

The maladies further down the list are the ones that pull doctors and families into an anguished moral quagmire. Two that most often pose hard choices are Down's syndrome and spina bifida. Both are often associated with retardation and physical handicaps, but severity varies widely from case to case. The doctors see spina bifida children in braces jumping about in their hallways. They see others in wheelchairs, or on stretchers. The doctors see Down's patients working in stores and restaurants. They see others at age fifteen, tearing their families apart, temperamental three-year-olds in adult bodies, screaming and demanding.

"Individualize," says Dr. Larry Platt at USC. "You have to individualize these cases. That's the only way to handle them. It's not just what the kid has wrong. It's who the parents are."

Platt does not hesitate to place his medicine alongside his Orthodox Jewish faith: "You cannot ask a religious question of an authority without knowing one thing—who is the person you are asking it for? Who is the individual? Tell me about the individual, the authority will ask. The answer you get from him may be different for two different individuals."

Platt's own views are rich in contradictions. "I don't know how to separate out the fifteen-week-old fetus whom I aggressively treat from one whose mother says, terminate. I have a hard time. I live in conflict," he will say. Moments later, he will also say: "I cannot allow my personal feelings to get in the way of my scientific knowledge. I don't believe other people making choices for themselves puts me in conflict. I learn to tolerate, understand other views in the world."

Everyone has personal boundaries. Platt knows there are religious scholars who argue that doctors should not even screen for Tay-Sachs disease. This is an invariably fatal disorder in which the child slowly loses muscle control and becomes blind, deaf, paralyzed and retarded, and usually dies by age five. Genetically caused, it is associated mainly with Eastern European Jews. There is no known treatment, so some see prenatal diagnosis for it simply as a search-and-destroy mission. So be it, Platt says. He has seen too many families, religious Jewish families, torn apart by the birth of a Tay-Sachs baby. He has seen families lose their religious commitment, come to doubt their God. In his dual role as a doctor and religious leader in his community, Platt hears the questions all the time.

Why did God do this to us? the families want to know. Why?

So Tay-Sachs has become a disease Platt would rather screen for, despite his discomfort with abortion. In 1970, about one hundred such babies were born in this country. In 1980, when prenatal diagnosis first became a widespread procedure, there were only thirteen. That is good enough for Platt. "You can pin me to the wall now in terms of what about this next birth defect," he said. "What about this sex chromosome defect or that metabolic problem? Some live and do fine. The Down's syndrome babies do better than the trisomy 13s and 18s. Who knows where to draw a line?"

Others wonder whether at least the treatable diseases should not be diagnosed prenatally. For example, in phenylketonuria, or PKU, an enzyme deficiency prevents the proper breakdown of an amino acid, phenylalanine, that is essential to health. The results can be severe mental retardation and other physical anomalies, but this can be avoided if a PKU newborn, diagnosed at birth, is placed on a permanent diet low in phenylalanine. Hospitals routinely check all newborns for PKU, but now doctors can also diagnose this disease in the womb. Because it is treatable, though, the only reason to diagnose it prenatally is to give parents the choice of selective termination.

Choices and ethics are the matter at hand, Platt points out, but so, too, is a practical question—limited health-care dollars. How much time and commitment should he give to a fetus that will likely not live, or live long, or live well? Platt's response: What does the parent want, and what does the parent understand, and what can the parent handle?

Platt still gets letters from one mother. Her unborn baby had hydrocephaly. Retardation was a certainty, but she did not want to terminate. Following her wishes, Platt's team simply followed and planned the delivery. In her last letter to Platt, the mother painted what seemed to him a beautiful picture. Beautiful, Platt thought, because she loves this child. The mother de-emphasized the handicaps. The baby is beautiful, the baby talks. Maybe she has a little problem with seeing, maybe a little problem with her gait. So for this family, saving the fetus with hydrocephaly was right, Platt believes. For other families it would not be.

Some of the doctors, though, once past the philosophy and guidelines, allow that they are still conflicted, with no resolution in sight.

When she looks at a couple agonizing over decisions and options, the young Yale physician Angela Scioscia cannot help but think: A few years ago, we wouldn't have detected this problem, and the baby would have died or been delivered. How many people do you alarm and worry in order to prevent tragedies? She cannot shake the ambivalence. She wonders if she is part of a search-and-destroy mission. Then she reminds herself that she is helping families at a difficult, painful, stressful time. Yes, there is conflict, but either you deal with it or avoid all gray areas and just hide in a nice, safe spot where you never have to confront anything. She would love a world where there is never abortion or malformations or gray areas. But that's not the world she or these families exist in.

"I don't know, you get sort of practical," she said one morning. "If I got too philosophical, I couldn't find my way out. I don't know what's right or wrong. When I started, I didn't expect this path. I thought I always would do good and right—and would know what it was. Now I don't know. My certainty grows less each day."

Not everyone is sure the rules can be left to the practicing doctors, to be decided case by case. John C. Fletcher, the bioethicist at the National Institutes of Health who has written widely about this field, asks a question: This may be okay for now, but what of the future? Can matters be left to the empiric tradesmen?

Fletcher is not so sure they can be, for on the horizon, he sees several major scientific developments that will greatly complicate the already muddy picture of fetal medicine. He eyes, particularly, the nascent but growing use of specific gene probes. Where scientists once used amniocentesis mainly to look at the twenty-three paired chromosomes, they now are zeroing in on a much finer target—individual genes that cause specific diseases.

The new diagnostic tests result from recent advances in biotechnology. Scientists have started identifying the specific aberrant genes that cause maladies such as hemophilia, sickle-cell anemia, cystic fibrosis, muscular dystrophy, Lesch-Nyhan syndrome and a rare eye cancer called retinoblastoma. Once these abnormal genes are identified, scientists can synthetically reproduce—clone—them. Because of the way DNA strands combine only with related strands, these clones then become precision probes for the doctors. Combined in a test tube with DNA extracted from fetal cells, the clones will seek out and combine with only those cells that contain similar genetic abnormalities. The science is ever evolving. Experts believe they eventually will be able, through such gene probes, to diagnose in utero those individuals who will be more susceptible to common diseases such as cancer, diabetes and heart attacks.

Fletcher wonders: Will there be selective terminations based on these diagnoses?

Doctors can now probe for diseases that will not manifest themselves until the fetus is an adult. They have a test for Huntington's disease, a degenerative, ultimately fatal affliction that does not reveal itself until the person is over forty. Presently the test is administered only at a patient's request, but it could get more widespread use, even with fetuses. So Fletcher asks: Should the person be told that he is carrying a bad gene? If the doctor does not tell a patient he's carrying, what about the patient's future children, half of which will inherit the disease? Should a fetus be terminated if it carries the gene, since that means it will develop the disease?

Riding in on top of these questions, Fletcher believes, will be the matter of selectively terminating fetuses because of their sex. This issue now only lurks in the background, but Fletcher thinks it will mushroom when chorionic villi sampling eventually replaces amniocentesis as the chief means of chromosomal and metabolic diagnosis. CVS results, after all, are available in the ninth or tenth week of pregnancy, before the fetus's movement can be felt, before the woman is visibly pregnant. With CVS, decisions to terminate because of the fetus's sex will be easier to make.

The USC ultrasound expert Greg DeVore once got blind-sided on this issue. A couple came to his office at the Genetics Institute in Alhambra, she an actress, he a lawyer, both on their second marriages. They had been referred to DeVore to scan for malformations, and he found none. The woman then asked about the sex of the fetus. DeVore looked on his screen—sometimes he can discern this, depending on the fetal position—and he told her it was a girl. The woman began crying, became nearly hysterical. I failed you, I failed you, she sobbed to her husband. Right then and there, they decided to terminate, and DeVore could not hide his anger. I thought you came here because of concern for malformations, he told them. I would never have scanned you for this reason. This is very inappropriate, completely inappropriate.

Yet DeVore knew this was not the first or last time he would see a couple terminate based on the sex of the fetus. If they're going to give you fake reasons, you're going to be set up sometimes. Every fetal doctor already has had isolated instances of this experience.

"The problems that have come along so far we've been able to master," Fletcher said one afternoon, sitting in his office at the National Institutes of Health complex in Bethesda, Maryland. "We have been able to trust the doctor-patient relationship to resolve problems. It's been a sort of home-grown, internal morality. The question is, can this simple structure carry the weight of all these new issues? I don't think so. Everywhere I look I see very weighty issues gathering and growing. What will happen when society gets involved?"

Fletcher sounds at first like an alarmed opponent of prenatal diagnosis and fetal medicine. As it happens, he is just the opposite. He argues that the problems the field creates cry out for an ambitious expansion of the science, not its restriction. His reasoning is in part practical. Modern working women in this era are having babies later and later, and this trend will continue. Whether it's a good or bad trend, it's in place, and there will be no give. People just are not going to change their ways of life. So there will be more and more high-risk pregnancies and need for prenatal diagnosis. Technology will have to shape itself to our life-styles. Technology, which dragged society into this quagmire, will now do society's bidding.

"There's going to be more and more prenatal diagnosis," Fletcher said. "The entire human genome [genetic makeup] will be mapped by the year 2000."

The question Fletcher poses: "Are we going to devote as much effort, money and time to developing therapies for these disorders as we have to the diagnosis . . . or is abortion going to become the way to deal with them?"

Unless we are willing to stand pat with abortion as therapy, Fletcher argues, fetal doctors must be given the go-ahead to stride into an even more controversial field—human fetal and embryonic research. Talking of this, he paused to choose his words carefully, knowing that what he was about to suggest would draw the anguished wrath of some. At centers that now offer test-tube fertilization service to infertile women, researchers already can, and do, detect the genetic nature of minuscule four-cell and eight-cell embryos before they are implanted in the women. Embryos that are developing normally get implanted; those that aren't are discarded. Would it be moral and ethical, Fletcher asks, to create such test-tube embryos specifically for the purpose of research? That research, Fletcher argues, should include the rapidly evolving field of genetic engineering. Scientists now tinker in laboratories, trying to change aberrant genes in mice, monkeys, dogs and sheep, hoping one day to do the same with humans. One lab has managed to alter the genes of a sheep fetus, with the help of Michael Harrison in San Francisco. The scientists' progress is slow, however, for the parallels to humans are sometimes shaky. They could learn much from gene-altering experiments with human test-tube embryos. Prenatal genetic diagnosis is inextricably linked to genetic engineering, Fletcher believes.

"Now is the time to get behind those research scientists," he said. "Unless you are willing to raise the rate of abortion and use that as the solution, you have to somehow learn how to do therapy. We must be committed to the idea that it is not wrong to experiment with in vitro [test-tube] embryos. Now is the time to face the music."

An ethicist such as Fletcher is not the only type whose thoughts touch controversy when contemplating the future. You want moral problems? doctors such as Larry Platt and Michael Harrison say. Let us tell you what we are thinking about.

They are thinking about anencephalics, those whose skulls never develop above the forehead. The fetus has no cerebral cortex, only a minute portion of brain stem on top of the spine. Technically, such fetuses are alive, since the stem produces a small amount of electrical activity, but they die quickly after birth, within hours or days. The other organs—the heart, kidneys, liver—often are perfectly normal. The doctors cannot help but think: These fetuses would be ideal sources of transplant organs. They could put the organs into needy babies still in the womb. Each year, an estimated five hundred infants need new kidneys, five hundred need hearts and five hundred to one thousand need livers. Each year, about thirty-five hundred anencephalics are born in the United States.

"The object of the game would be to take the organs out of the ones who can't be helped and put them into those that can be helped," said Harrison.

To do this, however, the doctors could not wait hours or days for the anencephalic to expire on its own, for as the brain stem fails, vital organs lose their blood supply and begin to deteriorate beyond the point where they could be used for transplantation. The doctors would have to intervene. The law in all states does not allow them to do this, since, technically, the anencephalic is not brain dead. Efforts are under way in some states, including California, to change the law.

Platt is a doctor who hesitates to stick a needle into a fetus, fearing the potential harm, and he resolutely will not do abortions. His eyes widen with enthusiasm, though, at the thought of fetal organ transplants. "The thing is, in utero transplantations are more exciting than after birth, because in utero is privileged time with the immune system. You don't have the rejection problems you get later," he said. "I personally have no conflict, no problem, with this idea. The anencephalic baby cannot live."

Fletcher, pondering a future full of gene probes, embryo research and fetal organ transplants, continues to ask his question. Can the doctors handle the moral burden on their own? They are doing the work, coping with the problems. But are they the ones to lead us? The doctors pose a different question: With so many divergent paths, none clearly more correct than the others, how do you lead others? How do you set firm standards?

This, finally, is the question that swirls around all discussion about the newly risen world of fetal medicine. For many of the doctors, it is a question without an answer. They believe this personally as well as professionally, for in their private lives, when the doctors had their own choices to make about pregnancies, they did not all respond in the same manner.

Harrison and his wife, both forty-three, had a baby six months ago. Amniocentesis at that age was clearly called for, and they had one. They decided before the procedure that if the results were bad, they would terminate the pregnancy. The results showed a normal fetus.

DeVore, father of seven, a Mormon bishop, did not hesitate to put an ultrasound transducer on his wife's abdomen for the last four pregnancies, when the technology was available. He agonized for weeks, though, over whether to do an amniocentesis during the last pregnancy, when his wife was over thirty-five. What would we do with the results? he and his wife asked themselves. Could they consider abortion? If not, why take the test? But if they didn't, there would be tremendous anxiety to deal with. At the twentieth week, with just enough time left to terminate if the results were bad, they opted for the test. Even then they did not know what they would do if they got bad news—they told themselves they'd decide when the results came back. They were spared that ordeal, for the results were normal.

Larry Platt swam in a sea of contradiction.

He is an unbounded defender of the choices and knowledge his medicine provides. The suggestion that fetal doctors are meddling with nature lifts him out of his chair. To not intervene, to let nature take its course? Why, you could say that about health in general. He orates, pacing his office: Let everyone just die, then. We progress in steps. You have to use the tools you possess to get to the next discovery. Put down your tools and you can't go on. Why, it's like getting to the moon, space travel. Space travel is even more fascinating than medicine. Yes, there was a catastrophic accident, contributed to by human error, but Platt would love nothing more than to be on the next space shuttle. He finds it amazing that man should even attempt to travel in space, to reach the moon. He watches every liftoff and touchdown he can. This is man using who he is, to build and to bridge. Just think of it.

There is, though, the matter of the second pregnancy of his own wife, Wendy, at age thirty-two. She wanted an amniocentesis. Platt said no.

Medically speaking, based on facts and statistics, it's not indicated until you're thirty-five, unless you have a family history of problems, he explained. The risk before then outweighs the likelihood of finding defects. This is what he tells medical students and physicians all around the country, and so this is what he was telling his wife.

Wendy pointed out that he did amnios for lots of other people under thirty-five, all the time, when they wanted it.

That's right, that's right, Platt said. But you don't need it.

Instead, over the months, he watched his ultrasound screen with anxiety. Their baby developed without problems. Meanwhile, though, Wendy's best friend, younger than she, gave birth to a baby with Down's syndrome. Platt believes that his wife, to this day, is upset with him.

He does not know why he refused her an amniocentesis.

"I would hate to admit to a denial thing," Platt said one morning. "But I guess it was partially denial. I guess I was avoiding something."

UPDATE

In the summer of 1989, after five years' practice on hundreds of sheep and monkeys and six failed attempts with humans, Dr. Michael Harrison at the University of California–San Francisco realized the goal he'd long pursued—operating on a fetus with a diaphragmatic hernia. In the first successful major surgery on a fetus, Harrison's team saved an apparently doomed fetus whose lungs were not developing because of pressure from abdominal organs spilling into the chest cavity through a hole in the diaphragm. Harrison cut into the mother's uterus, partly removed the fetus, opened its left side, pushed its abdominal organs back into their proper location, closed the hole in the diaphragm with a Gore-Tex patch, and returned the fetus to the womb. Seven weeks later

Blake Shultz was born healthy and breathing. In June 1990, after Harrison's team repeated the operation on a second fetus, and watched both infants flourish for months, they reported their results in *The New England Journal of Medicine,* garnering expressions of wonder from many quarters. Then in October 1990, in the British medical journal *The Lancet,* Harrison's team reported yet another success, this time the opening of a fetus's chest and the surgical removal of a malformed lung lobe.

The catalog of refinements and new procedures in the world of fetal medicine continued to evolve. Doctors experimented with earlier CVS and amniocentesis, and with placental biopsy, a form of late-term diagnosis that yields immediate results, so helps doctors make decisions about delivery and treatment of the newborn. Color ultrasound machines emerged with visualization so enhanced, doctors could discern the direction and turbulence of a flow, and whether it was blood or fluid. Lung and liver transplants were tried on a handful of newborns, using pieces of their parents' organs, and physicians talked of doing the same with fetuses.

Predictions for the future abounded. Doctors made plans to do plastic surgery on fetuses with cleft lips and palates, since fetal wounds heal without scars. Although a handful of early experimental attempts failed, doctors still talked with enthusiasm about gene therapy on fetuses with maladies caused by a single aberrant gene, such as thalassemia, cystic fibrosis, muscular dystrophy and Huntington's disease; the diagnosis would be made early by CVS, the correction by injecting self-replenishing bone marrow stem cells with the normal gene into the fetal abdomen or blood vessels. Experimental research continued on a revolutionary way to bring safe, routine fetal diagnosis to almost everyone, by isolating and growing large colonies from the few fetal cells that normally spill into the maternal bloodstream.

Other frontiers remained blocked, however. Talk about fetal and embryonic tissue experiments, and of mining anencephalic infants for fetal organ transplants, triggered a backlash among those concerned with the ethical implications, including the possibility that women would get pregnant so as to sell tissues and organs. The result was a withdrawal of federal funding, a retreat by state legislators, and a virtual moratorium in the field.

This opposition fueled by ethical questions failed to dim the doctors' expectations, though. After all, their world had already been transformed. The most meaningful recent advances were not the flashy pioneering of the UCSF team, but the increasing acceptance and use of more basic techniques in fetal medicine by an ever-growing number of physicians. Those with doubts simply could not hold back those with hopes. "A few of us were on the cutting edge," Larry Platt said at the start of 1991. "Now more people are catching up. That's the really big change."

Making the Leap

December 1987
Bethesda, Maryland

Late in the morning on Monday, December 7, 1987, two scientists faced each other, one sitting, one standing, in a small conference room at the National Institutes of Health in Bethesda, Maryland. W. French Anderson, fifty, director of the laboratory of molecular hematology at the National Heart, Lung and Blood Institute, had been explaining to a NIH advisory committee why he was seeking their permission to make the first authorized attempt at altering a sick human being's genes. Now he was leaning back in his chair, fielding questions from a committee member, Richard C. Mulligan, thirty-three, an MIT associate professor and lab director at the Whitehead Institute for Biomedical Research in Cambridge. Anderson that morning had traded his customary sweatshirt and moccasins for a tailored gray suit. Mulligan had found a gray herringbone sport coat to wear over beltless khaki jeans, a pink striped shirt and a red bow tie.

"I am curious, French," Mulligan said, drawing out his words as he paced before a chalkboard. "Do you think it would work if you tried it?"

Anderson forced a chuckle.

"That's the question," he said, hurrying through his response. "Do we think that it will work? We've asked that ourselves during pizza sessions many times. An even better question is, if it was my own child—"

"Let's keep it to the—" Mulligan began to interrupt.

"No one really knows," Anderson quickly replied.

Both men, eyeing each other after this momentary exchange, appeared satisfied, even triumphant. That they'd interpreted the meaning of their conversation so differently was not altogether surprising. After all, they saw most matters from widely varying perspectives.

The tension and conflict evident between Anderson and Mulligan that morning in a NIH conference room can be seen as a classic one between two types of lab investigators: the applied scientist and the basic researcher—that is, the medical doctors and the molecular biologists. Making such a distinction risks oversimplifying matters—the differences do not always break along such clear lines—but the two groups do tend to look at the world differently. Anderson is a medical doctor. Mulligan is a molecular biologist.

When is the right time to make a transcendent leap, and how to decide? Must we fully understand the basic science involved and feel certain we will cure the patient, or should we accept uncertainty and view the first attempts as part of the experimental research? How do we balance the dangers in premature application against the waste of undue delays? Asked such questions, Anderson and Mulligan do more than simply disagree. They grow mystified, and aghast, at each other's answers.

From afar, scientists in white coats in a lab appear all of a group. Closer up, the differences seem more evident than the similarities. The doctor's training in medical school and residency gears him to act, to apply science, to get results. In the classroom, he thumps chests and listens to hearts. The molecular biologist earns his Ph.D. in a lab, amid test tubes and vials and slides. There he learns technique and patience and a distrust for anything the hard data cannot prove. He seeks not results so much as a general understanding into the workings of genes and cells and viruses. How to do science? This is the eternal tension in the lab between these two groups. The answer often depends on where the scientists stand and who they are and in which direction they direct their gaze. It is, moreover, difficult at times to separate the scientists' intellectual differences from matters of ego and ambition and politics. Competition, after all, is the engine that drives the quest.

Many scientists are in the race to do human gene therapy, and they all want badly to prevail, but Anderson in particular does nothing to hide his abiding passion to be the first across the finish line. "I want to be the best scientist among my peers," he says frankly. "I get bored when there is no clear goal in sight. I want to win. I don't mind letting my colleagues know that."

Still, he defends his present petition for human gene therapy experiments in scientific terms as well. We always operate with uncertainty in medicine, Anderson argues. We don't know how aspirin works, but we use it. It is unethical to withhold treatment that might help. "What is the situation if it turns out we got into a patient and it cures him?" asks Anderson. "Then how are we going to justify that we sat on it for two years now? Should we sit on it another two years? What about four years?"

Others, particularly but not only the molecular biologists, shake their heads in dismay at such talk. We first need to understand, they reply. We need to do the basic science. The basic researchers ask the same questions over and over: How do you know this? What are the facts?

Talking to his postdoctoral fellows at MIT, Richard Mulligan finds himself at times posing just those questions. At thirty-three, he is something of a Wunderkind, winner of a MacArthur Foundation "genius award" and head of his own twenty-one-man lab. Why do you think that will work? How do you know? he asks his postdocs. Mulligan's tone at these times touches on the sarcastic. Do you feel it? Believe it? . . . Is it a religion? Is it intuition? . . . The fact is, you don't know. Where is the science?

"If I were an MD, I could see why you'd want to try anything," he said one day recently. "But let's just define what we are saying and doing. There is absolutely no shred of evidence that it will work. Maybe French just has faith in miracles."

Discussions with French Anderson about the science of genes do, at times, tend to veer toward the mystical. "Nature is a very formidable opponent," he said one day in his lab, when his experiments were faltering. "You must just keep pushing. We all get tired. Molecules are the same way. Molecules and cells have a mind of their own and so long as they can beat you they will. The only way you can beat them is just keeping going. Sooner or later they get tired."

Anderson likes the dark—the literal dark. He does not usually keep lights on when he sits in his suburban Maryland home, and his NIH office is a narrow cave, the window glass covered with blackout lining. The dark, he explains, reduces sensory input and allows meditation. Equally soothing for Anderson is tae kwon do, the ancient Korean martial art, in which he possesses a third-level black belt. For relaxation in the evening, he teaches tae kwon do in a gym across Wisconsin Avenue from his NIH lab in Bethesda. Tae kwon do, he explains, is something he can do subconsciously, almost in a transcendental state, the world focused right there in that moment.

It is important, he told his class one night in the gym, to keep some parts of your body relaxed, some parts tight. While speaking, he stood perfectly still, barefoot, in a white cotton martial arts outfit. Suddenly his rigid right arm shot out, the knuckles on his closed fist slamming into the gym wall. The sound echoed across the room. "Well, I guess that makes the point," Anderson said, his face expressionless, inscrutable. "Try not thinking of what to do. Just do it."

The next morning in his lab, he explained: I do science like I do tae kwon do. Science is also something best done without thinking, something transcendent and intuitive.

Told of all this some time later, Mulligan looked stricken. He just shook his head.

Anderson is a thin man of medium height, with fine silver hair swept straight back over an angular face. He and his wife of twenty-five years, a pediatric surgeon, are childless, having decided long ago they lacked the time for parenting. At times, he tends to stammer. A pediatrician by training who was graduated magna cum laude from both Harvard College and Harvard Medical School, and with honors from Cambridge University, Anderson has worked in the labs of Nobel Prize winners Sir Francis Crick and Marshall Nirenberg, who, respectively, cracked the mystery of DNA and the genetic code. Anderson can lay claim to several major breakthroughs of his own during a twenty-two-year tenure at NIH, but those lab triumphs came years ago. Most recent efforts have followed blind alleys.

That is apparent from a look at his calendars. There are those who might consider Anderson's meticulous calendars the product of an overly obsessed mind, but Anderson takes pride in this form of self-appraisal. Every half day he measures what he has done and assigns points. Good basic research gets two points, speeches and journal reading get one point, administration and nonscience get no points. Then he figures each month's total. Months with thirty or more points on the calendar get colored green, months between twenty and thirty get colored yellow, months below twenty get colored red. Anderson's calendars throughout the early 1980s feature long bands of red and yellow, interrupted only occasionally by a spot of green. These colors provide a reminder: There was a time not that long ago when French Anderson was less than a leading figure in the race to do human gene therapy.

That fact, and the manner in which he jumped into the pursuit, are not the least of the elements that irritate some of his competitors. This part of the story involves a good deal of rancor.

Around 1980, a handful of scientists—the chief ones being Howard M. Temin at the University of Wisconsin, Robert A. Weinberg at the Whitehead Institute and Edward M. Scolnick, then at NIH—began exploring a method of gene transfer that was both wondrously clever and astonishingly daring. They were then just coming to understand the nature of a particularly sinister class of viruses called retroviruses (the agent that causes acquired immune deficiency syndrome). Unlike more common viruses responsible for such diseases as polio or smallpox, retroviruses do not destroy an infected cell or occupy it only temporarily. Instead, they quietly incorporate their own genetic material into the cell and stay there forever, forcing the cell to make viral proteins along with its own cellular proteins. The first scientists in this field offered an extraordinary suggestion. Why not harness retroviruses to work for, instead of against, human health? Why not take advantage of the retrovirus's ability to insert genes into a cell? Why not strip a retrovirus of its own viral DNA and drop into it a human gene—a human gene that someone badly needs because his own is missing or defective? This gutted and remodeled retrovirus would function as a vector, a carrier—it would deliver the needed human gene to a host cell, which would treat it as its own.

Why not, the scientists also suggested, put the gene into the human bone marrow, which generates the cells that populate the bloodstream? In the bone marrow are the basic, self-renewing stem cells from which all the other blood cells arise—they are the cells responsible for replenishing the entire system. If the stem cells take up the new gene, that gene would continue to proliferate in the body forever. The process of actually doing gene therapy on a human would then work much like a traditional bone marrow transplant. Doctors would remove some of the patient's bone marrow cells and combine them in a lab dish with the retrovirus vector, which would infect the cells with the new gene. Then the doctors would put the altered cells back into the patient's body.

In time, a handful of scientists fixed on a gene that seemed most likely as the first candidate—the ADA gene. This gene codes for an essential enzyme that inhibits a poison found naturally in humans, a poison that can disable the immune system. Those born without an effective ADA gene suffer from a host of usually fatal immune-deficient diseases, including severe combined immunodeficiency (SCID), which was what afflicted David, the well-publicized "bubble boy" in Texas who lived in a sterile plastic tent until he died at the age of twelve.

ADA and retroviruses—that became the hot field in human gene therapy research. The early advances at the start of the 1980s came from the Toronto labs of Alan Bernstein and A. L. Joyner and from the San Diego labs of Theodore Friedmann and Inder Verma. Soon after, another team began to stand out, a team based in the Boston area, connected in various ways with MIT, the Whitehead Institute, Children's Hospital and Harvard Medical School. One member of that collaboration was Richard Mulligan.

First, Mulligan's team designed a particularly nifty retrovirus vector, safer and more effective than earlier versions. Then they used it to put a gene into living mice—a test gene not linked to any disease. In mid-1984, they started playing with a much more critical gene—the ADA gene. They were on a roll, and had few substantive competitors.

In those early years, French Anderson also was involved with human gene therapy, but his efforts largely involved a method called microinjection, which was not yielding fruitful results. As the retrovirus bandwagon gained force, he realized the need to switch paths, so in the summer of 1984 he formed a collaboration with the Princeton biologist Eli Gilboa, who was constructing retrovirus vectors. At this time Anderson also began talking by phone to other leading gene therapy researchers, since he was preparing a review paper for the journal *Science*, summarizing the state of the field.

On September 28, 1984, while updating his *Science* article, Anderson placed a call to John Hutton, a physician at the University of Cincinnati. Hutton had news. He'd just finished isolating and cloning the ADA gene—something only one or two other labs had within their reach. Now, on the phone, he seemed unclear about what he was going to do with it.

Anderson drew a breath. "John, you want to send it to me?"

"Sure," Hutton said. "Why not?"

The retrovirus technology had come from one quarter, the ADA gene from another. Others, searching for the right word, later would suggest that Anderson at the very least was being rather "opportunistic." Whatever way his entry was to be characterized, though, it was clear Anderson now was in the race. He was Mulligan's competitor.

In October 1984, Anderson had a conversation with a member of Mulligan's Boston team, Stuart Orkin of the Harvard Medical School and Children's Hospital, that can fairly be described as strained. "John Hutton has sent us the ADA gene," Anderson began, "so now we're going to join the ADA field. I appreciate all of the help you've given us in talking about your work for my *Science* paper, but I won't ask you for anything more, because now that we have the gene, we're competitors." Orkin said little. He is a serious and intense man, by nature taciturn, given to few words in even the most cordial of situations. But Orkin was disturbed. I wish the man could be a little more original, he thought.

Anderson understood he was arousing some irritation, but this did not give him pause. He knew much about, even embraced, the rougher, competitive side of science. While working in Nirenberg's lab in the 1960s, pursuing the genetic code, he'd seen more than one scientist lock his logbooks in a safe each night to keep them from competitors within the same NIH building. Anderson eagerly dived headfirst into the scrap.

By early 1985, Anderson's lab team had matched the Boston group's early accomplishment—they, too, had put a test gene into living mice. Both groups, however, were simply refining a method—the test gene was just a marker that did not cure a disease. They needed to get the ADA gene into mice.

Anderson tried to do this time after time in mid-1985, but it never worked. Other labs also failed—the entire field seemed blocked. The ADA gene just would not go into a living system. Anderson's two most trusted young lab lieutenants, Philip Kantoff and Martin Eglitis, felt disconsolate. We do not understand the basic science, they reasoned. We will have to retrace our steps and learn why we failed.

If there is a particular moment that has most fully characterized Anderson's unusually focused drive to change a human being's genes, it came now. Let's think ahead and look at the big picture, he suggested. When you do an experiment, you'll get either a yes, a no or a maybe answer, and that will lead to other experiments. But if you look down the road a ways, you might find you don't really need steps two and five. Regardless of what they say, you're going to do steps three and six anyway. So skip two and five. Just go straight to three and six. Why try to refine and refine the mice? We want to cure human patients. Monkeys are much closer to humans.

"Let's bag the mouse work," Anderson told Eglitis and Kantoff. "Let's go after the monkeys."

That's just what he proceeded to do. In collaboration with a team headed by Richard J. O'Reilly, head of pediatrics and director of the bone marrow transplantation program at Memorial Sloan-Kettering Cancer Center in New York, Anderson in mid-1985 began infecting monkeys with a retrovirus vector containing the ADA gene. Monkeys represented a much larger and more complex system than mice. Success here would be much more difficult, but it also would have much more meaning—success here would mean you could go into humans.

The monkeys, it turned out, reacted more favorably to the ADA gene than did the mice. In only one monkey was Anderson's team ever able to detect the presence of the human ADA gene directly, but in four of the five monkeys evaluated, the scientists could see that a few of the cells were producing the enzyme coded by the human ADA gene.

What exactly this meant has become a matter for considerable debate.

To Anderson, the experiments suggested a great deal, enough to convince him to write a paper reporting their results. He would submit it to *Nature* (the prestigious scientific journal published in Britain), he told his lab. As soon as *Nature* accepted it for publication, he'd begin drafting a protocol to go into a human. When the monkey paper got published, he'd submit the protocol to the human gene therapy subcommittee of the NIH's Recombinant DNA Advisory Committee (RAC). "This thing," he said, "is about locked up." To the dismay of some colleagues, Anderson also went public. At a NIH press conference in September 1985, Anderson, answering a reporter's question, said human gene therapy could come within a year. An avalanche of media coverage followed, including excited predictions and extended reports by virtually every major newspaper and magazine.

There were other scientists, though, primarily molecular biologists, who judged Anderson's monkey results quite differently. They did not simply think his results were weak—they thought the results represented a complete failure. Richard Mulligan was one of those who held this view.

By now, Mulligan had become something of a symbol in the Anderson lab. It is misleading to characterize the present conflict as a man-to-man rivalry between these two, for the divisions are more intellectual than personal, and involve many people spread across the country. But at some point Mulligan's name became a form of shorthand in Anderson's lab for all the competition, all the critics. A full generation younger than Anderson, Mulligan possesses a considerably different approach to the world than does the older scientist. Anderson shrinks from social settings and abstains from drink, while Mulligan enjoys beer, martinis, champagne, Hollywood parties, attractive women, good food and popular restaurants. Tall, bearded and lanky, clad usually in worn jeans, he looks more like a graduate student than the world-class scientist he is. He is often bemused by what he sees and hears. He does not hesitate to suggest that another scientist is "nothing," if that is his judgment. *Arrogant* is a term sometimes mentioned in the same breath with Mulligan's name. His comments on a PBS *Nova* program broadcast in 1985 particularly irked some doctors. "We molecular biologists are responsible in the technical sense for the whole method," he said. "We should not leave some of the scientific issues to the physician. I would feel very, very much more responsible than the physician for the patient if someone used a method I worked on."

Brilliant, though, is another word invoked often when describing him. He tends to work not by grinding out the lab hours, but by relying on "conversational science"—talking and thinking over concepts with others. Although this approach at times irritates some of his more traditional elders, it also attracts a considerable circle of admirers.

After their initial successes in human gene therapy research, Mulligan's team like all the others had encountered critical roadblocks. There might be a biological block, they came to believe, that we just don't understand. To Mulligan, faced with such complexities, Anderson's work appeared to be barely touching on this basic biology, and then only in a peripheral, shallow fashion. He resented Anderson's whole approach. He objected even to being grouped in the same field with him. He did not think they were so linked. It made him uncomfortable to say so about another scientist, but the fact was, he could not imagine Anderson's position scientifically.

Mulligan—and others—saw several fundamental problems with Anderson's monkey results. The levels of ADA enzyme activity Anderson found, after all, were just faint traces, certainly not enough to cure a patient lacking his own ADA. In only one of the monkeys could Anderson detect the presence of the human ADA gene itself. Having failed at this, Anderson had tried to test indirectly for the gene's enzyme activity. Even there, he had found nothing when he used the standard test. He had been forced to rely on a far rarer type of assay.

To Mulligan, though, there was an even bigger problem with Anderson's work. To do gene therapy, scientists had to get the new gene into the replenishing stem cells in the bone marrow, for only then could they provide a patient with a continuing source of the new gene. That much was clear. If you just got the gene into the more mature, already developed cells, the effect would be quite limited—when those cells died, so would the transplanted gene. But that was exactly what Anderson had done, Mulligan was certain, for the enzyme activity in Anderson's monkeys had lasted only a brief time. The activity had started declining after sixty to eighty days, and had disappeared altogether by day 170. Anderson must have hit some late, mature cells—cells that soon died. Anderson could not have gotten into the stem cells.

In truth, the whole business of stem cells was rapidly becoming the chief obstacle for all those pursuing the goals of gene therapy. Everyone just might be running up against a brick wall, Mulligan reasoned. The stem cells, after all, have been estimated to make up only a fraction of bone marrow cells, one in ten thousand. There is no way to separate them from the rest. They look like the other cells and behave like them. You can't test for them or select them out. So how do you show you can get into them?

Anderson had to be called on this, Mulligan decided.

Mulligan's opportunity came on October 15, 1986. That day the Institute of Medicine, an arm of the prestigious National Academy of Sciences, opened a special conference in Washington about gene therapy, and Mulligan was a featured speaker. The first morning of the two-day conference, at a breakfast reception, he moved about the hall at the newly opened J. W. Marriott Hotel, three blocks down Pennsylvania Avenue from the White House. Anderson approached him at one point. They chatted briefly, their tones cordial. Then Mulligan climbed the podium and began his talk.

The stem cells have to be infected, he said. You've got to see results long after transplantation—at least four months. And instead of testing for a gene's enzyme activity, they should be looking for the presence of the gene itself. French Anderson's lab couldn't detect the ADA gene, Mulligan pointed out. The enzyme activity they did see came only in a short window of time. Clearly, Mulligan argued, a test for stem cell infection needs to be developed. "In my opinion, such assays would constitute the appropriate final test prior to clinical testing in a human," Mulligan said. "If no such assay becomes available, a critical decision will have to be made as to how to proceed."

With that, Mulligan left the podium. He felt pleased. After this, he thought, there is no way researchers can claim breakthroughs unless they address the issues I raised. I have set the terms.

The next day, the other scientists had questions for Mulligan, but he was no longer there. The Red Sox were facing the Mets that afternoon in the World Series at Fenway Park. Mulligan had tickets.

Sitting in the audience, listening intently, French Anderson had stared at Mulligan as the younger man spoke. Occasionally, Anderson had slowly shaken his head—that was the only evidence of his feelings.

Anderson did not so much disagree with Mulligan as view the matter from a different angle. Mulligan, after all, was a basic researcher pursuing knowledge. Anderson was an applied scientist, oriented by his medical training toward putting his findings to a tangible use. Anderson completely agreed with Mulligan's claim that without the needed test for stem cell infection, a critical decision loomed. Unlike Mulligan, though, he was not inclined to search any longer for that test, since he did not think it could be found. He was ready to make the critical decision.

There finally was only one way to find out if you could get into stem cells and stay in, he believed. Go into a human patient, a human ADA-deficient patient. See if there you got results that lasted.

It should work. Even if you hit only a handful of stem cells, a fraction of them, that should do the trick. Those few cells, after all, would have a selective advantage over all the others.

At the heart of Anderson's impassioned endeavor was his belief in this theory of selective advantage. In an ADA-deficient patient, he reasoned, a few stem cells carrying the ADA gene, even if greatly outnumbered, would have this selective advantage over all the others because they alone would be immune to the body's poisons. They would proliferate while the others died out.

It was an intriguing notion, but Mulligan wasn't alone in thinking it at best a poorly reasoned and speculative theory, full of basic flaws. How, for example, could Anderson assume that the stem cells in the ADA-deficient patient were the defective ones? If they weren't, newly infected stem cells would have no advantage over all the other stem cells.

Who was right? There was no easy way to resolve these issues, since selective advantage could not be tested in monkeys or any other animal. Animals have their own ADA gene, and thus their own ADA enzyme activity. They aren't sick, as the human patient would be, so the newly inserted cells would have no advantage over the monkey's own cells.

That, as it happened, was precisely why Anderson believed you had to go into humans, why you had to make that critical decision. Of course, everything Anderson was shooting for hinged on the idea of selective advantage, so it's possible his thinking was also colored by more visceral forces. If his theory wasn't right, he told his colleagues, gene therapy was a long way off. For patients and for his own goals, the theory had to be right. It just had to be right.

It is here, where the pursuit of science turns on matters of theory and what a lab investigator desires, that the differences between the applied scientist and the basic researcher become most sharply apparent.

Molecular biologists do not traffic much in theories and desires. They talk a complex language, one deeply rooted in the hard nuggets of science, and they keep their eyes on the cells. In doing so, they see all sorts of unanswered questions. Which donor cells really get taken up into the body's system? How can we be sure those cells even exist in the marrow obtained from the patients and infected with vectors? What if there is something wrong with the cells the vectors are supposed to infect—maybe there won't be anything for the vector to hook onto. How do you know you won't have to kill off some of the patient's own cells to make room for the ones you are giving him? How dangerous would that be? Where will the newly added gene land on the host cell's chromosomes? Might it disrupt the cell's normal functions, or turn on a cancer-causing oncogene? What if the retrovirus vector or other viral material managed to escape the cell and become infectious?

"Suggestions that we go forward in the absence of the scientific information—I don't consider that very scientific," Mulligan argues.

It is also, the microbiologists fear, politically unwise. Scientists and their regulators are not unaware that the idea of changing a human's genes is startling and frightening to many, in its implications of playing God and in its potential to alter the essence of being human. They are deeply concerned about being perceived as moving too fast. This is what sets gene therapy apart from other medical frontiers such as cancer chemotherapy or AIDS drugs. Anderson's competitors worry that French, driven by ambition and ego into a failed experiment, might sour public sentiment and take them all down with him. They do not want Anderson or anyone else to provide ammunition to the outspoken critics of genetic engineering, such as the environmental ethicist Jeremy Rifkin. They also shrink from the specter of Martin Cline, who in 1980 unsuccessfully tried the first gene therapy using recombinant DNA techniques, operating abroad without getting proper approval from review boards. In the furor that followed, Cline resigned as chairman of his division at UCLA and the NIH terminated his two grants.

"Nobody wants to provide a target for the people to say, 'Gee, it doesn't work and what are we doing to the environment, and what else is going on here,' " said A. Dusty Miller at the Fred Hutchinson Cancer Research Center in Seattle. If an experiment fails, said the Harvard Medical School and Children's Hospital researcher Stuart Orkin, "lots of explanations will be needed. It will give ammunition to lots of critics. We would be dead for ten years."

These scientists pose a question: Why the rush? Gene therapy in general, far down the line even when the models can be applied to widespread disease, might eventually help many people, but there are only some thirty-five ADA-deficient cases of severe combined immunodeficiency (SCID) born each year in the United States. Approximately one-third of them will have a properly matched sibling donor, and so will be able to get a regular bone marrow transplant. That leaves about twelve cases a year eligible for gene therapy. Of those, some might be able to take an unmatched transplant. Others certainly are candidates for an experimental procedure called PEG-ADA just now being tested by Michael S. Herschfield at Duke University, in which the ADA enzyme—not the gene but its product—is injected directly into patients, much as insulin is given to diabetics.

The biologists enjoy pointing out that there are more labs in the field than patients. "The only urgency is the competition of labs," said Orkin. "There is not a crying need elsewhere. This is not like AIDS. These are rare diseases. Gene therapy is a stunt. Face it. Our position is to try to understand the science. If we learn enough, it will apply. Intellectually it is more interesting to understand. We are just plodding along right now. We don't know why or what works."

The difference between these observations and those offered by the physicians is striking. The sharp disparity exists at least in part because the medical doctors labor in a world apart from the basic researchers. Some of them sit across from patients as well as test tubes. Some of them listen to parents beg, sometimes demand, treatment. "I resent the fact that a few well-meaning individuals have presented arguments strong enough to curtail the scientific technology that promises to give some hope," wrote one such parent, Ola Huntley, mother of three children suffering from sickle cell disease. "Aren't they deciding what's best for me without any knowledge of my suffering? I am very angry that anyone would presume to deny my children the essential genetic treatment."

In early 1985, University of Wisconsin clinician Dr. Sheldon Horowitz looked at his six-year-old ADA-deficient patient, Erin McCarthy, and thought: We can't wait forever. We have gotten into trouble hearing that gene therapy might be available in six, twelve months, and trying to wait, and while we wait the kid gets some terrible infection and then we're really up against the wall. There came a day when Horowitz felt moved to sit down and compose a letter to the federal panel that must approve human trials. "Gene therapy may have only a small chance of success," he wrote, "but its risks are minimal compared with certain death."

You would not at first be trying to cure anybody, French Anderson and others say. You would be doing it specifically as part of the experimental research, using a small handful of patients with drastic, terminal illnesses, patients with no alternatives, patients who volunteer. Such Phase One clinical testing is not unusual. We test drugs and treatments all the time when treating terminally ill patients stricken with such diseases as cancer or AIDS.

Accepting and using imperfect science, uncertain knowledge—that, say the applied scientists, is what medical therapy is all about.

Anderson's collaborator, R. Michael Blaese, deputy chief of the metabolism branch and head of the cellular immunology section at the National Cancer Institute, talked one morning of why he thinks the science is close to justifying going into humans. He listed recent hard evidence pointing to more efficient methods and increased safety, but he also mentioned something else. "I go around talking to clinicians," Blaese said. "Often they are cancer specialists accustomed to throwing new drugs at terminal patients, realizing the chances are slim but the possible benefits so great. They are used to taking desperate chances all the time. That's how they make discoveries. . . . They keep asking me, what are you afraid of, why not try, why not go in? I sort of feel that way too. There's no hard promise it will help, but patients with terminal diseases are willing. . . . I remember when I was a student in the 1960s, doing work in a basic research lab. Then Christiaan Barnard started putting hearts in people, when the labs were suggesting it wasn't going to work. But it worked. . . . Then came kidney transplants, after the lab tests showed that skin transplants wouldn't work. I remember the basic lab people being very dubious, skeptical. But it worked."

Even those who must oversee human gene therapy efforts find it difficult to reconcile these sharply contrasting worlds. When Robert Cook-Deegan, a medical doctor with postgraduate training in molecular biology, directed a sweeping inquiry into the human gene therapy field, he chose to print an epigraph at the front of the resulting report, which was published in 1984 by the Office of Technology Assessment (OTA), an arm of the Congress. It was a quote from the Austrian philosopher Ludwig Wittgenstein: "Where two principles really do meet which cannot be reconciled with one another, then each man declares the other a fool and heretic."

One day recently, Cook-Deegan said: "We're at a real sticking point. There are certain kinds of information you can't get without going into humans. But at the same time you don't want to go into kids just for the hell of it, without some hope it will help. People will part company on this. I don't know how we will grapple with this."

In the fall of 1986, Anderson decided he would simply have to force the issue. He was tired of the selective-advantage issue just hanging there, unresolved, with no prospects for reaching an answer. He would have to put a proposal on the table. He would have to submit something to the panel that must approve clinical trials on humans—the human gene therapy subcommittee of the NIH's Recombinant DNA Advisory Committee. He would invite fire from all his competitors. What more do you want to know, he would ask them—and more important, how can we get the answers to your questions without going into a human?

Anderson began talking to his trusted lab lieutenants, Martin Eglitis and Philip Kantoff, about his plans. First they would publish a paper about their monkey experiment results, then they would put something before the RAC.

"Are you willing to go into a patient and fail?" Kantoff, dubious, asked Anderson one day at lunch, as the three shared a pizza in the lab's conference room.

"Sure," Anderson said. "If we waited until we were certain, lots of kids would die. Also, let's face it, it's a big scientific plum we're after. It comes down to selective advantage. We don't fail if that's right, and we can never know if that's right until we go in."

"Isn't ambition coloring our plans?" Kantoff asked.

"No more so than ambition influences a businessman or an athlete," Anderson said. "Every Olympian is overly ambitious."

"Why do it now, French?" Eglitis asked.

"Because then we will direct the debate. I know everyone on RAC and the subcommittee. I know what they know and what they don't know. They basically don't want to make a mistake. But they don't know what's right or wrong. Only we sit around and think about these things. So by putting a protocol on the table, finally everyone will understand—here's what we know, here's what we don't know, here's what we cannot know without going in."

But Anderson's plan—the monkey paper, then the RAC protocol—soon hit a sizable roadblock. Near the end of January 1987, *Nature* rejected Anderson's monkey paper. Two anonymous reviewers, other scientists in the field, had savaged his results. "Although the authors naturally wish to put their findings in the best light, most dispassionate observers would conclude that the experiments were largely a failure," wrote one. "I am left cold by this work."

What happened next may tell something about a world where judgments and perceptions claim as much territory as do hard facts and clear truths. When Anderson sent his monkey paper to another publication, *The Journal of Experimental Medicine,* the editors there readily accepted it. This magazine was not as prestigious or widely read as *Nature,* but it was a recognized professional journal. So when Anderson's article appeared in print in July, he had the stamp of legitimacy he'd so long sought, along with prominent newspaper headlines excitedly announcing another big step forward in human gene therapy.

In this fashion, the stage was finally set. Anderson now could try to force to the public table what previously had been a relatively private debate within a corner of the scientific community. He could raise the questions he wanted everyone to consider: Do you at times leap with incomplete knowledge into the unknown, powered on by faith that discoveries will be made and by the driving obligation to do something for a patient? Or do you progress step by step, keeping both eyes firmly focused on the data and the facts, guided by what is truly known?

After some consideration, Anderson decided he could trigger this debate by filing something less than a formal proposal. The five-hundred-page "preclinical data document" his team composed instead in the spring of 1987 was Anderson's own hybrid invention, not called for under any formal procedure. The thick volume included a detailed roundup of the state of the science, along with a draft version of a protocol for human trials—one that followed, essentially, the protocol he had used on the monkeys two years before.

Send this to all my competitors, Anderson told the RAC's executive secretary, William J. Gartland, Jr. Here are their names.

Mulligan got a copy. So did Stu Orkin, Dusty Miller and eight others. Anderson knew he was walking into a clearing and willfully drawing the fire of his critics. If they're correct, he reasoned, then I say so, and I haven't lost anything. If it turns out there are hidden agendas, which there will be, or just simply concerns . . . they can be answered. This would also be a dry run for the policy-making process itself. A "bellwether," Anderson called it, showing how the process handles all this. Can a system of government committees and regulatory bodies reach answers in this sort of matter?

The gentlest of the reviews that arrived on Gartland's desk in the summer and fall of 1987 were merely negative in tone toward Anderson's document. Others were withering. Noting the low ADA enzyme levels, the risk of viral contamination and the emergence of the alternative therapy involving PEG-ADA enzyme, all but one firmly agreed the time was not right for human trials.

Anderson, in turn, responded on November 20 with a letter to Gartland that can fairly be likened to the sort of long-planned move a wily chess master might make just when he appears cornered. "Overall we agreed with essentially all of the concerns raised by the reviewers," he began. By the time the letter reached its conclusion on page seven, however, Anderson was writing, "We now think, based on all the information that is currently available, that it would be appropriate to prepare a limited clinical protocol."

In the leap from the opening to closing thoughts soared the soul of a true—some would say fevered—applied scientist.

Our decision, Anderson wrote, hinges on the following consideration: In specific cases where all available therapies, including bone marrow transplants and PEG-ADA, have failed and there is nothing else to offer, "would it be ethical to deny the potentially life-saving gene therapy protocol in the face of certain death?" We would certainly be more comfortable if we understood the gene transfer procedure better, and had higher enzyme activity and less risk of viral contamination. But a clinical decision in this setting, as in other complex medical situations, should be based on an assessment of the risk/benefit ratio for the patient, which in this case involves the threat of impending death. We are aware of three infants who may soon fall into the last hope category. Because of that, we feel a limited clinical protocol should be submitted in the near future.

It was against this backdrop that the RAC subcommittee gathered on December 7, 1987, in Conference Room 9 of Building 31C at the NIH headquarters in Bethesda, Maryland. The day offered its share of unspoken undercurrents and subtexts. By design, the fifteen-person panel includes three each from the fields of basic laboratory science, clinical medicine, ethics, the law and public policy. Because the committee's highly respected consultant in retrovirology, Nobel Prize winner Howard Temin, could not attend, the panel had decided to add what they called an "ad hoc consultant" to the panel for the day, someone who could deliver the expertise that Temin normally provided. The ad hoc consultant they had selected was Richard Mulligan.

Anderson in his tailored suit and Mulligan in his sport jacket and bow tie both looked as if they were wearing someone else's clothing. Anderson sat with members of his lab in chairs along the wall, amid some two dozen other observers. Mulligan sat at the long rectangular table with the other committee members.

At first, Anderson's November 20 response to his critics appeared to be shaping the discussion. Anderson's letter shifts the idea from a full-blown clinical study to the idea of a limited, last hope protocol, suggested James F. Childress, an ethicist in the University of Virginia's religious studies department. Do the standards for approval change? Childress thought so. Is there a "boomlet for last chance" here? asked Alexander Capron from the University of Southern California Law School, who happened to be knitting as the meeting unfolded.

Mulligan was taken aback. What was this talk of last hope? He thought all candidates for this experiment were last hope patients. That's what this therapy was for. And why was that man knitting? "Excuse me," he said out loud. "As I understand it, French never was going to do more than two patients. So what's the difference? I don't see how the issue has changed."

Most likely, it had not. "Let me set your mind at ease," Maurice J. Mahoney from Yale University said dryly to Capron. "I don't think many here see the two situations differently."

Late in the morning, the conversation eventually turned to matters of hard science. It was Mulligan's turn to talk retrovirology. He rose and walked to the head of the table, holding a single sheet filled with notes.

"I think I will involve French in this if I may," he said.

Mulligan had questions. I am curious, he said to Anderson. Do you have data that shows infection of stem cells?

That is a crucial point, Anderson allowed. We have no evidence with the monkey or with ADA.

"So . . ." Mulligan said, drawing out his words. "It appears you're infecting . . . something."

Mulligan by now was busy with a grease pencil working on a board set before him on an easel. Soon it was covered with circles, arrows and cells.

He continued: Why was Anderson assuming he wouldn't have to kill off a patient's own bone marrow cells before adding the newly infected ones? "What's the evidence for that?" he asked.

Anderson began citing several studies, but eventually stopped. Pointing to Mulligan's chart, he said: "I have to admit there are black boxes up there."

What level of efficiency would he need to get selective advantage? Mulligan wondered.

"That's also a critical question," Anderson said. "There are data and studies, but they still don't answer the question. We don't really know."

Mulligan took two steps, digesting these responses, then stopped and bit off his next question: "I am curious, French. Do you think it would work if you did it?"

"That's the question. . . . No one really knows." Here Anderson paused noticeably. "I don't think it is likely."

Mulligan nodded slightly, his eyes gleaming. "Then what would we learn from this experiment?" he inquired.

That question, finally, represented the heart of the matter. Scientists are quite familiar with failed experiments, but they like experiments to provide answers whether or not they succeed.

"If there is any improvement, any selective advantage, we learn that that happens," Anderson said.

"And if nothing happens?" Mulligan asked.

"That's a good question," Anderson answered. "That's why we changed course, in the November 20 response, to a last hope protocol."

Both men seemed satisfied as the meeting drew to an end near three o'clock. Mulligan thought he had made it clear that there was no data or evidence to support a human trial. Anderson believed the issues were now sharply framed, the committee prepared to evaluate proposals.

"After listening to this today," Anderson told the panel, "my group will get together and draft a limited last case protocol. Then the committee will have to make tough decisions."

The first human trials will, in the end, also need approval from an institutional biosafety committee, the full RAC, the director of NIH, and the FDA, but the frontline deliberations will come from the members of this RAC subcommittee. It is not clear when they will face the decision Anderson intends to force upon them.

We want to approach this rationally, the panel's members say when asked. We want a reasoned process, a legitimate procedure. Most on the panel, however, also say they are generally inclined to rely on the critiques sent in by the ten reviewers. We must look, they explain, to what the scientists tell us. That the experts' judgments are colored by matters of training, philosophy and politics as well as by the hard facts is a condition that the panel must accept. It is partly an epistemological question, observed the bioethicist LeRoy Walters, the RAC subcommittee chairman.

"How do you know the truth?" he pointed out. "There is no alternative but to listen to the experts. Who are the experts? The experts are those who are acknowledged by experts to be experts. At a certain point, it gets to be a circle."

"There may be gray areas," Gartland added, "but at least we can agree that there are these gray areas and go ahead anyway. We can at least agree about what we are basing our decision on."

The type of question less likely to be agreed upon has more to do with the scientists than the science. It is difficult to watch the pursuit of human gene therapy without speculating about the people involved. Most particularly, it is hard not to wonder whether French Anderson's fiercely willed drive toward a finish line is a danger to science, or what is required in order to make transcendent leaps.

Just how do you reach the landmark discoveries? It is true that the history of science abounds with sudden, intuitive advances. Yet it is also true that many of those came not from acts of directed will, but rather from unplanned, unexpected random twists of fate in a lab.

One morning recently, a member of the RAC leafed through the scathingly critical reviews of Anderson's preclinical data document. He could not hide his puzzlement. The RAC had received not a single piece of paper, not a phone call, from any other scientist interested in filing a protocol. So he had a question. What was it with French Anderson? Was he a visionary, that far ahead of the others? Or was he something else? Was he off the wall?

That question was put to Anderson the same day.

"I don't know who is right," he said. "I don't know if I'm right or not. Was Lindbergh right? If he crashed into the Atlantic he would have been wrong. The simple issue is that if you're a pioneer, most pioneers by definition flame out. They fall off cliffs, their ship sinks, their plane crashes, something else happens. Were they right or were they wrong? If they were lucky and they got there, they were right."

UPDATE

On March 30, 1990, W. French Anderson's formal proposal to conduct human gene therapy was considered by the same NIH Human Gene Therapy Subcommittee that had listened so dubiously to his preliminary report more than two years before. Once again Richard Mulligan was in attendance, and once again, this group of experts from across the country peppered Anderson with a barrage of deeply skeptical questions, sounding unconvinced about the plan's efficacy and safety. One week before, the Food and Drug Administration had licensed the drug PEG-ADA, an injectable form of the ADA enzyme, for use in humans, so committee members now wondered why this simpler treatment shouldn't be used instead of complex gene therapy. By the end of the day, the committee members had decided that Anderson's proposal still left many questions unanswered. Anderson, acting neither surprised nor discouraged by this response, said he would revise the proposal and submit it once again.

This he did on June 1, 1990, at a meeting Mulligan did not attend. Anderson's modified proposal contained new data provided by collaborators in Italy and New York, data suggesting that when defective T-cells from children suffering from immune deficient diseases were infected with the ADA gene, then injected into mice, the cells survived for months in the mice's bloodstream. This evidence suddenly transformed the committee's attitude. If children receiving Anderson's gene therapy also received PEG-ADA, the committee decided, the procedure just might work. That same day, the committee startled the scientific community by voting unanimously to give provisional approval to W. French Anderson's proposal, with the stipulation that he meet eight specific criteria spelled out by the panel.

After years of enduring disparagement, Anderson now watched the official obstacles fall with stunning speed. Meeting again on July 30, this time with Mulligan in attendance, the subcommittee formally voted twelve to one for Anderson's proposal, with Mulligan the sole dissenter. The next day, July 31, the full Recombinant DNA Advisory Committee voted its approval, sixteen to one, with Mulligan again the only one objecting. On September 7, the director of the National Institutes of Health gave his approval. A week later, at 8:59 A.M. on September 14, so did the federal Food and Drug Administration.

Within hours on that same day, at one o'clock, the first human gene therapy patient, a four-year-old girl, was wheeled into the pediatric intensive care unit at the NIH clinical center in Bethesda. There, over the course of thirty minutes, some billion gene-altered immune-system cells, suspended in two ounces of sterile saline solution, dripped down a plastic tube into the child's left arm. Four months later, in January 1991, a nine-year-old girl became the second ADA-deficient patient to undergo gene therapy.

This was not the method Anderson's team had so long pursued, however. Discarded for the time being was the critical, unresolved notion of implanting the ADA gene into the self-renewing stem cells of the bone marrow, so that the cure would be permanent. Anderson's team instead had simply isolated and grown in large quantity a sampling of the little girls' T-cells, infected them with the ADA gene, then returned them to the patients by means of a conventional blood transfusion. The girls, scientists explained, would need to return regularly to the NIH for new transfusions, although they hoped the doctored T-cells would prove hardy enough to survive for months.

It is too early to tell whether the first gene therapy patient is cured, and no results have been published in professional journals. There have been signs of improvement, Anderson told reporters in the spring of 1991. There are antibodies she never had before, and normal, functioning immune cells. But it could take a year to know whether the treatment is working or the patient cured, Anderson added. What is more, because the girl shows no outward signs of disease and the current protocol involves relatively small doses of cells, any improvement that does occur may be difficult to document.

The central issues raised by Anderson's pursuit of human gene therapy therefore remained unanswered, despite the dramatic turn of events. Skeptical scientists still publicly scorned Anderson's work, saying he was driven by ambition rather than good science. "The main impetus [for the experiment] is the need for French Anderson to be first to do gene therapy in man," said Dr. Arthur Bank, professor of medicine and human genetics at Columbia University. Stuart Orkin called the attempt "a long shot that's highly unlikely to succeed. . . . I think the NIH team wanted to make the first strike. A large number of scientists believe this experiment is not well-founded scientifically. I'm quite surprised there hasn't been more of an outcry against the experiment." Mulligan agreed, with his customary bluntness: "They're misreading their own data. The possible benefits of the experiment don't outweigh the risks. It should be scuttled. The people doing this aren't scientists. The data they used to approve this are kindergarten stuff."

As always, Anderson held his ground in the face of his critics. "We feel that gene therapy is potentially a major new medical option," he said one day in the spring of 1991. "And the most important thing, with any new therapy, is to get started. Now we're getting started."

A Crafty Purpose

December 1985
West Lafayette, Indiana

In the summer of 1981, during a chance conversation between two scientists at an international conference in Strasbourg, France, Michael G. Rossmann, fifty-five, a professor of biological sciences from Purdue University, mentioned that he was looking for a new project and was thinking of tackling the polio virus. The goal he had in mind, to forge a three-dimensional model of the polio virus, was unprecedented and excitingly ambitious—none of the complex viruses that infect humans and animals had ever been so mapped. Listening to Rossmann describe his plan, however, Roland R. Rueckert, fifty-two, a microbiologist from the University of Wisconsin in Madison, could summon no expression of support or enthusiasm. In fact, he stiffened with alarm. Rueckert had good reason to do so—mapping the polio virus, after all, had long been his own goal.

Rueckert had first learned how to grow polio viruses in large, pure amounts at the University of California, Berkeley, virology lab between 1962 and 1965. He'd eventually found that they contained four protein chains, which was hard to figure—he'd imagined there would only be one protein in something so small. How did they all fit? he'd started wondering. That question, in turn, had kindled his interest in the structure of the polio virus.

For a long time, it had seemed an impenetrable topic. Scientists were able to map in three dimensions a few proteins and plant viruses through the technique called crystallography, but the procedure was relatively primitive—the subjects would be isolated, converted into crystals, then hit with X rays for hours, after which researchers would laboriously interpret the resulting photos for years before constructing a model. Animal viruses were much too large and complex to tackle in this manner. They'd have to be X-rayed for so long that the crystals would disintegrate before the job was completed. Even if scientists could collect the needed data, the task of making sense of it all would be overwhelmingly burdensome.

Methods had evolved, though. By the time Rueckert encountered Rossmann in France, there were emerging new high-power machines that could X-ray virus crystals in minutes rather than hours, and new supercomputers that could handle the complex computations in hours rather than years. Rueckert had come to realize that scientists soon could do crystallography on the polio virus. Since his own training was rooted in microbiology, however, he needed someone more familiar with the advanced X-ray techniques. He'd found a promising candidate in a graduate student named Jim Hogle, then working in a crystallography lab on campus, and had set him to work with a supply of polio virus. In time, Hogle had carried this project with him when he'd transferred to the Harvard University laboratory of Steve Harrison, the first crystallographer to map a plant virus's structure.

Now here was Rossmann, threatening tough competition for Hogle. Rueckert chose his words carefully. "Why don't you go after the common cold virus instead?" he suggested. "I'll help you. I'll provide samples of the cold virus I'm growing in my own lab."

Rossmann, curious, studied the man who suddenly was offering such assistance. The pair could not have been more different in character. Rossmann, wiry and wild-haired, seemed to dart rather than walk across a room. He budgeted his time ferociously and rushed back to his lab most evenings after dinner to work late into the night. Rueckert, by contrast, was stocky and low-key, and enjoyed long walks in the woods near his home. People who spoke fast or in a high-pitched tone tended to get on his nerves. The two scientists' knowledge, however, complemented each other's. Rueckert moved in a world filled with cells and amino acids and genes, while Rossmann, his training rooted in mathematics and physics, was one of the deans in the rarefied field of crystallography—he'd been second only to Harrison at Harvard in determining the structure of a plant virus, and had worked in the Cambridge lab of Max Perutz, who won a Nobel Prize for solving the structure of the hemoglobin protein.

For five hours Rossmann and Rueckert talked over the matter of cold and polio viruses, the one wavering and the other pressing. As Rueckert recalls it, Rossmann's reluctance to switch his attention from the polio to the cold virus was rooted largely in the personal. "Michael wanted the glamour of polio. The argument that turned Michael, I think, came when I emphasized that the polio project at Harvard was not Steve Harrison's. Michael was determined to show he was better than Harrison. After I explained it was Jim Hogle's, Mike agreed to study the cold virus. I would supply samples, and show them how to grow it."

In just such an inadvertent and self-interested fashion, these two unlikely collaborators found themselves bound together in a singular endeavor that would, before it was over, make scientific history.

Among those who soon signed on to pursue the cold virus project at Rossmann's lab in Purdue were two young postdoctoral fellows. Edward Arnold, twenty-eight, had trained in organic chemistry and crystallography at Cornell. Gerrit Vriend, twenty-nine, had studied biochemistry and computer science in the Netherlands. Rossmann was famous, they both figured, and his project looked interesting. This could be the place to launch their careers.

The team first needed to grow and crystallize viruses, which was not an easy task. Rueckert showed them what to do.

Viruses will not multiply by themselves. They are nonliving agents that can reproduce only by seizing a host cell. Beneath the hollow protein shell of a virus is a small amount of genetic material that, when released inside a cell, commandeers the cell's replicating apparatus, directing it to make duplicate copies of the virus. So the scientists began with a sample of rhinovirus 14 from Rueckert's lab—one of the more than one hundred known types of cold viruses—and added these to human cells, where they would replicate. Then they broke open the cells to get at the multiplied viruses, purified them, and combined them with a chemical that would draw out all water. If everything went well, Rueckert told the others, virus crystals would begin to grow within twenty-four hours. Within four days, they would expand to three-tenths of a millimeter, about the dimension of a black pepper grain and the size needed for X-raying.

But everything did not go well in the Purdue lab, at least not at first.

Sometimes, the cells died. Other times, the process produced fine "crystal showers" too small to be X-rayed. Once, after a series of failures, they spent days rechecking everything from the virus to the machinery before learning that the problem was with the building's water supply. "It's not so much fancy stuff here at this stage," said virologist Marcia Kremer. "But there are so many places where simpler things go wrong."

Once the process did work, and he had his virus crystals, Rossmann did not want to expose them to his lab's conventional X-ray generator. A crystal would have to be hit with the rays for more than eighteen hours, and by then, he reasoned, it would be quite dead. Rossmann thought instead about leasing time on Cornell University's High Energy Synchrotron Source, essentially a particle accelerator that provides a thousand times stronger X rays than conventional generators. Rossmann wasn't sure whether sensitive virus crystals would hold up under such intense rays, but if they did, a crystal that normally had to be X-rayed for eighteen hours could be shot in four minutes. Rossmann liked those numbers.

He and Eddie Arnold first visited Cornell in 1983. The data they collected then were not useful, for the crystals they brought were a disordered, inconsistent lot. They did, however, establish that they could get high-resolution photos. So the next year, in May 1984, Rossmann and a team of six returned to Cornell with one hundred crystals carefully mounted for X-raying. To make best use of the limited and expensive synchrotron time, they worked around the clock for five days, with three-man teams alternating on twelve-hour shifts. They repeated this process again in June and November.

Each photo produced by crystallography appears essentially as a circle containing many dots. Clear distinct dots are a thing of beauty to a crystallographer. By the end of the year, Rossmann had them.

The most complex task of all, however, still lay in front of the team. They had to convert those dots back into the three-dimensional virus from which they originated. "What we start with and what we want is the virus model," Vriend explained later. "The process takes us to those dumb dots, unfortunately. So then we have to do all sorts of things to the dots. If you do it all correctly, you get what you started with. We are undoing what our own experimental process did to us."

The scientists knew that those dots represented waves of light from X rays that had scattered, or refracted, as they passed through the crystal. If they could properly measure those refracted waves, they could begin to figure out the atomic structure of the virus crystal that had scattered them. Using an optical film scanner, they calculated the degree of brightness and darkness of the many dots. From this, they could determine the character of the light waves. No single shot, however, can yield a portrait of the virus. The film is flat, and the crystal is three-dimensional. Moreover, a single shot can involve no more than 40,000 dots—otherwise the photo would simply be all black—while the team needed 580,000 distinct dots to generate their virus model. So each shot represented only a slice of the virus, reflecting the angle and position of the crystal in relation to the X ray. To form a complete picture, the scientists needed to combine the data from eighty-six separate shots.

First, they had to assemble as many light waves as possible and place them in the proper position relative to one another. This difficult procedure, called phasing, confounded even some of the scientists. Those who knew the workings of the cell gave way to those who grasped the complexities of higher physics. Yet phasing alone did not provide enough information, for at best, the scientists could match up less than one-third of the needed waves.

In the end, the fate of the Purdue team's years of work hinged on a controversial theory that Rossmann had first advanced as a young man. His paper, published in January 1962 in an arcane journal called the *Acta Crystallographica*, had attracted many doubters. Rossmann never forgot the reaction and never let go of his desire to prove them wrong. If you know that you have a twenty-faced symmetrical object such as a virus, Rossmann in essence had reasoned, you do not need all the data. You can extrapolate the information from a subsection to the rest of the object.

"Michael had predicted it would happen," said Vriend. "Scientists simply lacked the computer power and courage to start it."

The Purdue team had no alternative. In early March 1985, they turned to the university's Cyber 205 supercomputer. In essence, they asked it to average what data they did have and apply that to the whole virus. The result provided a few more matched waves and a clearer map, so they pressed on. Forty times, they asked the computer to average and reconstruct the map. What followed, for the scientists, was wondrous. On the screen, the computer began to build, atom by atom, a three-dimensional structure. Tubes, arms and hollows took shape. Arnold could, in some early images, see the canyons and ridges of the virus. He could not yet see the protein chains fully resolved. For the scientists to be right, everything would have to match and fit together —structure, proteins, chemical formulas. Arnold knew that their type of scientific pursuit often reached a dead end after years of labor. Still, he couldn't help but feel excited.

"It was like looking at a beautiful picture from far away," he said later, "and then from closer and closer."

In Wisconsin, meanwhile, Rueckert and a graduate student, Barbara Sherry, were not sure they were heading anywhere with their part of the inquiry.

Since 1982, they had been working to identify where human infection-fighting antibodies attach themselves on the virus's protein chain —such sites are called antigenic binding sites. Because they'd observed that all the antibodies grouped at one of four places, they knew there were four antigenic sites. To learn precisely where those sites were situated on the virus protein chain, the scientists had then looked at mutated viruses that were resistant to the antibodies. Their reasoning: Whatever had mutated in those viruses was preventing the antibodies from attaching and doing their job, so the mutations must be at the sites where the antibodies normally attach. If they could find those mutations on the protein chain, they would have found the four antigenic sites.

The only way to find those mutations, however, was to compare the lengthy protein chains of normal viruses with those of the mutated, resistant viruses and look for the minute differences in their sequences. The limits of their science and their resources required that the Wisconsin team do this search at a painstaking crawl. The laborious task took three full years.

When they finished in January 1985, it at first seemed the occasion for considerable celebration—Rueckert and Sherry had found the mutated sites. Looking closer, however, it soon became apparent that what they'd come up with did not make sense. Some mutations sat off by themselves, much farther down the protein chain from where the rest of the mutations were clustered, and where antibodies appeared to bind. Rueckert and Sherry were dismayed. "They should have been together, where the antibodies indicated they were," Sherry said. "We drafted a paper reporting this unsolved problem and were about to publish it. We never did, though."

Before they could, the phone rang in their lab one morning. Rossmann was calling. He had his breakthrough.

. . .

From early March to early April, the Purdue team had harnessed forty percent of the supercomputer's capacity, feeding it six million distinct pieces of data. Without the supercomputer, the month of calculations would have taken ten years.

This was not the science of old. Scientists not that long ago used little more than logic and chemical formulas to imagine what a gene or protein looked like. Then they built oversize structures with twists of wire and plastic, much as a youth assembles a model airplane, studying and adjusting the parts until the triumphant moment when everything seemed to fit. Now, the supercomputer did much of that work. As monumental a task as any for the scientists was to design the software programs that guided the Cyber 205.

On Saturday night, April 6, Arnold asked the computer to plot out the map as it then stood. This the computer did in a series of separate frames, for the image was too complex to integrate into one snapshot. On Sunday, Arnold printed out the series of separate frames and converted them into transparencies. He then stacked these transparencies one on top of another. If they contained a complete and accurate map of the virus, they would all match. As the scientists looked down through the pile of transparencies, they would see a single unified image, with the structural borders and protein strings forming continuing lines rather than overlapping. The protein would be discretely resolved, and the mathematical and chemical formulas would fit with the structural shape. Everything would make sense.

Just as likely, though, they would see nothing. For most of the team, that would mean they had wasted three or four years. For Rossmann, it would mean that for twenty years his vision of the biological world had been fundamentally wrong.

When the team gathered in their basement lab in Purdue's molecular biology lab at four o'clock Sunday, Rossmann said later, "I frankly was very skeptical. There had been so much doubt about my molecular replacement idea I thought maybe they were right. This was just supposed to be a diagnostic test to make sure we were not up a dead end. I was just seeking encouragement to continue. In fact, we had plans to go back to Cornell the next Thursday to shoot more crystals."

Vriend was the first to look down at the stacked transparencies. He did not know what to think. "I had never seen such a map before. I thought, well, that looks nice."

Then Rossmann looked. He said nothing at first, preferring to study what was before him. After four years, a few more minutes did not seem to him a long time. He knew, though, what he was looking at, for he had worked many times with such transparency maps. He had it. The job was done. "This is the most beautiful map possible," he wrote on the blackboard.

If there was any doubt, the team had only to look at Rossmann a moment later—he was dancing on the conference table. Soon after, team members and their spouses were down the street at the China Palace restaurant, pouring champagne.

One last critical step remained before the four-year pursuit of the cold virus could be considered completely successful. The Purdue team's model had to match with Rueckert's and Sherry's information about antigenic sites, or something was fundamentally wrong. Both teams, after all, in essence had been working only with parts of the whole. The Purdue team had a structure that looked good but existed in a vacuum, as an object to marvel at. The Wisconsin team had biological insights that tapped particular secrets of the virus but could not explain it as a complete entity. Each needed the other.

On May 1, Rueckert and Sherry arrived at the Purdue lab to compare findings. At the start of the morning, they knew only the locations of their antigenic sites on a linear chemical protein chain. They had no idea where they were in the virus's three-dimensional structure. Most important, they had no explanation for their oddly situated mutations. "They hadn't sent us data because they didn't trust what they had," Rossmann said. "I expected their data not to fit. There was tension as we looked at each piece of data. I didn't want to see, but I had to."

Point by point, slowly, they checked what they had. When Rueckert and Sherry's four antigenic sites were matched with Rossmann's structure, the sites turned out to be just where they should be—on the elevated ridges above the canyons. The scientists could see where antibodies bind to the virus. Tension gave way to excited cheers. "It was like when you laugh so much your sides hurt," Rossmann said. "I just felt I couldn't take any more happiness. I had to leave and walk around."

Then, as they looked longer, it became clear why Rueckert and Sherry found mutations far from where they should be on the protein chain. In the three-dimensional structure, they saw that the protein chain was folded and curled over itself in such a way that the two distant spots actually were positioned together. This time, it was Barbara Sherry who danced on the conference table.

"It was not just a confirmation, it was the ground-breaking next step," said Arnold. "Without this, we would see a structure but not know what to make of it. We would just know it looked sort of like a plant virus. Our work was a monument. Their work made the rhinovirus 14 come to life."

Rueckert considered the day one of the most exciting moments of his life. "When you get a breakthrough like that . . . the feeling that you can explain everything is very appealing. You feel like you can control the universe."

Many weeks would pass before Rueckert and the others became aware that their sense of omnipotence was largely illusory. It was true they had before them, in exquisitely fine, atom-by-atom detail, one of the world's most resilient agents of disease. It was true they could see how it was structured, how its various parts fit together, how it attacked the body and how the body reacted. But they still could not see how to master the indestructible cold virus.

That had always been an elusive goal for scientists, and for good reason. Because there are one hundred different types of cold viruses, and they regularly mutate, no one antibody can neutralize all of them. In fact, the body needs a different antibody for each type of cold virus. Scientists have long searched for an unchanging structural feature common to all cold viruses, believing they then could develop a single vaccine that would generate antibodies to attack this target. Peering through electron microscopes, however, they had never been able to spot such a common feature, since they saw the cold virus only as a vague, fuzzy ball.

With his newly clarified model, Rossmann was certain he could do better, and he was right. He could see that the fuzzy ball was actually composed of twenty triangle-shaped sides, marked on the surface by ridges and canyons. Looking closer, Rossmann believed he even could see the long-pursued common feature. It was the part of the virus that grabs onto a host cell, he surmised, and it lies deep within the virus's canyons.

But what he saw did not provide him a solution. What he saw, rather, was an explanation for why the cold virus has remained unvanquished. The answer, Rossmann in time came to realize, was simple. Although the cold virus did have an unchanging common feature, the human body's infection-fighting antibodies couldn't reach it—the antibodies were just too big to fit into the virus's narrow canyons. They instead had to attach to the ridges above the canyons, ridges that regularly mutated. This made the cold virus a much tougher opponent than the deadly polio virus, which does not often successfully mutate. And this explained why colds still plague mankind while polio does not. A preventive cold vaccine now seemed more unlikely than ever.

Rueckert and Rossmann could not help but feel bemused. Out of a chance meeting and decidedly uncelestial human motives, they'd shifted from a glamorous scientific subject to a commonplace one, but in the end, the cold virus had turned out to be a much more exciting target than the polio virus. Exciting to them, at least—the cold virus's triumphant design filled them with wonder and delight rather than a sense of defeat. Rossmann and Rueckert had found no cure, but they had revealed a natural world of elegantly simple order. They had, in other words, achieved their goal.

"How crafty, what purpose to the design," Rossmann said of the cold virus when it was all over. "Cold viruses have taken a long time to fine-tune themselves. It's interesting how random selection creates something of a higher level. Very pretty. It all makes sense. That's what our work presupposes: When you get it right, it will all make sense."

Portrait of a Dinosaur

March 1991
Montecito, California

There is a sequence of events that unfolds with regularity most weekday mornings in Montecito, the affluent hamlet of nine thousand that overlooks the Pacific Ocean just south of Santa Barbara. At precisely 8:30 A.M., a forty-five-year-old man clad in a wash 'n' wear shirt and pair of slacks emerges from his house, hoists a tan canvas backpack over his shoulders, climbs on his twenty-year-old bicycle, and begins pedaling down the private lane that leads from his home to East Valley Road. There he turns left, heading toward the east. He glances with unhappiness at a huge half-built house—he's appeared at county planning commission meetings to protest this neighbor's proposed five-car garage. Pedaling on, he waves to familiar workmen, shopkeepers and pedestrians as he passes a telephone company switching station, a hardware store, a real estate office, an antiques store and the San Ysidro Pharmacy and Coffee Shop, where the chic locals taking breakfast at outdoor tables playfully shout questions—"Why can't you afford a car?"—and offer thumbs up signs, as if watching a marathoner on his stretch run. Just past the pharmacy, he turns left on San Ysidro Road and cuts across a parking lot to a one-story, six-room wood and stucco converted house.

After a two-block journey, Dr. Anthony A. Allina has arrived at his office, ready for another day of work.

Usually, it is a full but not hectic day, for Allina has little taste for what he calls "assembly line medicine." He is a general practitioner, a category of medicine he chose largely because it provided the opportunity to counsel patients and hear what they had to say. Some of his patients are a mite quirky, healthy but convinced they are dying or freezing or otherwise afflicted. Some are in genuine need, although troubled mainly by anxiety or depression. A fair share have back pains or aching knees or viral infections that are quite real but defy effective treatment. All will be able to talk freely, though, at least if they so choose, for the doctor keeps a white-noise generator in his waiting area to blur words coming from the two private examination rooms. That is about as fancy a piece of equipment as there is in Allina's office, for he has no laboratory, not even an X-ray machine. By design, his suite of rooms (shared with a psychologist) more closely resembles a person's living quarters than a doctor's office. My patients, Allina likes to joke, are more likely to sniff for dust than feel intimidated.

Here, in short, is what looks to be the portrait of a man doing exactly what he wishes, a man living a life of his own choosing. "If you see him pedaling along, you think he's the happiest man in town," one neighbor says.

Such a portrait is not complete, however. If the image of Tony Allina bicycling daily to his office represents a doctor who's forged his own world, it also represents one who is now clinging quixotically to that world while it rapidly disintegrates about him.

As the medical profession moves inexorably toward systems involving prepaid care delivered by large corporations or groups of doctors, Allina has declined to participate, withdrawing last summer from the health maintenance organization (HMO) that insures more than a quarter of the local Santa Barbara market and once provided him with twenty percent of his patients. Even though the population is aging and senior citizens make up a quarter of his practice, Allina two years ago stopped taking new Medicare patients. Paperwork burdens, bureaucratic hassles and reduced fees all played some role in his decisions, but mainly, he objected to both the public and the private programs' encroachment on his professional autonomy. Put simply, he did not wish financial considerations, his or others, to influence how he treated a patient.

"I am increasingly anxious and disturbed about what it is like to be a doctor and a patient," he explains when asked about this decision. "Patients are just pawns in a huge system now, and doctors are employees on an assembly line."

Partly because of this attitude and partly because he as a general practitioner doesn't perform the lucrative tests and procedures that draw big payments from insurance companies, Allina's earnings are low for a doctor in an affluent community—under fifty thousand dollars last year. Having boxed himself into a corner, he watches his potential pool of patients relentlessly shrink as more and more in that pool join HMOs or become eligible for Medicare. So watching, an unavoidable question looms. Just how long, he not infrequently asks himself, will I be able to continue my way of doing medicine?

Not for long—that much seems certain. The transformation of medicine has come with astonishing speed, much of it occurring in just the past five years. After watching health care costs increase ten to twenty percent annually, after watching the nation's total health bill approach six hundred billion dollars a year, after watching physicians fail to police themselves, after watching patients demand and expect to excess, those who have footed the ever-rising bill—governments, insurance companies and corporate employers—have simply seized control of the ball game from doctors and their patients. The traditional doctor-patient relationship, in which patients go to physicians of their choice and doctors order tests and bill as they see fit, is gradually disappearing. This erosion of unfettered fee-for-service health insurance plans began in 1983 when Medicare started paying hospitals predetermined rates based on patients' diagnoses, not on the actual treatment rendered or the length of the stay. Then rules arose about when a patient could be hospitalized, and for how long. Curbs were placed on tests ordered, medicines prescribed, services delivered. Doctors' fees were limited to what Medicare deemed reasonable and customary. Soon the private insurance companies were following the government's lead, setting up oversight boards, review committees, utilization panels and fee caps. When all that did not satisfactorily contain costs, more and more corporate employers began switching their health care coverage for employees to even more tightly managed plans.

One type involved preferred provider organizations, PPOs, in which patients could only go to certain doctors who'd contracted with the health plan to provide services for discounted fees. Another involved HMOs—prepaid group health plans that, for a fixed monthly sum per patient, agreed to deliver all needed medical care to its enrollees, but retained the right to determine which treatments were truly needed and where they should be obtained.

Prepaid group health plans weren't new, of course. The earliest ones, among them the Ross-Loos Clinic and the Kaiser Foundation Health Plan, began in the 1930s. A Minneapolis physician, Dr. Paul M. Ellwood, Jr., coined the term *health maintenance organization* in 1970, and the U.S. Congress passed a federal act in 1973 that provided encouragement and regulation for HMOs. The original idea was to provide a means both to insure patients against the costs of health care and to provide that care; the traditional HMO employed full-time, salaried physicians to deliver medical services in its own central location, and sometimes even in its own hospital. Many of the HMOs established in the past half dozen years, however, bear little resemblance to the original prepaid group plans; they have simply contracted with outside physicians or groups of physicians to provide care for the plan's enrollees in the doctors' private offices, alongside non-HMO patients. Consequently, the differences between the various PPOs, HMOs and increasingly regulated fee-for-service insurance plans have started to blur.

However they are organized and whatever they are called, the cost-controlled group plans are expanding their reach. More than a quarter of the country's population is now covered by either an HMO or a PPO; there are some 37 million people enrolled in HMOs alone, almost fourteen percent of the population and double the level in 1984. California, with twenty-nine percent of its insured population in HMOs, has led the way.

Doctors, like it or not, have had to follow that patient base. Many have taken jobs at clinics or health care companies or hospitals—in 1989, for the first time ever, more doctors were working as salaried employees than were operating their own practices. Others have retained their private offices but banded together in loose associations, which in turn have contracted with employers and insurance companies to provide services, usually with limits and rules attached, either on a discounted fee or on a prepaid per-patient basis. Plenty of doctors are bucking the trend, particularly those with affluent patients able and willing to pay their own way, but the pattern is apparent. Leaf through the most sober medical journals these days and you find much the same prediction time and again: The private, independent, autonomous primary care physician such as Tony Allina, calling his own shots in the interests of his long-term patients, spending as much time as needed with each one, is doomed. Depending on the community and the circumstances, health care experts estimate, such doctors might make it for another five years, or ten, or maybe even fifteen. But they cannot last. "The physician who desires to hold on to the traditional notions of the physician-patient relationship might very well find that this requires battle with windmills," is how *The Journal of Legal Medicine* put it in one article.

The result of all this is bitter disenchantment in a profession that is customarily regarded both as prestigious and psychically and financially rewarding. It's evident in surveys of doctors—almost forty percent now usually tell pollsters they'd definitely or probably not enter medical school if they had a career choice to make again. It's even more evident in personal conversations; inviting doctors to discuss their profession these days is a guaranteed way to unleash a flood of grievances.

The first time I felt the direct force of this unhappiness, it so happens I was sitting in my own doctor's office. Dr. Kenneth Matsumoto, a Beverly Hills internist, has been my physician for twenty-two years, a circumstance I'd more or less taken for granted until my employer recently began considering changes in its health plan, changes that might make it difficult for me to continue seeing him. Only then did I start giving thought to a certain change of mood and pace that had colored Matsumoto's office in recent years. I recalled that once, some time ago, he'd called me, agitated, to denounce the latest twist in the Medicare rules. Another morning, as I was leaving, he'd tossed me a long article, torn from a professional journal—"Medicine: The Death of a Profession" was its title. Most recently, I'd noticed fourteen cardboard boxes stacked against the wall in his office. Eventually, I realized that these were all signs of a staunch holdout, a doctor who was refusing to join an HMO, a PPO, a clinic or any sort of group whatsoever. Although he still has a large practice and healthy income, Matsumoto has lost fifteen percent of his primary care patients in the past five years. A fair share of the fourteen cardboard boxes lining his office wall contain files of patients who have recently left his care. The farewell letters and calls he receives all have a familiar ring. My company has changed health insurance plans, they begin. I now have to go to a doctor in an organized group. Could you recommend one from this list?

"Everything is bottom line and profit today," Matsumoto said when I finally told him that soon my file might be in one of those boxes. "How do you bill Medicare or one of the groups for two hours of thinking about a patient's condition, especially when maybe you don't get an answer? There are no procedure codes for thinking about your patient. I am very concerned about what all this is doing to the philosophy of medicine."

My talks with Matsumoto in time led me to other doctors, and to similar expressions of discontent, and finally to Santa Barbara, where I had the notion of looking at how all the changing conditions in medicine had played themselves out over the past decade in one relatively small, confined community. What I found there was a health care scene that has been thoroughly transformed within a handful of years by the arrival in town of a single powerful HMO, Health Net, the second largest in California. I found doctors who have adapted happily to the changes, and doctors who have adapted but not so happily. And I found doctors such as Tony Allina, who refuse to adapt.

Profile of a dying breed, profile of an anachronism. That was how I cautiously explained to Allina my interest in writing about him. I thought he might take offense at such a description, but he did not. "That's what I am," he said. "A dinosaur."

There was a time just ten years ago when doctors in Santa Barbara County considered it improper to compete for one another's patients. Some 350 physicians practicing in their own private offices coexisted in relative peace with some 200 doctors who practiced together as partners in one of two large, shared facilities, the Sansum Clinic and the Santa Barbara Medical Foundation Clinic. By dint of their size, the clinics wielded a certain influence, but in essence they were simply large doctors' offices, open to all patients on a fee-for-service basis; they did not offer their own health plans. When one of the clinics happened to woo private practitioners' patients, the independent physicians would not hesitate to write letters to local professional journals suggesting that the two organized groups in town were "disturbing our patient relations." It's fair to say most doctors did not then possess a particularly sophisticated appreciation for the changing times. Terms such as *targeting markets* and *competitive products* were as yet a foreign language in medicine.

This was the world Tony Allina entered when he first hung out a shingle in 1978. By then he'd developed a particular interest in the relationship between physical health and people's emotional states. One day he managed to link an elderly woman's unexplained diabetes flareup to stress caused by a recent doubling of her rent. Another morning he provided relief to a patient with mysterious pelvic pain by teaching her autogenic training, a form of biofeedback without machinery that he'd learned from a psychologist. If Allina's waiting room often was empty in those early years, he at least had the type of practice he wanted. He spent up to an hour with each patient, and billing was informal—handwritten, amusing, personal notes from Allina's wife Rebecca. Although he must have had some dealings just those dozen years ago with insurance companies, they apparently were unintrusive ones, for Allina does not remember them.

"Every time I walked into the examination room in those days it was a new opportunity to use my healing techniques, my mind, my tools," he recalled. "I had three to five patients a day—as busy a day as you could have. Most of the patients I was seeing had complicated problems."

At first, the signs of the coming change were isolated and gradual—just a patient here and there asking that his file be transferred to the Santa Barbara Medical Foundation Clinic. Allina did not feel particularly concerned. But in talking with other Santa Barbara–area independent doctors during the early 1980s, he found they were losing even more patients to the clinic than he. The trickle had built into a flow.

Health Net, an HMO based in Woodland Hills, was making its presence felt. Then a separate division of Blue Cross of Southern California, now an independent company with some 750,000 enrollees in California, Health Net was among the new breed of HMOs that contracted with outside doctors rather than operate their own health care facilities. It had established a beachhead in Santa Barbara in 1979 by signing an exclusive contract with the Santa Barbara Medical Foundation Clinic to provide care for Health Net members on a fixed, prepaid, per-patient basis. At first, the HMO's presence had been little more than a curiosity, but soon, helped by aggressive marketing, it had started to grow. First one, then another, large employer in the area—Raytheon, the University of California, Delco, Martin Marietta—began offering Health Net to employees as one choice among other health plans. It proved to be a popular alternative because its premiums were cheaper than those of most other plans, about sixty-seven dollars a month per single subscriber.

From a relative handful of Santa Barbara County members in 1982, Health Net quickly rose to more than twenty thousand and kept expanding. By 1985, some local independent doctors had lost twenty percent or more of their practice to the HMO. There was, meanwhile, talk of Blue Cross launching its own local HMO and of Medicare shifting entirely to some form of a prepaid per-patient group program. It was assumed that both would contract with the Santa Barbara Medical Foundation Clinic to provide services, since the clinic was organized, experienced and had elaborate facilities. In the face of all this, it's not hard to see why the once-friendly mood within the Santa Barbara medical community grew strained. The town's independent physicians were no longer colleagues but competitors with those who practiced at the clinic. The battle now had to be joined.

"We were starting to bleed," one prominent independent physician told me. "It was immense and quick. We were losing patients we'd known for a long time. You look around for who's left and the room is pretty empty. Our emotions, in order, were fear, anger, disappointment —and then a sense of reality. Doctors are not trained as businessmen, but some of us were interested in these elements. After the anger and fear wore off, we started to see what could be done to recover."

To compete with the clinic and cut their own deal with various insurers and HMOs, the independent Santa Barbara doctors somehow had to band together, at least on paper. An early effort was California Preferred Providers, Inc., essentially a "clinic without walls" that enabled the private doctors to negotiate discounted fee-for-service schedules directly with insurers, unions and local employers. Allina hesitated but joined—"It was an alternative to Health Net and it was a way to keep my ear to the pipeline," he explained. Another effort was the Cottage Independent Physicians Association, which was pursuing not discounted fee-for-service arrangements, but its own contracts with HMOs and Medicare to provide prepaid per-patient health care.

In the fall of 1986, that's just what it got. Health Net, deciding to reach beyond its exclusive arrangement with the Santa Barbara Foundation Medical Clinic, forged a second deal, this time with Cottage IPA. Health Net enrollees now could choose to see doctors at the clinic, or any independent doctor who was a member of the Cottage IPA.

Allina was not entirely unprepared when he began receiving letters inviting him to join the Cottage IPA. By then, he'd been inundated, in bulletins, meetings and private conversations, with dire warnings about HMOs' imminent claim on forty percent of the market. Private physicians, the newsletters kept advising him, had to offer "competitive products" and be "packaged in many forms."

At a meeting on September 10, 1986, Allina listened as Cottage IPA organizers and a Health Net vice-president explained how it all would work. Health Net would pay Cottage IPA approximately thirty dollars a month for each Health Net member who chose a Cottage IPA physician as his primary care doctor. Of that amount, Cottage IPA would pay one-third—about eleven dollars a month per patient—to each primary care physician, who in exchange would provide all basic medical services, regardless of how often the patient sought his care. The primary care doctors would also serve as "gatekeepers," deciding when to request approval from Cottage IPA's utilization review board for more sophisticated tests, procedures and referrals to the group's specialists. Cottage IPA would pay its specialists on a fee-for-service basis, and would budget forty percent of its fixed payment from Health Net for that purpose. If Cottage IPA kept to its budget for specialists, it would do fine. If it went over budget, it would have problems.

In other words, the financial risk of skyrocketing health costs would be partially shifted from employers and insurers to the doctors who actually made most of the medical decisions. When Cottage IPA primary care physicians considered whether to order tests or make referrals, they would have to weigh their own organization's financial condition along with their patients' needs. Where once doctors had a financial incentive to overuse the system, they now had a financial incentive to underuse the system.

Allina wavered. He no longer was running such a small-time operation—during the early 1980s, his practice had started to grow as he became better known among the young, affluent families of Montecito. With insurance and Medicare forms requiring knowledge of complicated diagnostic and procedural codes, he'd found it necessary to hire a full-time clerk—his wife's friendly handwritten notes no longer would do. His revenue had to keep pace with his mounting overhead. Health Net, now with more than thirty thousand local members, looked promising.

"I'm starting more and more to focus on the business of medicine," he recalled. "I resent this, but I have to. The feeling was I better get on the wagon, that if I didn't, I'd get left in the dust. I also thought it might not be so bad. I talked it over with other doctors. They said 'Let's see, maybe it will be okay.' So I decided to give it a try."

For almost two years, it indeed wasn't so bad—Allina did not feel at all compromised. When he referred Health Net patients for tests or consultations, they got them. He could afford to see his HMO patients often and at length, for the fixed prepaid fee he received each month was generous. In fact, after some calculation, he realized that the payments he received for these HMO patients were larger than what he'd get if he were billing them fees for service. In 1987, his first year with Cottage IPA, Allina's gross income jumped from less than $140,000 to more than $170,000, his net earnings from almost $50,000 to more than $70,000.

The entire enterprise seemed to be flourishing. By the end of 1987, Cottage IPA doctors were treating almost two thousand Health Net patients, and by the end of 1988, almost eight thousand. When they saw their old physicians on the HMOs' approved list, some former patients who'd left for the clinic returned. Soon, HMO patients were accounting for up to a quarter of the Cottage IPA doctors' practices. The biggest problem was a three-month backlog of unpaid specialists' bills, the result of a booming business overloading a limited claims-processing system. If they'd had "some bad luck"—as a Cottage IPA newsletter described the birth of premature twins who'd required 119 days in a hospital intensive care unit—they'd been able to absorb that burden with only a sixty-thousand-dollar loss. "It looked charming," said Dr. Dan Secord, Cottage IPA's president. "We thought we had the world by the tail."

It would take months before the doctors came to realize they were spending far more money than they were receiving from Health Net. Only when an outside claims-processing firm opened the piles of boxes sent it by Cottage IPA, and paid off all the past due debts, did it become apparent that the doctors' organization had lost $348,000 in 1988 and almost $500,000 in the first eight months of 1989.

Later, Cottage IPA doctors would offer a number of explanations for their misfortune, some related to their own mismanagement, some to Health Net's marketing ploys and low lump-sum payments. But it's fair to say that the Cottage IPA doctors basically had been naive about the fundamental concept behind Health Net's plan, and the HMO system generally. Cottage doctors hadn't fully embraced the notion that to survive financially on Health Net's fixed payment, they had to restrict their patients' use of tests, procedures and specialists. Allina had found no restrictions to his practice because there were none in those first years; the utilization committee routinely approved most of what came before them. Specialty care, allotted forty percent of Health Net's payment, was claiming closer to fifty-five percent.

"The gatekeeper role was hard," said Dr. George Weston, Cottage IPA's former medical director. "Patients come in, say they want to see a physical therapist or a psychiatrist or a dermatologist. It was a very difficult role to say no. We never played it before. We had no paid management. We were amateurs running an eight-to-ten-million-dollar operation. We didn't know it was a bad deal."

Soon enough, the freshly enlightened doctors began to adapt to their new world. In June 1989, Allina received a newsletter signed by the Cottage IPA board of directors. "Over the past several months it has become apparent that the Cottage IPA is having a problem with over-utilization . . ." it began. "At the present time, it appears that our incurred expenses are exceeding our income by approximately 10 to 15 percent each month. . . . Until recently, CIPA has been very lenient regarding referrals for specialty and ancillary care. This policy has now been changed. The Utilization Review Committee (URC) has instituted and will enforce strict regulations regarding referrals."

Two months later came an even harsher newsletter. "Perhaps it is too early to see the results of these new regulations," it read. "[But] the reality is that the total cost of all primary care, referrals, follow-ups, procedures, tests, ancillary care have continued to increase. At the present time, our expenses now exceed income by nearly 20 percent or nearly $50,000 per month. . . . To protect the financial viability of CIPA, the Board of Directors has had to institute some rather extreme measures. These consist of newer more strict regulations regarding referrals for specialty care and a decrease in reimbursement to our providers."

From there the exhortations cascaded. Newsletters that Allina received increasingly talked about the "financial implications" of doctors' "practice habits." At a Cottage IPA meeting one night, Allina listened as a speaker went on at length about "rationing" health care services and distinguishing between patients' "desires and needs." Emphasis had to be placed on "the judicious utilization of services" and "not just philosophical goals of the traditional primary care physician." Doctors who practice "cost-effective medicine" should be "recruited and rewarded," and those who do not should be "discontinued." Doctors who find the gatekeeper role difficult and uncomfortable, who object to the tasks of triaging and rationing and policing, should be "discouraged" and "weeded out."

During this time, Allina also began receiving official notices from Medicare that sounded similar themes, but in less abstract terms. One day a Medicare form letter arrived announcing that a ten-dollar blood sugar test he'd administered to a patient with diabetes was "not reasonable and necessary." Allina sent copies of his indignant response to his congressman and the California Medical Association: "This service, a fasting blood sugar, on a diabetic just started on insulin is certainly necessary," he wrote. "I demand a review. . . . I also insist that you send a letter of apology to my patient. I expect a written response to this letter and not a form letter." In return he received another form letter once again denying the test. "Blood sugar determinations are REQUIRED to monitor diabetic patients," he wrote back. "Please stop sending these ridiculous notices!" He eventually won that battle, but months later Medicare sent another notice, this time saying that Allina's two sixty-six-dollar home visits to a ninety-one-year-old semicomatose woman suffering cardiovascular and musculoskeletal collapse due to kidney infection were "not justified." Allina began his response calmly. "When I first saw this patient . . . she was nearly dead," he wrote. "I do not feel the services were unnecessary." By his third letter, he was fuming: "The patient was moribund, hypotensive and semicomatose. How you can reject a claim for medical services in this situation is mystifying. If you do not reverse this decision and send an apology to myself and my patient . . . I will be sending copies of all these correspondences to my lawyer, the California Medical Association and appropriate political representatives demanding a reversal."

What was once a vague uneasiness on Allina's part about the changing face of medicine by then had solidified into disenchantment. He'd always thought of himself as a quite conservative practitioner, even a minimalist. He believed he regularly performed an appropriate gatekeeper role with his patients, based on his own judgment. But now there was this coercion from the group. The one way suggested good medicine to Allina, the other the work of a comptroller.

Questions he'd always wrestled with daily took on an added complexity. Should he send the woman with unexplained neck pain and a tender thyroid to an endocrinologist or put her on antibiotics? Should he order X rays to see why the teenage girl's leg fracture was still hurting after three years? One day, when a patient came to him describing symptoms of anxiety and depression, Allina found himself prescribing the antidepression drug Prozac instead of referring the man to a psychotherapist, even though he felt this wasn't dealing with the core problem.

"I was functioning as an agent of the organization as much as a healer or advocate of patients," Allina told me recently. "I felt I had to stand between patients and some of the more costly medical care that might benefit them. I would go to these medical meetings, read the reports, and feel exhorted to support the aims of the IPA, to hold down costs. I started to feel I must put off certain things I'd normally do with a patient. For example, a person comes in with a cough and fever. I listen to his lungs, it sounds like pneumonia. There are two approaches I can take. I can take a sputum culture, do a microscopic exam of it, give the patient antibiotics and wait for the results. Or I can take a chest X ray, complete blood count and blood culture, and hospitalize the patient. Or I can do gradations in between. It is an ambiguous, uncertain area. The tendency, given the IPA's pressure, is to wait. There are likely to be times, doing this, that you're going to make a mistake and fail to put in the hospital someone you should have. You are going to put someone's life at risk."

Feeling he'd lost his role as advocate, Allina soon began sensing that he instead was the patients' adversary. Sitting across from them, exchanges that once were healing consultations now sometimes became arguments over services he'd not allowed. The most disturbing moment came when a thirty-four-year-old woman who'd recently had a biopsy and mammogram for a benign breast lump wanted more tests; when Allina denied her request, she told him he was withholding necessary care. This patient ended up not only transferring to another doctor, but also sending Cottage IPA directors a full-page letter denouncing Allina—"He was not interested in following up on one of the patients for whom he had primary care. . . . His obvious lack of concern for this patient has made it impossible for me to see him further."

Months later, Allina would still thumb through his files and stare at that letter. "This was not what I'd expected when I got into medicine," he said one day, holding the letter before him. "Of course, you could say that life generally is not what we expect."

Complex is the buzzword usually invoked by people discussing the matter of health care in this country today, and for good reason. The lines between cause and effect, victim and villain, tend to blur. Doctors, for instance, have benefited greatly from the third-party involvement that now causes them so much grief. Medicare's arrival in 1965, and the gradual expansion of private fee-for-service plans in the following years, ushered in a two-decade-long golden era for physicians in which their practices mushroomed while they successfully resisted any form of outside regulation. People who once hesitated to visit doctors unless seriously ill now started to come regularly—Dr. Matsumoto, deluged, saw his practice quintuple among patients over sixty-five. With the patients' rising expectations came an increasing pressure on doctors to order sophisticated tests, and an ever-present threat of malpractice suits against those who did not. Health care costs, consequently, rose not just because of expensive, newly evolved high-tech procedures, but also because both doctors and patients were insulated from the true expense. Someone else was paying the bill.

Medical costs, which have doubled in the past decade, are expected to double again by the year 2000, to $1.5 trillion annually. Health care costs rose 21.6 percent in 1990 alone, even with strong cost-containment measures, and claimed 26 percent of the average company's net earnings. Such skyrocketing expenses are one reason why some thirty-five million Americans currently cannot afford or do not qualify for any health insurance. Clearly, trade-offs and rationing and low-cost health care are necessary, not everything that's available can be provided to everyone, and human lives must be balanced against economic cost.

Every doctor I spoke with readily acknowledged this, even while complaining about the particular way such circumstances have affected their lives. Most even agreed that doctors and patients had largely brought the present circumstances on themselves. Over and over, I heard stories about patients who'd angrily left doctors because they wouldn't approve particular tests and procedures, and surgeons who'd opened up patients mainly because they had a liberal insurance plan. I was told about doctors making millions by running Medicare clinics or kidney dialysis mills, and of orthopedists recommending surgery because of their outsize mortgages. I was told about the "worried well" patients who endlessly travel a circuit of doctors, insulated from the cost by private insurance or Medicare, which together now pay for roughly seventy-nine percent of all health costs. When I visited Health Net's headquarters in Woodland Hills, its medical director, Dr. Leonard Knapp, groaned about his perpetual need to close "loopholes" and serve as "broker" between doctors "gaming" the system and patients clinging to unreasonable expectations.

Spending a week inside the office of my own physician, Dr. Matsumoto, looking to document his fights against the restrictive measures of Medicare and third-party payers, I mainly saw his struggle to keep patients from overutilizing the system. An older woman on Medicare who'd already been to six other doctors about her shoulder pain wanted Matsumoto to take another look; a younger man was convinced he had stomach cancer despite normal results from a battery of X rays,

CAT scans and gastroscopies; an eighty-seven-year-old with a vague numbness in his foot wanted an array of procedures even though his circulation and muscle strength were normal. Let's let it go, let's let nature take its course, Matsumoto would tell them, as they shuffled out, often as not on their way to try another physician.

So it isn't hard to see why some doctors, including many connected with Health Net and Cottage IPA, are not nearly as concerned as is Allina about ambiguous decisions and dual roles. "We have to tighten belts and make hard choices," Dr. Dan Secord, president of Cottage IPA, told me when I came to visit him in the comfortable suite of offices he occupies in downtown Santa Barbara. "The successful management of a [prepaid per-patient] plan requires being extremely cost-effective and -conscious. You may not provide everything that is out there. Certainly, there are ambiguities. Plus there are litigious patients, malpractice threats. But we must do this." Dr. James Shaw, Cottage IPA's chief financial officer, thought it good for doctors to quit the HMO if they found it uncomfortable to be in an adversarial relationship with patients. "Managed care is not for every doctor or patient," he said. "But I don't mind being a gatekeeper. There are only a few gray areas, not many. It's usually mental health and physical therapy issues where there's lots of agonizing. Back pains, things like that. Not when you have lung cancer. In most cases I'm usually sure of my decision. There is a conflict of interest, no doubt. We do have a financial interest in limiting care. But I do have a conscience. I don't think this limits the quality of health care." Dr. Knapp at Health Net put it directly: "Doctors are not used-car salesmen," he reminded me.

All the same, it was easy to find some doctors in the Cottage IPA who shared Allina's concerns. One of them was the former medical director, George Weston. "When we started cutting down on the use of specialists, we started taking more risks," he told me. "There's lots of judgment involved. You say no to a request for an ophthalmologist and soon enough, the optometrist will miss something serious. You say no to ninety-nine requests for a dermatologist, but the hundredth one may have a cancerous lesion. There's a lot of waste and overutilization, but not all. You are slicing lean meat, not just fat. You have to affect the quality of care. We are pressured by utilization boards and low fees and competing marketers. The market has forced this."

It is not possible in this sort of exchange to sort out who is right or wrong, of course. The matter turns on specific cases, after all, and is clearly more a tangle of nuance and interpretation than of absolutes.

For every complaint I heard about the gatekeeper role, there was a reminder that HMOs such as Health Net encourage preventive health care and allow annual physical exams. For every string of cautionary anecdotes I heard about cost-cutting policies, I found a study that says HMOs and Medicare cutbacks haven't much affected the quality of health care. And yet, for every such study I read, I also found researchers acknowledging their limits and complaining about a dearth of measurable data. After weeks of listening and watching, what I thought mostly about, going over everyone's comments, was a story offered by Dr. Secord as I was leaving his office. It seemed he'd hurt his knee while skiing up in Whistler, north of Vancouver, and had had it treated without fancy tests in a local doctor's office, mainly because there was only one magnetic resonance imaging machine in all of British Columbia. But when he'd returned to Santa Barbara, he explained, he'd gotten an MRI test "because my buddy runs the machine. . . . I could have done without, but I wanted to see what was going on in there before they did arthroscopic surgery." The doctor or health care administrator, in other words, is much less likely to embrace uncertainty and rationing when he is sitting in the patient's chair.

All the same, patients probably will have to do just that in the future. Whatever the permutations and shake-outs still to come, some sort of sea change is looming both for doctors and patients, like it or not. The doctor-patient relationship, once based on an unspoken understanding, a trust on the patient's part that the physician would do what was best for him or her, is being transformed into a contractual business relationship in which the physician provides a specified, measurable service at a negotiated price. If you are willing or able to pay more, you can get more—this is what's meant by a "multitiered" health care delivery system. "Who is to make the final determination whether I should stay with my patient all evening in the Cedars-Sinai emergency room?" Matsumoto asked me one morning, complaining about a Medicare ruling that had denied him payment for five hours of tending to a critically ill woman with an uncertain diagnosis. However unpalatable to some, the answer is now apparent: Those who are paying the bill.

By the end of 1989, Tony Allina was fed up. His letters to Medicare and his congressmen were multiplying. So too was his paper work for Cottage IPA—its ever-tightening restrictions on tests and referrals meant more forms, more denials, more appeals, more phone calls. Meanwhile, patients waiting for decisions were showering Allina's office with inquiring phone calls, until his receptionist's workload had increased tenfold and he found it necessary to hire a second clerk. Everything had to be processed through him even when the patient had been referred to a specialist.

And just as his costs were climbing, Allina's income from the HMO was dropping. In the fall of 1989, out of financial necessity, Cottage IPA had cut the per-patient monthly fee to primary care physicians from more than eleven dollars to just eight dollars. Eventually, Allina began losing money—a thousand dollars in one particularly bad month, he calculated. Spending time talking and listening to patients was now something he could not afford to do. When considering whether to hospitalize a patient, he couldn't avoid thinking that if he did, he'd have to visit him—a full hour round trip minimum—without getting paid anything extra. He came out ahead only if he didn't treat patients very often, or in much depth.

"I spend lots of time explaining things to patients," Allina said. "I'm slow. I spend time trying to get to know patients. But then I didn't want that. I was very happy just to have them come in, get a throat culture, penicillin, good-bye. Fine. I couldn't afford more. It was a business now. And I wasn't enjoying it. As I would sit talking with such patients, I'd think: This is a money-losing activity."

The experience that most forcefully influenced Allina's attitude began when a seventy-eight-year-old man appeared in his office one morning complaining of feeling weak and tired. A complete physical exam in the office yielded nothing unusual, but a standard blood panel showed low thyroid activity, which would explain the tiredness. Allina prescribed a thyroid medication, then hesitated. The test results also showed a below-normal level of albumin, an integral protein in the blood and tissues. Allina believed something was wrong, but he did not know what. Low albumin was a measure of inadequate intake of protein, or reduced production of it by the liver, or overutilization of it within the body, so suggested a wide range of possibilities—deficient diet, liver disease, problems with absorption of food, infection or any form of malignancy. But the patient's liver function and white blood cell counts were normal, and older patients' lab tests can yield off-readings sometimes. Given the parameters of the Cottage IPA–Health Net system and the absence of a diagnosis, Allina didn't know what specialist or test to order short of a full-scale exploratory workup. He thought of sending the man to an internist for another opinion, as he would with non-HMO patients, but he believed such a referral for this

Health Net member would be denied by Cottage IPA, since its internists were all primary care physicians themselves.

Something's wrong, Allina told his patient, but I don't know what's causing it. Let's wait two months and I'll check you again.

Allina never got the chance, for the patient, rather than appear at his next appointment, instead visited an internist outside the Health Net plan. By then he'd developed some numbness in his left hand, and a CAT scan and other tests revealed a tumor growing in his neck. The diagnosis would have been difficult before the numbness developed, but the unhappy patient nonetheless withdrew his entire family—including his wife, daughter, son and grandchildren, all longtime patients—from Allina's practice. The wife called one day and simply asked for their files to be transferred to another doctor.

"My inability to make a diagnosis made him lose confidence in me," Allina said. "And I agreed with the man. He made the right choice. That's what made this so onerous to me. The primary care provider cannot be your advocate when he is the gatekeeper for a doctor's organization."

Allina wavered for months. He'd lose patients—but by then he knew so few by name anyway and had to rush through his visits with them. He'd be letting down his colleagues—but his practice had lurched far from his original notion of close, personal medicine. He'd lose valuable sources of income—but it had never been his primary goal to make money, and he could survive without a large income now because he'd made some investments and had consciously chosen to live simply. He owned a spacious home in an affluent community, but it was bought relatively cheaply years ago, and sitting on its driveway was nothing fancier than a five-year-old Honda Accord.

Allina backed away from the federal government first, deciding in 1989 to stop taking any new Medicare patients, even though those he still treats regularly refer their friends to him. When Medicare referrals called, he'd refuse them, explaining it was because of the Medicare system. This is part of my protest, he'd tell them.

Then, in July 1990, Allina completed his retreat by writing a letter of resignation to the Cottage IPA. When his departure from that organization became official on October 17, Allina lost nearly twenty percent of his practice, and a guaranteed monthly payment of more than eight hundred dollars, which is a fair share of his office rent and a not insignificant amount considering his income level. Allina's net earnings, ranging between $50,000 and $70,000 in the previous three years, had always placed him at the lower range of general practitioners' incomes. But because of the increased overhead and lower Cottage payments, 1989 had proven even less lucrative than most, falling below $50,000. Without new Medicare or Cottage patients, his income in 1990 declined yet again.

Just what meaning Tony Allina's act of resistance has beyond his own world is hard to say. He's not the only one to quit—from a high of more than 220, the number of Cottage IPA doctors has fallen to 135—but Cottage IPA doctors continue to treat some seven thousand Health Net patients. Overall, about eighty-five percent of Santa Barbara's insured population is in either an HMO or PPO, and very few major employers are even offering the option of an unregulated fee-for-service insurance plan any longer. For Health Net, dominating the region with more than forty thousand members, there is an abundance of doctors perfectly willing to take Allina's place, not the least because there's a relative glut of physicians compared to twenty years ago. The younger doctors everywhere in the country seem particularly amenable—forty percent of male doctors and sixty percent of female doctors under age thirty-five are working for HMOs.

If the battle being fought by doctors such as Tony Allina appears futile, it also could be seen as irrelevant. In light of those millions currently without any medical insurance, it could be argued that what's needed is not the preservation of independent physicians partial to close patient relationships, but a system that can deliver basic health care to vast numbers at low cost. There is a role, in other words, for bare-bones HMOs, even if their services are limited. Private, autonomous medical advocates might be a luxury only the most affluent can afford.

Allina and the other doctors I spoke to were well aware of these considerations, and they did not entirely dispute them. Asked what was being lost in the present transformation of medicine, most, rather than overstating the case, had difficulty putting their thoughts into words, referring vaguely to "a change in philosophy" and "the value of intangibles." Theirs finally was more a lament for a vanished past, for a loss of what once was valued and rewarded in medicine, than a call for a particular course of action now. "If we turned the clock back, lots of people wouldn't get needed medical care. There is no solution. I just wanted to vent my spleen," Matsumoto told me at the end of our week together.

For the time being, Tony Allina's finely ordered world remains intact, the forces of change held at bay. Allina generally sees some fifteen patients a day, nine or ten of them briefly, the other five or six for longer periods up to an hour, which is about two-thirds the load of his fully active colleagues. At twelve-thirty or one, he pedals home and joins his wife Rebecca for lunch, usually the previous night's leftovers. At three o'clock, if it is Wednesday or Friday, he plays tennis a half mile away at the Knollwood Tennis Club, an activity that also occupies much of his weekend. When there is the need, he makes hospital rounds. By six, he has seen his last patient for the day, and is at his desk, finishing paperwork. Unless there are house calls, he arrives home by seven and plays with the family's dog Nellie for the few minutes before dinner is served. Most evenings he spends helping his two daughters—Crystal, twelve, and Amy, sixteen—with their homework. He is in bed, asleep, by ten-thirty.

It is only occasionally, quite infrequently in fact, that Allina awakes in the middle of the night, torn by conflict over the path he has chosen. Then, in those rare moments at four o'clock, staring at his bedroom ceiling, he wonders: Has he made the right choice? Or is he tilting at windmills, failing to adjust to a changing world? His answers vary. At times, he feels optimistic—"I expect a rebound. Patients unhappy with the way medicine is delivered will be willing to pay more. Companies will seek alternatives. I am hoping for the best. I hope I can continue." At times he feels defiant—"If practicing triage because of financial pressure is where medicine is going, then I'll find something else to do." Most often, though, he feels realistic. "I don't know if I would have the courage to quit medicine because I don't know what else I could do," he told me one day in the fall of 1990. "The thing is, I can see getting out. But I also can see having to acquiesce."

UPDATE

In the spring of 1991, Tony Allina decided to start accepting Medicare patients once again. Economics, as he'd feared, had hampered his effort to make a statement.

"I couldn't afford it," he explained. "I didn't want to make it more difficult on my practice than it already was."

IV

Matters of Man, Matters of Nature

Passing the Laugh Test

July 1987
Washington, D.C.

The matter at hand involved uranium mill tailings, tens of thousands of tons dumped in towering piles throughout the West, leaking radiation. Cover them with dirt, the Environmental Protection Agency decided. Seal off the radioactivity. But then came the question of how much dirt.

The lingo at regulatory agencies such as the EPA includes the term *best available technology.* Well, reasoned Milton Russell, then an EPA assistant administrator, the best available technology here is to pile on more dirt, and more dirt and more dirt. It would be impossible, though, to pile on an infinite amount of dirt, or to reduce the radiation risk to zero. So where, Russell wondered, would be the stopping point?

Russell didn't really know, but that didn't stop him from reaching a decision. Making such choices, after all, was his job. For three years and eight months, until he stepped down in March 1987, Milt Russell served as assistant administrator for policy, planning and evaluation at the EPA. Put more simply, he was what is now called a "risk manager."

Russell, fifty-three, is a Republican appointee and an economist who talks like one, describing pollution as an "externality of production," so environmentalists more often than not have found themselves at odds with him. Yet it is fair to say that risk managers in any form would not be popular figures. A risk manager is in the business of recognizing trade-offs. His underlying premise is that not every good thing can be done. He balances human lives against economic cost, among other considerations, performing a sort of environmental triage. He traffics in imponderables about the value of human life and the morality of knowingly imposing involuntary risks on people.

He also presides at a shotgun marriage of science and law, something that fails to satisfy either the scientists or those who advocate, draft and administer environmental law. Many laws presume the possibility of zero risk and assign liability where that is not reached, but science's increasingly sophisticated ability to detect and finely measure dangers renders the world a minefield of risks, some unavoidable. Put simply, science cannot provide the certainty of protection demanded by the statutes.

"You can't wish some problems away," Russell had taken to telling people by the time he left the EPA. "Every problem doesn't have a solution and the solutions to those problems which do have solutions are not necessarily nice. . . . There is something about the American character that seems to assume there is a good solution to every problem, and that just ain't true. I mean, there are just some problems for which there are no easy, much less right, much less perfect, solutions."

Risk managers of Russell's sort did not exist a decade ago. Looking back now, there are those who trace their emergence to a moment in 1972 when radioactive tracer studies for the first time found residues of the carcinogenic growth promoter DES in livestock. The traces, of course, had been there ever since the use of DES began—they just hadn't been noticed until the detection methods grew sufficiently sensitive. The discovery all the same presented something of a crisis to the Food and Drug Administration, since the agency was then operating on the presumption that no level of a carcinogen could be regarded as safe. There was no way around it—the FDA had to ban DES, and at once.

The staggering ramifications were immediately apparent to Peter Hutt, then the FDA's general counsel. If DES could be detected in livestock at low levels, certainly traces of other carcinogenic drugs and feed ingredients could also be found. The FDA, it seemed clear to Hutt, faced the prospect of banning all carcinogenic substances from animal feed and drugs. That would sweep bare most supermarket shelves, a prospect that Hutt considered enormously impractical, if not impossible. He asked himself a question: What the hell are we going to do?

It was then, just days after the FDA withdrew approval of DES, that Dr. Richard Lehman of the FDA Bureau of Veterinary Medicine walked into Hutt's office one afternoon. Lehman had something in mind that he thought might be helpful in handling Hutt's problem. "Quantitative risk assessment," Lehman said.

The idea of quantifying human risk from carcinogenic substances, on the basis of mathematical extrapolation from animal feeding studies, had been examined by scientists for more than twenty-five years, but it had remained an inquiry for scholars, not a tool for regulators. Now, suddenly, the practical use of risk assessment seemed quite apparent to Hutt and others. Since they presently were going to find trace elements of carcinogens throughout the food chain, they needed to draw differences between "significant" and "insignificant" levels, if they did not want to end up banning the whole food chain.

In the July 1973 Federal Register, the FDA proposed regulations that for the first time would quantify human risk from a carcinogen and establish a "safe" level of exposure. From that beginning point, the risk-assessment business, responding to the needs of the times, became a booming industry. As the years passed, scientists refined techniques, wrote mountains of research papers, hired themselves out both to regulatory agencies and private industry, and eventually opened a good number of their own risk-assessment consulting firms, many with offices furnished in high-tech chrome and glass.

During this evolution, however, there always were certain sizable limitations connected with the business of risk assessment. The calculations produced by the process, most agreed, were uncertain at best and very possibly meaningless. Even those doing them allowed that they were transcending the bounds of traditional science, making judgments and assumptions to reach a number. The leap from low-dose animal exposures and other sorts of data to human risk estimates, after all, is made by mathematical models that depend on a host of inferences and assumptions piled one atop another as the calculations continue. Mistaken judgments can get magnified exponentially. The National Academy of Sciences, for example, has cited ten statistical models that yield strikingly different predictions about saccharin and bladder cancer—all the way from 0.22 to 1,144,000 lifetime cases of bladder cancer resulting from consumption of one bottle of diet soft drink per day by 220 million persons over a lifetime.

Seen in this light, it is not surprising that, whichever way the scientists juggle their figures, industrialists, unions and environmentalists end up having considerably different opinions of the results. The calculations are variously lambasted as wildly overestimating risks, as failing to measure most risks and as a mathematical sham designed by corporate interests to dilute regulatory efforts.

The descriptions offered by those who actually do the risk analyses are not much more appreciative. Joseph V. Rodricks, a toxicologist by training, spent fifteen years at the FDA, the final two as chief science adviser to the FDA commissioner. Now head of the consulting firm Environ, he has conducted dozens of risk assessments for private clients and government agencies. He is a founder of the Society for Risk Analysis and the author of more than seventy scientific papers in the field. Talking about his line of work, he said: "We can't pretend to get scientific results. Science is fifty years behind what the public wants us to provide. Someone has to go beyond the data. Someone has to answer the question of where to draw the line. Pure science would say 'we don't know if saccharin causes bladder cancer,' but someone has to fix on an answer. The whole regulatory operation depends upon it."

So emerged the risk manager.

Offering the EPA position to Milt Russell in mid-1983, Al Alm, then the deputy administrator, had explained the job: When decisions loomed, he and William D. Ruckelshaus, then the agency's administrator, did not have the time to ask whether the analyses were right, whether the assumptions were checked. They wanted never to have to worry. Russell, by his own description, was more an analyst than an ideologue, experienced in government after a stint in the midseventies as senior staff economist for the President's Council of Economic Advisors. Alm thought Russell could make sure that they would never have to worry.

It was Russell's notion that his new job could be executed in an organized and sensible process. He was not naive—he understood that the final decisions would require judgments—but he believed they could be reached through what he admiringly called "a rational framework." He set up a formal "development plan." He set up an "option selection process." He set up meetings to consider "cross-media implications." After six months of this, Russell felt a sense of accomplishment. A sensible system was now in place.

Beginning with the risk-assessment figures, he would ask certain questions: How sure is the scientific evidence? What is the degree and distribution of risk? What is the investment necessary to reduce it? Does this investment make sense, given all the other demands on our economy? What kinds of social and personal disruptions will regulation bring?

These seemed to Russell impeccably logical questions. Others, however, disagreed. At public gatherings, his critics would rise, stabbing the air with accusing fingers. How can you stand there, they would ask, knowing there is a risk and not stopping it? How could you decide that some people will die of cancer? Thus began the education of a risk manager.

One of Russell's first lessons came three years ago, in the case of the uranium mill tailings.

Uranium milling produces powdery, sandlike tailings that release radon, the gas that is the second deadliest cause of lung cancer (after cigarettes). Before this danger was fully understood, the sandy tailings were used as fill dirt and building materials in house construction, particularly in the Rocky Mountain states, and also were simply dumped at rural sites scattered throughout the West. When Congress passed a law in 1978 requiring the government to find and eliminate this contamination, thousands of homeowners, many centered around Salt Lake City, Utah, and Grand Junction, Colorado, saw their basements, gardens, patios, garages and foundations torn up and replaced. It was less clear, however, what should be done with the tailings that simply remained dumped in soaring piles. Upon reflection, the EPA fixed on the idea of covering the tailings with dirt. And in that fashion, Russell found himself facing the question of how much dirt.

The tailing piles left untreated and uncovered, the EPA estimated, would probably produce six hundred extra cancer deaths in a century. This is the rough equivalent of six deaths a year (although mathematical purists would say that such extrapolations from lifetime estimates are problematic). If the EPA spent $500 million, it could pile enough dirt on the tailings to reduce the risk by ninety-five percent, from six hundred deaths a century to twenty, from six deaths a year to one death every three and a half years. Or alternatively, the EPA, by roughly doubling the amount of dirt, and spending another quarter of a billion dollars, could reduce the risk even further, by ninety-nine and a half percent. Instead of one death every three years, there would be one extra death every thirty years.

There were plenty who thought the EPA should take that second option. Some were members of environmental groups. Some were inside the EPA. Some were on Russell's staff.

There is no right answer here, Russell thought. There are always people who have different values.

Russell sought to put the six deaths in perspective. Roughly 125,000 people die of lung cancer each year in the United States, the vast majority due to cigarette smoking. Still, no one had asked for this radon risk. Cigarettes are far more dangerous, but people don't inhale uranium tailings voluntarily. Then there was the matter of proportion—although the total incidence of cancer from the tailings was relatively low, the risk was considerably higher to the tiny population living close by the piles. How, Russell wondered, to balance large risks to very small populations against the general public interest? Russell knew also that these tailings were the product of milling uranium for the nuclear power industry. There was anger and resentment in the community about that, coming from serious people, not kooks. You could say, somebody made this mess; the power companies, they ought to pay. And yet, Russell also thought, whether you should build more nuclear power plants is a very different issue from what to do now with these tailings. You could close every nuclear power plant and every bomb plant in the country tomorrow, and the tailings would still be there and you would still have to decide what to do with them.

Then there was the unadorned matter of money. That extra quarter of a billion dollars needed to get the risk down from ninety-five to ninety-nine and a half percent—in a world of limited dollars, is that the best place to spend it for improved health? You could buy a hell of a lot of kidney machines and ambulance cardiac-care units for that. If you're worrying about lung cancer, why not spend the quarter-billion to buy off tobacco farmers, or for an antismoking ad campaign, or on programs for early detection of lung cancer?

Finally, there was something else, something far less esoteric, notably distant from the economic textbooks at the University of Oklahoma where Russell once studied. Russell grew up on a farm in Texas. He knew about heavy equipment, knew how dangerous that stuff was to operate on the narrow dirt roads out there in the West. They would be moving millions of tons of dirt over long distances, stirring up dust, clouding visibility, filling lungs. You cannot put a price on those three or six lives lost to radon, people told him. But those lives to him were just statistical creations, dubious extrapolations on a page. Russell was thinking of real guys driving real bulldozers with real families. You could not factor that into the computer, Russell thought. But it's there.

The pressure came from all sides. Congress had passed an amendment threatening to hand the matter over to the Nuclear Regulatory Commission if the EPA did not act. A congressman, chairman of the House Armed Services Subcommittee on procurement and nuclear systems, had lashed out at the agency for setting standards that were too tough, considering that the dangers of radon were unproved. Then, when the EPA moved to relax those standards, a fellow at the Environmental Policy Center said he found the shift "disturbing."

The EPA eventually decided to spend half a billion dollars and pile on enough dirt to reduce the estimated risk by ninety-five percent. It did not make sense, the agency decided, to spend a quarter-billion dollars more to get the risk down by ninety-nine and a half percent. Russell had come to regard part of his job as applying the "laugh test" to decisions. After all the technical analysis, in other words, does the decision hold up under common sense? This one could pass the laugh test, Russell figured.

There were lawsuits. Ruckelshaus took the brunt of the vilification, of course, but Russell caught his share at small community meetings. He was uncaring, they said, unconcerned, a monster. He was allowing unconscionable risks that could be remedied.

Well, Russell thought, that's just one of those kinds of decisions you end up making. He also thought: Making a decision with your eyes open and in front of everybody is going to be very difficult. It's easy to make decisions. It's difficult to make good decisions and to make them in the light of day.

Ruckelshaus soon came to Russell with a suggestion: Go out there and do something about creating reasoned decision-making in the American public. Go out there and educate. So Russell took to the road, delivering speeches. He knew where he stood and felt willing to spell it out.

Acceptable risk is an uncomfortable term, he would say at the podiums. The popular notion is, no risk is acceptable. But public officials who talk about delivering zero risk perpetuate a comforting myth. On the other hand, to question that myth opens one to charges of being callous and uncaring. Not an appealing prospect. Little wonder that "acceptable risk" is a topic public officials most often reserve for quiet conversations with intimates.

"To risk managers and those comfortable with modern technology, pollution is an externality of production," Russell said in one speech. "Its reduction is a goal of public policy to be pursued vigorously, to the point that it maximizes the total public interest. To others, reflecting more traditional, deeply held values, it is a violation of personal rights; hence its production is an evil and its reduction a matter of moral principle. For them, to speak of an optimal level of pollution is like being told that each community should have an appropriate number of child molesters. . . . When you pierce through the fog of posturing and politics and special interests, the profound dichotomy between pollution risk as a factor of production and pollution risk as an evil lies at the root of much environmental debate in the country."

Yet Russell understood that he was laboring amid ambivalence. Up on the podium, he also said: "The idea of some risk for the greater good conflicts with the position that each individual is infinitely precious. This is one of the eternal conundrums of man in society. I doubt that it will be resolved by the EPA."

The EPA tried a different approach in Tacoma. The old copper smelter there had sat on the shores of Puget Sound, smack in the middle of the city, for about ninety years. Arsenic only recently had been discovered to be a volatile human carcinogen. EPA analysts figured that emissions from the plant, unregulated, were causing four additional lung cancer deaths each year. To eliminate the arsenic emissions would require controls so stringent, the plant would just close down, unable to operate profitably. That would mean the end of 570 jobs, a $30 million payroll. You could instead cut emissions almost in half and keep the plant open, but the smelter would still cause one extra lung cancer death beyond the norm each year.

Looking around Tacoma, where economic conditions were noticeably distressed, Russell thought: You take away those jobs, it's fairly well documented you end up with increases in alcoholism, child abuse, spousal abuse. You also end up with fear. That itself is a public health concern. And yet: The wind blew from the plant toward an affluent suburb where people had no need for smelter jobs.

The EPA opted for an experiment. The agency would communicate all the options and alternatives and uncertainties to the community. The agency of course would make the final decision, but first it would let the people indicate where they would make the trade-offs.

So Russell found himself at a public hearing. First, a fellow in his seventies rose to speak. He'd been working at the smelter for forty years, he said. He'd consumed so much arsenic in his day that his sweat was green. How can you say this arsenic is hurting anybody? He had lived with the stuff, he'd eaten it, he'd drunk it. What are you talking about? Then a young, frail woman rose, wisps of hair falling on pale skin, eyes full of tears. Her child had died of leukemia. That stuff in the air had killed her child. What was the government going to do about that?

It occurred to Russell that he was facing people different from himself. He was a man of rational analysis listening to people of faith.

The agency did not want the matter cast as a jobs-versus-health issue in Tacoma, but that was how it seemed. One day the crowd showed up at a hearing wearing newly produced buttons. "Both," the buttons read. If we had succeeded in explaining all this, Russell thought, the buttons would have said: "Some."

The EPA never did have to decide this one, for before the agency could act, the smelter owners closed down the plant. The market for copper had gone so bad, it wasn't profitable under any circumstances. The EPA, nonetheless, got blasted. Why is the EPA asking us to make these types of decisions, a good number in Tacoma asked. They're the experts. Why can't they make the decision? This is confusing.

This is confusing to us too, Russell would respond.

The EPA officials were no longer the people wearing the white hats. There were no objective right and wrong, yes and no answers. They had to make value judgments and expose their own uncertainty. They could no longer regard themselves as experts. And that, Russell observed, is a dangerous thing for the psyche.

In the end, it was another issue—lead in gasoline—that provided Russell with his greatest sense both of triumph and of frustration while at the EPA.

Lead-free gasoline had been introduced in the 1970s to accommodate newer cars with catalytic converters. The lead levels in regular gasoline had been reduced, but you could still find gasoline with lead at the pumps in the early 1980s. Some used it for older cars without catalytic converters, and some used it illegally in newer cars with converters. Leaded gasoline, after all, had more octane and was cheaper. Of course, it also had far more deadly pollutants. Lead in gasoline, emitted from tailpipes, fouled the air, the water, the street surfaces. The streets had a particular import. Kids pick up dust from the street, stick their hands in their mouths, end up ingesting the stuff. The relationship was so direct, Russell found he could correlate the kids' blood levels of lead with the increased driving during summer months. He could also draw lines between the blood levels and horrible maladies—brain dysfunctions, behavioral disorders, biophysical problems.

This one was not ambiguous to Russell, for once. His own department had initiated and pushed the research. When they toted up the pure cost-benefit figures, the benefits came out roughly three times as high as costs. That was without even trying to put a price on things like pain and suffering and the decline in children's IQs. The decision was easy. They laid it out before Ruckelshaus, took just an hour and a half. Let's roll, the administrator had said.

There were no denunciations or lawsuits this time. But there also was no applause. What Russell considered the most significant protective action during his tenure, one that salvaged hundreds of thousands of lives, was largely met by public indifference.

Russell felt he understood. Getting the lead out was going to raise the price of gasoline at the pumps and take away some octane, for an issue people didn't know was serious. "It's not baby seals," he said later. "And who's the enemy? There was no place that anybody could trumpet victory or describe evil. It was a classic case of a social benefit, social good, for which there were no villains and for which there were no heroes."

The risk manager's frustration was understandable. Public perceptions do differ markedly from what science says are the biggest risks. Hazardous waste sites trigger intense reactions, but scientists say that radon naturally seeping into homes from the soil, air pollution and the destruction of the earth's ozone layer pose far greater threats. The public, when polled about risks, tends to list such items as nuclear power and food preservatives near the top, while statistical analysts would put those items far down on a list that is headed by smoking, alcohol, automobiles and handguns. States sent state troopers to clear supermarket shelves of foods sprayed with the pesticide EDB, a risk measured in parts per million, while the everyday world is full of comparable risks. Drinking a half liter of wine increases the chance of death over a lifetime by one in a million. So does living two days in New York or Boston, traveling ten miles by bicycle, eating forty tablespoons of peanut butter or one hundred charcoal-broiled steaks.

It could be said, though, that Russell's rationality had come up against something more than a perception problem. It could be said he was bucking the perplexing force of human nature.

Those who study such matters report that the risks people care about have their own type of logic, a logic that transcends the data. People are personally offended when someone is imposing a risk on them. A small risk involuntarily imposed is more objectionable than a much larger risk voluntarily assumed. One study, in fact, indicated that people are willing to accept a risk one thousand times greater if it is of their own choosing. They elect to ride a bicycle or smoke a cigarette. They do not elect to ingest EDB. Equity is the issue.

People will also accept controllable or familiar risks—swimming, X rays—over what is beyond their control or unfamiliar. Paul Milvey, a senior analyst for the EPA, an expert in risk calculations with a doctorate in biophysics, once related a telling story about himself along this line. He was in a Washington area hospital, facing the need to undergo a CAT scan with contrast media. Because the test involved injection of an iodine-based dye, his doctor explained, there was a slight risk of death if his kidneys failed. They could instead take a nuclear magnetic resonance picture, a test that was not invasive and did not carry any risk, but this would require a trip to another hospital in the Washington area.

By all means, Milvey said, he would prefer going for that other test.

Then his wife pointed it out to him: The risk of death in a traffic accident while traveling by ambulance to the other hospital was greater than the risk of the CAT scan.

I'd still prefer the ambulance ride, Milvey said.

In the end, he needed neither test, and the doctors decided that he was healthy. But he could not get over his reaction. "Even though I knew instantly my wife was right, I nevertheless preferred the option of the ambulance risk to the unknown danger," he said. "It amazed me that although I'm trained to look at these things objectively, I couldn't do it, I couldn't convince myself otherwise."

The message here is one that Russell, however reluctantly, in time came to acknowledge. Ever the analytical economist, he saw it as part of his equation. "It is perfectly reasonable and acceptable, the way the world is, that some kinds of risk are cared about more than other kinds of risks," he said. "That's a datum for the EPA, and data points are not something you argue about. Whether they are rational, irrational, good or bad, they are data points. They have to be dealt with."

In mid-March of 1987, one week before he left the EPA, Russell traveled to Charleston, West Virginia, to give a farewell address of sorts before the National Institute for Chemical Studies. "There are myths each of us live by," he said to that group. "Let me alert you to some of these myths. There is the myth that risk numbers represent reality. There is the myth that there can be zero risk. There is the myth that environmental quality comes free. And then there is the myth often held by economists and public policy professionals such as myself. That is the myth that facts and logic provide 'answers' when it comes to environmental protection."

This insight had evolved gradually, by degrees. There was no blinding epiphany. But Russell during his tenure at the EPA had arrived at a conclusion that marked something of a journey from where he began.

A challenging new opportunity now beckoned at the University of Tennessee and the Oak Ridge National Laboratory in Knoxville. The pace would be less intense. He had found the EPA job fun, challenging, exciting. There had been a certain measure of satisfaction. It had been a very good three and a half years, full of amazing changes, things accomplished. But it did seem as though he had been there forever, and people in his type of position do get tired. He was not naive, but he had underestimated the resistance to dealing with matters in a systematic way.

"Now," he said, "maybe it's time for somebody else to make the decisions."

Lobstermen and Weathermen

March 1985
Boston, Massachusetts

There was a time, just fifteen years ago, when veteran New England lobstermen such as Robert Brown still put to sea much as they had for decades, relying on instinct, experience, their barometers and the collective wisdom of fellow skippers. Even then, aware of nature's sudden swings in mood, they never strayed more than fifteen miles from shore, close enough to retreat to land if the weather threatened. But when Robert Brown's twenty-eight-year-old son Peter left Hyannis Harbor late on Friday morning, November 21, 1980, guiding the *Sea Fever* toward Georges Bank for one last fishing trip before Thanksgiving, he did so in a manner that differed considerably from his father's ways.

Peter Brown had state-of-the-art VHF radios, radar, depth sounders and loran navigational position finders, which allow masters to plot their course through satellite readings. He had a special single-sideband radio capable of receiving broadcasts more than one hundred miles out to sea, much farther than the normal VHF radio's range, which stops at the horizon. And he had unusually sophisticated weather forecasts to hear on those broadcasts. As a result of projects adopted in the mid-1970s by the Weather Service's parent, the National Oceanographic and Atmospheric Administration (NOAA), the forecasts by 1980 were generated through a complex national computer system that drew information from all manner of sources—high atmosphere balloons, satellites twenty-two thousand miles above the earth, ships at sea, and thirty-eight special buoys that transmitted to the computer hourly reports on wind speed and direction, sea-level pressure, air temperature, sea surface temperature and wave height. With the guidance provided by these powerful new tools, lobstermen such as Peter Brown now could venture far past the old fifteen-mile limit. They could follow their prey as the lobsters migrated in winter to the continental shelf.

That was precisely what Peter Brown had in mind in late November 1980—pursuing lobster far out to sea. On the morning his forty-six-and-a-half-foot wood-hulled *Sea Fever* was due to leave Hyannis Harbor, the weather forecast called for what are fair conditions in the world of lobstermen—twenty-five-knot winds and five- to ten-foot waves. Brown, after hearing that report, headed out of Hyannis Harbor, traveling alongside a companion vessel, the fifty-two-foot steel-hulled *Fairwind,* piloted by Bill Garnos. Brown and Garnos's custom was to monitor continuous weather service forecasts on Channel 16 of their VHF radios until they were past the VHF range of forty to fifty miles, then switch to the single-sideband radios, which provided forecasts on a fixed schedule every six hours. On their single sidebands, the lobstermen customarily listened to the 5:00 A.M., 11:00 A.M., 5:00 P.M. and 11:00 P.M. broadcasts out of Portsmouth, Virginia, which were repeated twenty minutes later on another broadcast out of Boston.

The weather forecast on the 11:00 A.M. broadcast that Friday predicted that a low-pressure area off the South Carolina coast would intensify and move northeast to a position south of Nova Scotia. A marine warning might be needed south of Nova Scotia for Friday night and Saturday, the broadcast said, but the Georges Bank area, adjacent to this region, would get nothing more extreme than showers. Listening, Brown and Garnos felt reassured. The *Sea Fever* and the *Fairwind* now turned to the open sea.

Twelve hours later, when they approached the Georges Bank buoy, Brown listened to the 11 P.M. forecast, which still predicted acceptable weather. Brown later said he would have turned back then if he had heard a storm warning. Instead, he went to sleep. It was the 5 A.M. forecast Saturday morning that for the first time predicted gale-force winds in the Georges Bank area. The on-duty crewman awakened Brown with the news, but the vessel's master needed no radio forecast to see that the winds were already at forty knots, with waves up to twenty-five feet and heavy rain. By late morning, the winds were howling at eighty knots, with waves reaching fifty feet. The lobstermen were in considerable trouble.

Brown headed the *Sea Fever* into the wind, trying to maintain stability, as did Garnos on the *Fairwind.* At 11:30 A.M., as the *Fairwind* tried to ride up a giant wave, the storm forced the vessel around and down the slope. When its bow hit the trough, the boat somersaulted end over end. Three of the four crew members perished, including Garnos—only Ernest Hazard survived by reaching an inflated life raft. Then at one in the afternoon, the *Sea Fever* found itself also surfing down the face of a sixty-foot wave. When the vessel reached the trough, it veered broadside to the wind. The wave broke on the boat and flooded the pilothouse, washing crew member Gary Brown into the sea and to his death.

In all, four fishing vessels sank around Georges Bank that morning, but the *Sea Fever,* in the eye of the storm, managed to ride out the tumult and head home Sunday morning. "If anyone knew it would be so bad out there, we never would have gone out," Peter Brown said when he reached shore. "None of the fishermen had ever seen anything like it."

For commercial deep-sea fishermen who regularly test the harsh vagaries of nature, the deaths at sea were an all-too-familiar tragedy. This time, though, along with the customary grief came a less familiar response. The bereaved families of the dead fishermen chose to rage not at the cruel seas but, rather, at the National Weather Service for failing to predict the storm accurately. The families filed lawsuits charging negligence, and asked for $3.2 million in damages. The plaintiffs in *Honour Brown et al. v. United States* had more than money in mind. Theirs was a cry against the way in which modern technology had both empowered and enslaved their tradition-bound men. For the lobstermen were doomed not by fate or nature's caprice or their own mistakes, the widows argued, but by the trust they unknowingly had placed in a broken wind sensor atop a solitary buoy, bobbing on the open sea one hundred miles from shore.

The decision by the grieving families to blame the government rather than nature for the tragedy began with the brother of Gary Brown, the crewman washed from the *Sea Fever.* He called Michael Latti, a lawyer for whom he sometimes worked as an investigator. Latti's specialty is admiralty law.

When Latti first filed a negligence suit under the federal Suits in

Admiralty Act on behalf of Gary Brown's widow, Honour, in February 1981, U.S. District Judge Joseph Tauro privately thought the lawyer was crazy. "Am I being requested to rule that the weather can be predicted?" the judge asked Latti in chambers. "Does the Weather Service have a duty to get it right?"

Latti, however, had something else in mind. Through sources at the National Weather Service, he'd picked up an interesting piece of information. There apparently had been a continuing problem with a particularly critical Weather Service buoy. And the problem's history, Latti noted, was nicely documented.

During 1980, Rodney Winslow, then the meteorologist in charge of the Weather Service office in Boston, had written three strongly worded memos to his superiors reporting trouble with the wind sensor located atop the buoy at station 44003—Georges Bank. The sensor had stopped reporting in the spring, and then the buoy itself was hit by a vessel in August. At-sea repairs were made on August 11, but the wind sensor failed again on September 6. Winslow, concerned and believing the buoy's data critical, had regularly campaigned for repairs. "This buoy is extremely important to us . . . ," he'd written. "It serves as one of the few reliable observation points in an area where a tremendous number of fishing vessels operate daily. I urge every effort be made to bring and maintain these buoys on continuous operational status. Must we once again open ourselves to political repercussion because of the failure of an important piece of equipment?"

NOAA officials, however, that year as always were faced with considerations about budget and manpower limits. A buoy costs two hundred thousand dollars to install and maintain for a year. During the hostile winter weather season, an average of three of the National Data Buoy Program's thirty-eight buoys need repair at any one time. So rather than replace or repair the broken device on the Georges Bank buoy immediately, NOAA officials had decided to wait until January, when the buoy was already scheduled to get a new, improved type of wind sensor.

Reviewing these facts, Latti immediately thought of the Indian Towing case. *Indian Towing Co. v. United States* was one of the landmark cases in maritime law. A Coast Guard lighthouse broke down, and a tug with a barge in tow ran aground without the lighthouse guidance. The barge company sued, charging negligence. The Supreme Court in 1955 ruled that the government had no obligation to provide a lighthouse at all. But by providing one, the high court said, the Coast Guard had made skippers reliant upon its guidance, so the agency then had a duty to keep the light in good working order.

Latti felt he had a comparable situation. "It was only in the past ten years that offshore lobstermen started going past the fifteen-mile limit," Latti said recently. "They did this because of the special radios and forecasts. The lobstermen came to rely on that, and the government, by providing that service, induced this reliance. So the government then had a duty to keep the service in good working order." By failing to repair the broken wind sensor on the Georges Bank buoy, Latti reasoned, or at least give warning that it was not functioning properly, the Weather Service had breached that duty.

To make such a point in court, of course, he would have to prove that the faulty sensor was one reason why the forecasters had failed to predict correctly the monster storm. It did not have to be the only cause, but it had to be a substantial factor. So it came about that the trial of *Honour Brown v. United States* did, indeed, become in part a heated inquiry into how accurately weather can be forecasted.

In the courtroom, Latti made much of the three memos written during 1980 by meteorologist Winslow. He also called to the stand as an expert witness William Haggard, a consulting meteorologist who'd spent years working for the Navy and the NOAA in the field of marine and aviation forecasting. The Weather Service's tracking of the storm had been off between ninety and one-hundred fifty miles throughout its journey, because the forecasters didn't have the Georges Bank buoy data on wind direction and speed, Haggard testified. With that data, he said, the Weather Service could have issued a storm warning in its 11:00 P.M. broadcast Friday, in time for the vessels to turn back. The failure, he said, came not from the lack of one particular reading at a single moment in time, but rather, the absence of information over many hours. Without this flow of data, the isobars, or lines of pressure, that the forecasters plotted on their weather map were skewed. "Had they had the wind direction and speed at the buoy . . . ," Haggard said, "they would have realized that a piece of their jigsaw puzzle was turned at a wrong angle. And if they believed that piece was significant, then they would have to rearrange the puzzle to fit that piece."

To David Hutchinson, the U.S. Department of Justice trial attorney defending the government, Latti's entire case seemed ludicrous. It didn't matter whether the Georges Bank buoy wind sensor was working, he argued, because when the doomed ships passed nearby at about the time of the 11:00 P.M. broadcast on November 21, the weather there was just as it had been forecast. If working, the wind sensors would simply have confirmed the forecast, and what the lobstermen could see firsthand. To Hutchinson, the idea that the lack of data over many hours had skewed the forecasters' isobar map seemed absurd, an obscurely indirect cause not at all comparable to the lighthouse breakdown in the *Indian Towing* case. Besides, the fishermen weren't out one hundred miles because of the Georges Bank buoy anyway. That buoy hadn't been installed until 1977, some time after lobster vessels had first started venturing far from shore. The introduction of the sophisticated loran navigational system was what had empowered the lobstermen to pursue their catch in the dead of winter.

Above all, though, the government's lawyer repeatedly argued that weather forecasts simply can't be relied upon. The lobstermen in their own testimony, he pointed out, had acknowledged they knew this all too well. To underscore this point, Hutchinson produced his own expert witness, meteorologist Frederick Sanders, a retired Massachusetts Institute of Technology professor, who testified that the killer storm was not the low-pressure center tracked from the Carolina coast at all, but, rather, a second low that had formed suddenly in the Georges Bank area early on Saturday morning. This second low, Sanders said, absorbed the Carolina low that forecasters had been watching and exploded in what he called a "weather bomb." The Weather Service's computer guidance could not have predicted the weather bomb, Sanders said, and the Georges Bank buoy data would not have helped either. In other words, the lobstermen were lost "as a result of the risk fishermen fishing in the offshore waters of New England have been exposed to for years, an 'act of God.' "

Those most caught in the middle in *Honour Brown v. United States* were the Weather Service forecasters. On the one hand, they were on record as greatly valuing the data provided by buoys. On the other hand, they felt both a cautious protectiveness about their agency and an acute sense of the limits of their craft, regardless of what information they possessed. This conflict was reflected in their testimony. The forecasters said they weren't at all sure they could have predicted the storm even with the buoy data. Rodney Winslow and Dave Feit—who had issued the Friday morning forecast—agreed with the government's expert, saying that a new low had formed and explosively deepened in the vicinity of Georges Bank. "I would have to say that it [buoy data] probably would not have changed the forecast because of the way this storm developed . . . ," Feit said. "We did not consider the possibility of a new low off Georges Bank. . . . The explosion of this storm, I did not believe then and I do not believe now, was forecastable." The surprise storm, Feit added, "was not the first and it won't be the last. People must always be prepared for the weather to go sour."

If the meteorologists' comments about the Georges Bank storm sounded reasonable, though, their more general explanations about their work seemed to stun the judge. To Tauro, predicting weather suddenly sounded a good deal more like an amateur art than a professional science.

Buoy data, the meteorologists explained in court, were one part of the puzzle among many that they put together to formulate a forecast. Their importance varied depending on how many other data were available. Without the Georges Bank information, for example, the forecasters had used data from the Nantucket Light wind sensor forty miles away. Moreover, different forecasters rely more on one element of the puzzle than do other forecasters. "It's not total subjectivity," Winslow said, "but each forecaster has all the information at his disposal and he uses it as he deems necessary. . . . The puzzle may not fit exactly the same from one forecaster to another."

Judge Tauro, nonplussed, asked a question: While being trained, were not all forecasters instructed in certain basic procedures?

"No, sir," Feit said.

Tauro: "Are you telling me that meteorologists are free to follow whatever course—whatever design they feel is appropriate on an individual basis in determining what the weather is?"

Feit: "Yes, sir."

By the end of the seven-day trial, Tauro could not disguise his impatience with what he saw as inconsistencies in Feit's testimony. The meteorologist had seemed both to blame the lack of buoy data and to say the data would not have helped. Tauro also made clear he found the testimony of Latti's expert the most persuasive. In a forty-page decision issued December 21, the judge embraced the plaintiffs' case in its entirety. The federal government was liable for damages, the judge ruled. Yes, the dead fishermen's bereaved families could rage at the National Weather Service for failing to predict a storm.

Eight months later, Tauro fixed the exact amount of the damages: One and a quarter million dollars, to be distributed in varying amounts to the families of the lobstermen who were lost at sea.

▪ ▪ ▪

Over time, even though various lawyers cautioned that its reach was limited and subject to appeal, Judge Tauro's decision made for a number of front-page headlines across the country. In interviews, Michael Latti called the ruling a "landmark" and happily told reporters "it's very significant because it's the first case where the United States was held responsible for basically an inaccurate forecast. We're delighted."

If *Honour Brown v. United States* has a lasting importance, though, it most certainly will be limited to the lawbooks, for it doesn't appear that Judge Tauro's findings in a Boston courtroom will much affect the ways of New England lobstermen. Whether the fatal Georges Bank storm was an unforeseeable act of God or a predictable event, the last decade's technological advances and the lure of their prey are now just too strong to keep men hugging the shore.

Peter Brown appeared in court only for his one day of testimony, then promptly returned to the sea, where his father before him had toiled for twenty-five years and where he has spent much of his life since finishing high school in 1975. Lawyers scrambling to prepare for the damages portion of the litigation during a February snowstorm in Boston vainly tried to reach him, but he was aboard the *Sea Fever,* working his lobster traps—one hundred miles from shore.

"What can you do about it?" Brown told a reporter before departing. "Maybe it was one of those things that just come up, or maybe they missed it. Either way, Gary and the guys on the *Fairwind* are still dead."

UPDATE

On May 13, 1986, the First Circuit Court of Appeals reversed Judge Tauro's decision, ruling that the manner by which the National Weather Service chooses to predict the weather—what it relies on, what it chooses to repair or replace, what degree of sophistication it employs, how much money it spends—is a discretionary function of government and thus exempt from liability. It was not up to courts to tell the government what resources must be invested or skills brought to bear in an activity such as weather prediction. "The Weather Service is a particularly unfortunate area in which to establish a duty of judicially reviewable due care," the appellate panel wrote. "A weather forecast is a classic example of a prediction of indeterminate reliability, and a place peculiarly open to debatable decisions, including the desirable degree of investment of government funds and other resources. Weather predictions fail on frequent occasions. If in only a small proportion parties suffering in consequence succeeded in producing an expert who could persuade a judge . . . that the government should have done better, the burden on the [government] would be both unlimited and intolerable."

Because other courts of appeal had rejected this view when ruling on similar cases, Michael Latti appealed the reversal of *Honour Brown v. United States* to the U.S. Supreme Court. On January 20, 1987, the High Court declined to hear the case, despite a written dissent by Justice Byron R. White, joined by Justice Harry A. Blackmun, that expressed a desire to "grant one of these petitions [in order] to resolve the conflict" among various courts of appeal.

Latti and his clients, short of funds, reluctantly gave up their fight. No further litigation is planned.

Paper Games

May 1991
Lonsdale, Minnesota

To his surprise, Bob Schmidt now realizes there are details he cannot easily recall about recent years. The sequence of events, the numbing meetings with bankers and lawyers and relatives, the loud auctions and final notices, the tearful hugs in empty fields, have become a blur. Even the most critical dates remain fuzzy—when the family learned the bankers were pulling the plug, when exactly they lost their 1,572-acre farm, when they moved into town. The spring of 1985 is the best Schmidt can offer for one event. Or the summer of 1985. Or the fall of 1985.

"You know . . . ," he says. Then he pauses. Schmidt, forty-four, is an unhurried talker with a soothing, nearly hypnotic tone, whose words flow so slowly, his teenage daughter Sarah swears it takes her dad a weekend to deliver a sentence. The effect can seem either mellow or withholding, but both impressions mislead. Soon a deliberate grin full of corked intensity takes hold, spreads, deepens. "It just amazes me," he finally continues. "There are so many blank spots in my memory."

It does not really matter to him. Schmidt's halting efforts to recollect, after all, are taking place as he lounges at dusk on the porch of his farmhouse in the rolling hills of western Rice County, some fifty miles south of Minneapolis. Before him is a comforting sight—a 1,005-acre farm that in 1990 produced six thousand hogs, thirty thousand bushels of corn, $850,000 in revenue and more than $100,000 in operating profit. Upstairs, on the desk in his office, sit plans for a $200,000 physical plant expansion that would raise annual hog production to ten thousand.

The story Bob Schmidt is telling only partly concerns how his family lost their farm. It is also about how they won it back, at a bargain-basement fire-sale price, from the very lenders who pulled the plug on them four years before. The Schmidts now own most of their original farm but carry a mortgage only one-quarter as large.

Such a tale is not all that rare in this part of the country. Lenders who called in loans during the great agricultural depression of the mid-1980s quite often found themselves saddled with hundreds of farms they could not sell. Watching the value of their holdings tumble unchecked, faced with calving cows and feeding hogs and harvesting corn, the lenders soon were eager to sell the farms back to their previous owners at cut-rate prices, usually after the families had worked the farms rent-free for up to two years. One survey reported that almost thirty percent of the dispossessed farms sold by the Farm Credit System in 1987 went to the farmers who'd lost them. Charles Born, a crop farmer who lives thirty miles south of the Schmidts, puts the current figure higher. His sideline, a seed corn business, keeps him visiting farmers regularly. He figures that among the dispossessed farmers he knew, three out of five eventually bought their land back cheaply. Born, in fact, is one of them—he lost land mortgaged at $2,000 an acre and bought it back at $300 an acre. Now it's valued at close to $1,200 an acre.

Some of those perceived as victims five years ago, in other words, have emerged as victors. After four good years in a row, the farm economy once again is healthy. Livestock prices are high, land values have rebounded and the average profit in 1990 of farmers in southern Minnesota was up one-third, to more than $62,000. Meanwhile, the financial institutions that called in farmers' loans are in worse shape than ever. The places the lenders put their money when they retreated from agriculture—the bond market and commercial real estate—have proved far more disastrous investments than farmland.

People in the rural Midwest, as a result, can't help but chuckle a bit these days. Even though the farmers who aggressively borrowed and expanded weren't blameless victims, even though agriculture was over-extended and collapsing, there are plenty in this region who still don't think the lenders' ways made much sense. Why didn't banks just restructure loans and ride out the bad times, they ask, instead of selling farms at ten cents on the dollar? Wasn't it all a paper game anyway? Didn't they sort of panic? For that matter, aren't they doing exactly that again now by dumping all those shopping centers and office buildings?

Whatever the answers to those questions, on one point everyone agrees: The lenders took a shellacking, more so than some farmers.

"In reality, this was good for us," Charles Born said as he sat, like Bob Schmidt, on a porch overlooking the land he once again owns, this time with one-third the mortgage. "We would have been willing to keep paying at two thousand dollars an acre. It was the right thing to do. But the lenders wouldn't let us. . . . The thing is, they jumped when the feller went to the gun closet, not when he got out the gun."

Thinking back now, talking of the past or reading yellowing minutes of his family farm corporation's annual meetings, Bob Schmidt sometimes flinches. There were good reasons for the rapid expansion and heavy debt burden, he tells himself. But still, certain decisions haunt him. They'd started in 1969, after all, by buying just two hundred acres of land at $200 an acre—$40,000 cash.

They weren't even farmers then. Schmidt's father, Robert D. Schmidt, was a highly paid executive at Control Data who'd grown up on a Minnesota farm and always dreamed of retiring to one. Bob Schmidt was a newly married English literature major at the University of Minnesota whose wife Sheri worked as a systems programmer at Univac. Bob had attended high school in southern California, worked odd jobs at Paradise Cove and rode the surf at Malibu before reluctantly leaving the beach when his father got transferred to Minnesota. When asked his goals, he talked of being a teacher, but that was just something to say. He did not know.

One day in the fall of 1968 Schmidt's father invited the family to visit a plot of land he was thinking of buying in southern Minnesota. Bob Schmidt thought the place beautiful.

That he'd been on a farm only twice before in his life no doubt colored his judgment. In truth, the farm they were inspecting was something of a mess. There were no usable buildings. The house on it had been abandoned. The land, largely unfenced and uncared for, was what agricultural bankers politely call "marginal"—rugged, hilly, full of clay. Those gentle slopes climbing to thick stands of maple and oak were lullingly pretty, but they did not easily accommodate the bulky machinery needed to cultivate, plant and harvest.

Still, it was cheap. Schmidt's father, looking around, thought of walnut orchards, beef cattle and tax writeoffs. Bob Schmidt thought of reinventing himself. Escrow closed on January 17, 1969.

On weekends that spring, the whole family—including Schmidt's two younger brothers Bill and Peter, his sister Susan and her husband, Steve Jedlund—would drive down from Minneapolis to clear brush and talk over their plans. There was much to discuss. Times were changing in agriculture just then. Old boys who'd run small dairy farms all their lives, working thirty cows and putting the milk cans out on the road every night for pickup, were now selling their land and getting out. Why not, they figured, what with people like the Schmidts paying $200 an acre for land they'd always valued at $100.

The tempting offers from neighboring farmers soon started rolling in, and the Schmidts began expanding: The 240-acre Uhler farm and the 159-acre Edel farm in May 1969, the 126-acre Duffney farm in October, the 160-acre Simmonson farm the following January. Within months, the Schmidts' holdings had grown to 885 acres. By now Bob Schmidt was cutting classes at the University of Minnesota.

"We had decided to do a little farming," he recalled much later. "It was outrageous. Over eight hundred acres and still we barely knew what dirt looked like."

Most of the Schmidt clan lived at the farm that first summer of 1969. They bought two tractors, a disc, a drag, a planter. They cleaned and repaired. They planted corn and soybeans, even though their neighbors said they were too late into the season. They rented land to another farmer, asking for half the hay crop instead of cash. Bob had only a vague idea of what to do with the hay, other than put it in the barn, but he had a mind to learn.

"I made an arrangement with the renter," he said. "As he planted corn and oats and hay, I could ride with him in the tractor and pick his brain."

Late that summer, after the rest of the family had returned to the city, Bob and Sheri enrolled in the Faribault Area Vocational Technical Institute's Adult Farm Management Program, which opened all sorts of doors to them. Teachers came to evaluate their operation and took them on tours of other farms. They read textbooks, attended agricultural functions, studied comparative computer analyses. "It was like finding a gold mine," Schmidt said. "We could see what these farmers had done, were doing, were planning. We could see all the things we didn't have a clue about. And these farmers were so friendly and encouraging. We made friends and contacts. We got access to information."

By the end of summer, Bob Schmidt had decided he was not going back to school. He and Sheri were going to stay on the farm, and Sheri would commute to her job at Univac. When Bob's father urged him to finish school, Bob flatly refused. "No," he said. "I don't want to."

To farmers just then, the future looked limitless. International markets were ballooning—the Communist bloc had opened its doors to American farm products, drought-stricken developing countries had turned to the United States for food, and the Nixon Administration had devalued the dollar, making American farm goods cheaper for foreign customers. The secretary of agriculture, Earl Butz, had encouraged farmers to "plant fence row to fence row" to feed the world. U.S. farm exports, $8 billion in 1971, were beginning a rapid climb that would reach $43.8 billion within a decade. Bob Schmidt had caught a perfect wave.

The early 1970s were a blur of work. The senior Schmidt's brother-in-law, Mike Weltsch, joined the operation, and the Schmidt family formed a farm corporation named Tal Bauernhof—German for "farmhouse in the valley"—with Bob Schmidt as general manager. They bought black Angus calves and started a beef cattle operation. They bought sows and started a pig finishing operation. They planted soybean, corn and hay crops, not to sell but to use as feed for their livestock. They learned about artificial insemination and vaccinations at school, then started crossbreeding Herefords with Charolais, Simmenthal, Limousine, Main Anjou. They increased their cattle herd to more than five hundred head, including purebred Pinzgauers from the Austrian Alps. They installed three seventy-feet-tall silos and built a six-hundred-cow feeding facility. They bought more land, first the 220-acre Spiker farm at the fire-sale price of $180 an acre, then the 120-acre Vranek farm, which at $792 an acre for the first time did not come cheaply. At 1,225 acres and $300,000 in revenues, Tal Bauernhof by 1975 was among the largest farms in the county.

The farm wasn't making a profit, but with all the cost of expansion and improvement, the Schmidts were not greatly alarmed. A new mortgage with Travelers Insurance and short-term line of credit with First Bank Minneapolis kept the cash flowing, while Schmidt's father took the losses as tax writeoffs and poured his hefty bonuses from Control Data into further expansion.

In 1979 Schmidt decided to double the annual corn yield to eighty thousand bushels and move into the cash grain market. A year later, he doubled the hog production to five thousand with construction of a state-of-the-art modular hog barn. By now land was not at all cheap, but it looked to be going only higher, so the Schmidts in January 1980 bought the 192-acre Dalby farm for just over $1,042 an acre, then in July 1981 the 155-acre Bottke farm for $1,700 an acre. Then they leased five hundred more acres on a three-year contract. To work the new land, they leased equipment—a combine, two tractors, a plow, a cultivator, a planter—in deals that carried floating interest rates.

Schmidt shakes his head thinking about it all now. "We were going big time," he said.

They still, however, were not realizing a profit, and for good reason. Over time, the family had built a sizable debt as they rolled more and more of their expansion costs into short- and long-term loans. An already considerable $664,000 mortgage and $360,000 short-term debt in 1979 had grown to $1.4 million and $1.2 million respectively by 1984. Meanwhile, interest rates, fueled by the federal government's budget deficit and credit crunch, had ballooned—at one point Schmidt found himself paying twenty-four percent for leased equipment.

The Schmidts' interest bill was $37,000 in 1975 and $115,000 in 1979. By 1982, including leased equipment, it was $400,000. A year later it was $585,000. Such payments easily swallowed what otherwise would have been operating profits. On revenues of $900,000 in 1982, the farm lost $167,000. On revenues of $823,000 in 1983, the farm lost $503,000.

If such figures suggested a certain lack of control, even recklessness, they also reflected a not uncommon business strategy during the farm boom. The losses were largely on paper, after all—with tax writeoffs, the senior Schmidt essentially was channeling his considerable income into an ever-appreciating farm rather than sending it to the government. That's how the game was played, however unwisely. Many family farms lost money, only a handful made more than a few thousand dollars, and most survived on substantial incomes from nonfarm vocations. If the Schmidts were financially unrestrained, so were a good many farmers in those years.

"The Schmidt cash flow was tight and they were aggressive, but they weren't all that different from others," said Mike Taets, then a First Bank Minneapolis assistant vice-president and one of the Schmidts' loan officers, now an executive with a private bank holding company. "In fact, without doubt they were not among the worst. They were not as leveraged as some. I'd put them at the thirtieth or fortieth percentile on that scale, in the middle to back of the pack. They were smart and they were good people. They had a very, very well-run operation."

In the Schmidts' case as with most farmers, at any rate, both the lenders and borrowers were looking not at profits but at the rising value of the assets. Theirs was a joint march into treacherous territory, with both the banks and the farmers gambling that a continued appreciation in the worth of land would make them money and keep the operations afloat. With an appraised value in 1984 of $5.68 million, a debt of $2.79 million and a net worth of $2.89 million, Tal Bauernhof's asset-to-debt ratio looked good to everyone involved.

"When you're in the middle of a farm economy that's going gangbusters, and everyone else is paying out more, extending schedules, those kind of things start to multiply," said David Guimond, then a First Bank Minneapolis vice-president and another of the Schmidts' loan officers, now a vice-president at the regional stock brokerage firm of Piper, Jaffray & Hopwood. "You loan on land value. Two years later, you look like an idiot because land values have fallen. You're asked, 'You dumb stick, how could you do that?' You look like a dummy. But as you're going through it, you just lend."

By the early 1980s the risky game being played by both farmers and lenders had started to blow up in their faces. International markets were drying up, due in varying degree to Jimmy Carter's 1980 grain embargo of the Soviet Union, increased competition from farmers abroad, tightening credit to underdeveloped countries, and the rising value of the dollar. Meanwhile on the domestic scene, federal tax cuts without corresponding spending reductions were creating a growing budget deficit and mushrooming interest rates. For farmers, the cost of doing business was rising just as commodity prices were falling.

Still, to the Schmidts, busy with their hogs and cattle and relatively isolated on their fifteen hundred acres in southern Minnesota, these problems felt distant, even as late as 1984.

"At the time, I wasn't unaware of farm troubles—there was lots of talk in the press," Schmidt recalled. "But we didn't have the context of what was happening in the overall economy. We were in the middle of it, not looking at it later from the sidelines. We didn't see the big picture. Those going down around us, we thought of them as bad farmers, poor managers. It was not our problem."

Schmidt, in fact, felt on the upswing. They'd nearly halved their losses and interest burden from the previous year. They'd started backing away from row crops and emphasizing livestock, which their type of land better accommodated. They'd been honored as Minnesota's Commercial Beef Producers of the Year at the Minnesota Beef Cattle Improvement Association's annual gathering. They'd been spotlighted by the *St. Paul Pioneer Press* in a long feature article complete with several color photographs. As late as October 1984, Schmidt was even thinking of buying another farm over near Onatonka, a thousand-acre beauty, all crop-diversified in soybeans, corn, carrots, potatoes. The owners wanted $3 million and Schmidt had not a clue how they'd pay for it, but he was working on his projections.

Given such aggressive optimism in the face of deteriorating conditions and their own financial problems, it is hard to feel unqualified sympathy for the Schmidts, or view them as blameless victims. Land has to have cash flow—that is the bedrock axiom that many farmers' grandfathers learned in the 1920s and 1930s, as did many commercial developers more recently. Unless there's enough money coming from crops or rents to pay at least the interest on the mortgage, then borrowing and lending both are risky endeavors. There are those in southern Minnesota, accordingly, who use terms such as *foolhardy* and *irrational* when talking about farmers who rapidly overexpanded. Even the Schmidts at times use words such as *stupid* to describe some of their actions in those days.

However, the Schmidts also believe there were legitimate reasons for their general approach, if not each particular decision.

"Some would call us greedy, power hungry, crazy," Schmidt said. "Some are angry at people like us. But if you don't grow, you're going to get buried in time. There's the economies of scale, the need to have the most efficient operation, the need to produce at the least cost. Our situation revolved around my dad's income and the tax situation in that era. We were improving the farm, riding up appreciation, and also expecting eventually to make a profit. We were making all our payments. We were never late. What we were doing all made sense."

Whatever the judgment on this issue, this much seems clear—the Schmidts were playing by the same rules they and their lenders together had always observed and sanctioned. They were, that is, until their lenders decided they no longer wanted to play.

In February 1984, Bob Schmidt placed a phone call to Mark Blake, his contact at Travelers, to discuss the $1.2 million balloon payment coming due when their fifteen-year mortgage expired at the end of the year. Blake was reassuring.

"No need to worry now," he told Schmidt on the phone. "We'll just roll it over. No big deal. Sometime near the end of the year, we'll get together. Check with me in September."

In late September, when Schmidt again called, Blake said, "We'll just roll it over. . . . There might be some expenses but not too bad. I'll be talking to you by the end of November. I'll come down there to visit the farm."

Schmidt sensed a problem, but set it aside, for it was now time to renew his short-term line of credit at First Bank Minneapolis. In mid-October, Schmidt drove to downtown Minneapolis to make the annual presentation to his loan officer. This time it was not Guimond but the younger Taets, one year on the job, who was handling their farm account.

"I gave him the projections, the whole history," Schmidt recalled. "It was not much different from past years. Mark seemed positive. 'Looks good, Bob,' he said. 'I got to take it to the committee but I don't see any problems.' He was looking me in the eye. I was pretty happy with my numbers. I was confident of next year. I thought it was a done deal."

Schmidt returned to his farming. A week passed without the banker calling, then another, then a third. Finally, Schmidt called Taets. "I'm kind of surprised I haven't heard from you," Schmidt said. "Is there some kind of problem?"

Taets apologized for not getting back sooner. As a matter of fact, he said, yes, there was a problem. He'd been trying to solve it, he'd been trying to work it out. That's why Schmidt hadn't heard from him. But he hadn't had any luck.

"What's the problem?"

"Well," Taets said, "you have to find another bank."

Schmidt digested the news in silence.

"What the hell are you talking about?" he said finally. "Find another bank. How the hell are we going to find another bank? You know as well as I what's going on out there. . . . What are you doing? Are you calling our loans or what?"

"Actually," Taets said, "the powers that be are closing the bank's entire agricultural loan department. They think all you farmers should be banking out in the country. They don't want to have an AG business here downtown."

"Well, I just can't believe this," Schmidt said. "What are those guys doing? It doesn't make sense."

"Well, they've just decided they shouldn't be in the AG business downtown," Taets replied. "They should be in other things."

"How much time do I have?" Schmidt asked. "What if I can't find another bank?"

"I don't know. All I can tell you is, you don't want to be around here by next June," Taets said. Then he hesitated. "Don't let this screw up your deal with Travelers," he added.

"No, man," Schmidt said, drawing out his words. "I'm sure it won't bother Travelers at all that we no longer have a line of credit."

Schmidt soon would learn what did or did not bother his mortgage holder. Just two weeks later, a few days before Thanksgiving, Mark Blake finally appeared at the Schmidts' farm to talk about the balloon payment coming due at year's end. With him was a stranger, a heavy-set man named Ross House, introduced as a "Travelers farm manager."

They sat in the farmhouse living room, Schmidt across the table from Blake, House off to the side on a couch. Schmidt knew Blake, had been working with him for two years now, but he wondered who this House fellow was, why he was there. House was saying nothing, just listening. Schmidt tried to include him in the conversation in order to get him defined, but he remained aloof.

Blake began outlining the requirements for renewal of the mortgage. There will be an eight-hundred-dollar application fee, he announced.

Why? Schmidt asked. All we're doing is rolling over a loan, not seeking a new one. We're a customer.

Well, it's not just a rollover, Blake said.

That's what you told me, Schmidt said. Just a rollover.

Well, it's a policy of the company, Blake replied.

Looking back later, Schmidt had trouble recalling just what else was said that day and what was said later, on the phone, in the following weeks. What he did remember was that Blake kept coming back at him with more requirements.

First the interest rate was to be raised from 10 percent to 13 percent. Then it was to be 13.75 percent. There would be a one percent origination fee—$12,000. Then there would also be a three percent deposit up front, earnest money that the Schmidts would forfeit if they rejected the Travelers loan offer. By now they were up to $48,800 in payments before even getting the loan, which would come at an unworkable rate anyway.

"Well, Mark," Schmidt said one day, after hearing the terms revised for a third time, "it sounds like what you are telling me is, you want to own the farm. . . . Now what would you do with my farm?"

This was no idle question. He could not fathom Travelers' intent, or First Bank's. For legal reasons, no one was directly telling them, "No, you can't have a loan." They were just making it impossible to take the loan. But what was the point? The family was making its payments. Why pull the plug and take their land? Did Travelers really want the land? Did Travelers know of valuable oil or mineral rights? Or were they just out to get the Schmidts?

Years would pass before Schmidt would fully come to understand that the lenders' actions had little to do with the particulars of Tal Bauernhof's operation. The lenders were retreating not from Schmidt, but from agriculture.

There'd been plenty of hesitation and pullbacks by lenders since the start of the decade, but when the country's farm income suddenly dropped sixty-four percent in 1984, these concerns deepened, and for good reason. Given falling commodity prices, even if farmers were making payments now, projections suggested some couldn't in the future. With rising interest rates, the debt burden alone threatened to devour any operating profits that were realized—in 1982, for the first time in United States history, farmers cleared less ($19 billion) than they paid out in interest ($21 billion), and interest payments were eating up sixteen percent of total farm expenses. Agricultural land no longer looked at all valuable to lenders or buyers, nor farming profitable. As a result, appraisals for farms, machinery and livestock plummeted, and loans soon were worth less than their collateral.

"A confluence of events caused the banks to pull out," said Guimond, the Schmidts' former loan officer at First Bank. "From the bank's perspective, land prices were down, cattle prices down, hog prices down, expenses up. How can you sell the same product and still expect to repay the loan? It wasn't just lower land prices that was the problem. It also was the occasional farmer who got caught, who couldn't make his payments."

First Bank was closing out more than the Schmidts' loan and a single downtown agriculture department. Faced with a burdensome exposure to the sagging farm economy, the parent corporation, First Bank System, was developing plans to sell twenty-eight banks in four midwestern states, one-third of the banks it owned, as a means to halve its loans to farmers.

Other sectors of the economy simply looked much more alluring. Between 1982 and 1984, First Bank System had added more than $1.3 billion to its syndicated loans, which feed credit lines maintained by large corporations. Led by its president Dennis Evans, a shining star from the capital markets, it had also started betting on interest rates by building what in time would become an $8 billion bond portfolio.

"My own impression was that some less profitable areas of the bank were thought to be nonuseful," said Guimond. "If farming looked weak, you were to shift out. For a while, we were told if there's even a whisper that a loan might go bad, let's get rid of it. That didn't necessarily mean only farmers who were missing payments. It also could mean those who don't show they can pay back in their cash flow. They weren't separating out those with alternate incomes or security. They just wanted out of agriculture."

Travelers Corporation, meanwhile, was moving heavily into the commercial real estate market. Hotels, apartment buildings, office buildings and shopping centers beckoned, particularly in the booming Southwest.

"I had no set plan when I went to that meeting with the Schmidts," said Ross House, the curiously silent Travelers farm manager, who is now self-employed in a farm sales and management business. "The mixed and staggered signals Schmidt was getting were the result of several layers of bureaucracy. The borrower tends to see conspiracy, but the lenders and their attorneys are really just so goddamn incompetent. Travelers simply wanted out of agriculture. There were not enough Indians out there to say, let's run down and rewrite the Schmidts' loan. If Schmidt was only one problem, the focus, we could agree to rewrite. But the Schmidts were one of thousands."

The Schmidts could not accept the terms of the new mortgage Travelers was offering and could not find another bank to provide the short-term credit First Bank was withdrawing. The turnaround had been stunningly rapid. In mid-October the Schmidts had been talking about buying another thousand acres. By the first week in December, they were talking about handing over their farm to Travelers Insurance, their equipment and livestock to First Bank. On March 20, 1985, they decided they had no other alternative.

That day, Bob Schmidt drove to downtown Minneapolis to report the decision to their lenders. He'd wanted to get them all together in a room, but couldn't reach Blake of Travelers, so ended up sitting across from Taets and Guimond at a First Bank conference table. There was the usual premeeting banter, then Schmidt began.

"We've come to realize there is no way we can get financing. We can't service our debt, even with more cash from my father. It won't work. We don't like it, but we have to face it. So I've come to turn over all the assets. We want to help you recover your loans. We'll help liquidate. But you can't just dump everything. It will take time."

Schmidt looked at his bankers. Taets seemed to be taking the news pretty coolly, but Guimond had turned white. He looked sick. Schmidt hadn't quite expected that.

Driving home that night, Schmidt avoided the city and the interstate. He wound south on country roads lightly dusted with snow, passing through Chaska, Shakopee, New Praque, following no precise route, just a direction. He knew only that he was heading south. He could not recall ever feeling worse in his life.

Negotiations over how to proceed dragged on all that spring and summer. The Schmidts proposed to stretch the liquidation and reduction of debt over five years while they leased and worked the land. Travelers wanted two years at the most. Then the Schmidts proposed to avoid official foreclosure by handing over to Travelers a deed to the farm in lieu of the debt, and leasing the farm back for two years. Travelers never would commit. "The reality is, we were standing there trying to shove a fifty-five-thousand-dollar lease payment at them and they wouldn't take it," Schmidt recalled.

First Bank proved no more accommodating about the livestock and machinery that served as collateral to the short-term debt. It just didn't make sense to Schmidt to auction off everything right away, since there was no one out there with money to spend on cattle and combines.

"In effect, you're writing off the debt to two hundred strangers," Schmidt vainly argued to First Bank's officers. "Why not write it down to us instead? We've been good customers for a long time. Why write it down to two hundred strangers? That's what's going to happen. You're going to get twenty-five cents on the dollar."

Schmidt was proved wrong about that. The equipment auction on August 20 yielded closer to ten cents on the dollar. The cattle auction on September 7, advertised and staged on the farm as a select production sale of breeding stock, brought in just about what the bank would have gotten if the cattle had been shipped directly to a commercial auction house.

Days later, Travelers officials, following their lawyers' advice, officially rejected the offer of the Schmidts' deed in lieu of the debt. The formal foreclosure notice arrived in November. One night that month, Bob and Sheri walked far into a field that was once full of corn and was now stubble, to watch the moon rising huge in the sky. Hugging each other and crying, they decided to give up the fight.

In early November 1985, Bob took a job at Ballistivet, a fledgling company he'd invested in two years before that was trying to market biodegradable medical pellets for animals. He began commuting to the company's office in the St. Paul suburb of White Bear Lake, and criss-crossing the country to promote and service its product.

The next June, the Schmidts made the break with the farm complete when they bought a house in White Bear Lake. A month later, Sheri found a job in St. Paul, as operations manager at Volmela Specialty Company, an industrial graphics manufacturer. In August, they moved to their new home.

That was quite a day. Four pickups and a cattle truck full of the Schmidts' belongings and friends rolled through their new suburban neighborhood, a pleasant and pretty quarter of town full of gracefully aging frame homes. After everything had been unloaded, the Schmidts and their friends gathered over beers in a strange backyard. Bob slouched in his chair, studying the fence that marked the boundary of his new home. He was no longer a farmer. That part of his life was over.

"God," he said. "I hate this place."

Although public chronicles about agriculture in the mid-1980s usually ended with farmers mired in bitterness and displacement, this was not always the true outcome. Often, the seeming victims eventually emerged as victors, while the lenders who pulled the plugs on them ended up in far sorrier positions. The financial institutions simply did not know what to do with the farms they owned, and couldn't get rid of them, so not infrequently they let the foreclosed farmers stay on their land.

Largely for this reason, the Schmidt family never did lose physical possession of their farm.

After taking almost all of 1985 to decide to foreclose against the Schmidts, Travelers Insurance was required by Minnesota law to wait another year before seizing the land. So the official foreclosure sale notice didn't arrive in the mail until November 1986, and the land wasn't put up for sale until February 1987. Then it just sat for two more years without a buyer. Meanwhile, it had to be maintained, so

Schmidt's brother Bill and his wife Wendy were allowed to remain on the farm, working the hog and reduced cattle operation in a rent-free, interest-free and tax-free partnership with Schmidt's father, who around this time left Control Data, where he'd risen to vice-chairman, to start his own company. They called their new operation Fox Den Farm, and with such low overhead, it made money.

During this period, the Schmidts also managed to dissolve their huge short-term debt with First Bank Minneapolis. Forced liquidations had reduced the $1.2 million balance to $985,000, and Bob's father had paid down that amount to $400,000 by signing over his bonuses and stock shares from Control Data. In early 1987, sensing the bank would be inclined to write down the remaining balance, the senior Schmidt offered $40,000 to settle the account—ten cents on the dollar.

Bob Schmidt couldn't see how his father had the nerve even to make such a puny offer, but the senior Schmidt, who'd opened up the Soviet Union for Control Data, well merited his reputation as a crack negotiator. The bank jumped at his offer. What to the Schmidts was ten cents on the dollar, after all, could be regarded by the loan officers as fifty cents on the dollar, if they added the $40,000 to what had been paid off previously. Not such a bad recovery, considering this was by now essentially an unsecured loan.

"Their performance would look okay on paper," the senior Schmidt observed recently. "That was important to them. The lenders aren't looking at the situation as you are."

If this outcome was strange, it was not at all uncommon, particularly in Minnesota. Lenders getting squeezed from all directions had to deal where they could.

"There was a period there when you couldn't give a farm away," recalled Ross House. "In Minnesota alone Travelers owned two hundred of them, about eighty to ninety thousand acres. In 1985 and 1986 we were getting five or six new farms a week. There was literally no market."

"No one knew what to do with these farms," said Dave Guimond. "The dispossessed farmers are saying, stick it in your ear. It's not like taking over an office building and shutting off the lights, closing the pipes. You have a living, breathing organism. It needs caring for. Typically what we did is turn around and rent back to the farmer we took it from."

Then the Minnesota legislature in 1986 passed a "right of first refusal" law that gave the original owner of dispossessed property the right to match any potential buyer's bid. A farmer who had borrowed heavily to buy land at $2,000 an acre, as a result, could default on his debts, accumulate cash by working his land rent- and tax-free for the twenty months it usually took the lender to put the farm up for sale, then buy it back at a deflated price, perhaps $550 an acre.

Don't fight and don't quit, the shrewder farmers came to realize. Hang in there, don't leave your land. Sit tight. Try a little guerrilla warfare if need be.

When Norwest Bank pulled the plug on the Schmidts' neighbor John Derham, he just handed over the keys to the farm. Then he asked his loan officer a question: "Who's gonna feed your seven hundred head of cattle?" The banker had no answer. Four days later, Derham called him. "Well, nine of your cattle are dead and a couple others don't look so good," he reported. After a few weeks of such exchanges, the bank agreed to pay Derham a thousand dollars a month to care for the livestock. He accepted, but only after the bank tossed in extra cash for feed, feeders and two full-time farmworkers.

"You don't tap-dance with a gorilla," Derham advised recently, flapping his arms as he stood on the land he has now bought back from the bank. "Better to get away, kick at his shins from a distance."

In time lenders grew more than happy to take whatever they could get for the farms, livestock and machinery they owned. Rushing in concert to dump property on an already depressed market, they managed only to drive down prices further.

"We didn't know where farm prices were going to bottom out," Guimond recalled. "It turned out four hundred thirty-five dollars an acre was the bottom. But we didn't know. Some guys were saying two hundred dollars. So suddenly, you're happy for forty cents on the dollar."

"The idea at Travelers first was to hold the land, rent it to farmers, watch it bottom out, then sell it when the market went up and not until then," House said. "But then they panicked. Travelers had cash flow problems and needed money. Let's try to sell the dogs, they said at first. Within six months, they were trying to sell everything. In 1988, they were selling land for one-third to one-half what the loan was—thirty to fifty cents on the dollar. And eighty percent of the sales went to local farmers, even to the former owners."

In that year, 1988, however, the Schmidts were not among those who bought back their farms. Travelers's price was still too high for them. They occupied the land, but lacked the means to make an offer. Potential buyers, meanwhile, had started approaching and hovering.

It was then that Bob Schmidt decided to make his move.

The job Schmidt had taken as director of marketing at Ballistivet had soured for him, what with operational problems in the home office and long weeks on the road in budget motel rooms. It was hard to say what he disliked most during those trips, the dinners with talkative marketing men or the solitary tours of dusty towns to fill empty weekends.

In March 1988, just when it seemed to him farmland was close to bottoming out, he left on yet another long business trip. It did not go well, because of product distribution problems. Then, the day he returned to the firm's suburban St. Paul office, a series of employees brought him complaints. That evening the director of manufacturing called to say he'd had enough, he was resigning.

The next morning, after a sleepless night, Schmidt argued loudly with the company's general manager about the stewardship of the firm. The exchange escalated, accusations were hurled, warnings issued, lawsuits threatened.

"I expect your resignation," the general manager finally shouted.

"You got it," Schmidt snapped.

He was standing in his kitchen that night when his wife Sheri returned from her job at an industrial graphics manufacturer. Before he could speak, she did.

"Guess what," she said. "I was promoted to director of operations today. I'm getting a twelve-thousand-dollar-a-year raise."

Schmidt's response drew from both of his now-distanced pasts. "That's bitchin'," said the former California surfer. "I'm going farming."

Within days, he began commuting in reverse, from his suburban White Bear Lake home to the farm. Usually he spent the work week at Fox Den, coming home only on weekends. After discussion, he and Sheri bought into the partnership that had been formed by Bob's father and brother Bill. Together, they signed a ten-month lease with Travelers to work the farm into mid-January 1989.

That's all they could do, though. Travelers's asking price, $525,000 for 685 acres of the original farm, was still too high for them.

While they waited that summer and fall, realtors began bringing around potential buyers—three or four in all. Watching with increasing agitation, Schmidt began blocking out operating plans, cash flows, projections. They had the right of first refusal, but that wouldn't matter if the price offered was too high.

"We had to know what we could operate with," Schmidt said. "We weren't going to do it no matter what. We weren't going to commit suicide again. We'd only match the price if it made sense."

One potential buyer kept returning. The people from Benson-Quinn Hogs over in Owatanna looked serious, and asked lots of questions. They even sent their consulting veterinarian to inspect the hog barn.

Looking back later, it is hard to say precisely when the question of personal and real property on the farm first arose. Most likely, it was in October 1988, just as Benson-Quinn's interest was peaking.

One day the Travelers farm manager, Ross House, mentioned to Schmidt that they should sit down and agree on what was real estate, what personal property, particularly in the state-of-the-art hog barn. Travelers, after all, owned only the real estate. Then the Benson-Quinn people started making similar suggestions. To Schmidt the matter was obvious: The totally separate, movable things (office equipment, scales, washers) were personal. The fixed stuff (the furnace, the farrowing crates, the feeders) was real property. So one morning, when the Benson-Quinn people came calling, Schmidt shrugged and reached for a piece of paper. Soon after, his visitors left, clutching the list he'd compiled.

"That's how naive we were," he said. "I didn't grasp what this was about."

Two days later, a Benson-Quinn fellow called Schmidt, asking if they could get Schmidt's signature on that list. They needed Schmidt to guarantee exactly what was real and personal property, he explained, because Travelers wouldn't guarantee anything.

That, Schmidt would say later, was when he finally wised up. "I didn't entirely understand what was going on, but I figured we must have some cards in our hand that we didn't know about."

They did. Schmidt, in fact, had Travelers over a barrel.

"This offer for the Schmidts' farm had come in from Benson-Quinn in late 1988," Ross House explained recently. "But they wanted a bill of sale on all the stuff inside the hog barn. We told them we'd go back, check the records, get the fixture filing. Then we go and look, and lo and behold, there's no fixture filing. Oooh, I think. We have a little problem. We've got a pig in a poke. You don't have to be a rocket scientist to see someone is not going to plunk down five hundred thousand dollars for a shell. Nobody's going to buy this farm without a warranty. The Travelers lawyers decide the risk of an unwarranted sale is not worth it. It isn't worth getting into litigation. We should bite the bullet, they say. Cut whatever deal you can with the Schmidts."

For a while, House vacillated.

"I know Bob doesn't know what's going on. But I represent Travelers. I can't tell Bob to wake up, smell the roses, you have them by the short hairs. But Bob didn't come down with yesterday's rain. He finally figures it out."

This time, when the Schmidts went shopping for financing, they found an interested lender.

The tiny State Bank of Faribault, with just ninety million dollars in resources, had always played its hand fairly conservatively, avoiding loans to the more leveraged farmers. As a consequence, they'd ridden out the farm depression fairly well. They never had pulled out of farm loans. Where necessary, they'd restructured and extended terms of loans until conditions improved.

The bank's senior vice-president, Tom Laughlin, with whom the Schmidts now do business, recently explained his thinking:

"Many farmers could have survived if the lenders had reduced interest rates to their borrowers and restructured, but most lenders pulled out or raised rates. Theoretically that's what you do, but such an approach guaranteed that everyone would lose. Yes, land values were going down, and farmers just had too much debt. But the loans were already out there. For those who were still making their payments, why pull out? In that situation, we'd ride it out. Just the other day I reset the loan on one farmer where we'd reduced the rate for four years. At one point during those years, the value of the farm was less than the loan. Now the value exceeds the loan."

Making a commitment to the Schmidts, he said, "was not a real difficult decision. The Schmidts had done their homework. They had the papers to show cash flow. They would have a much smaller debt. And we felt comfortable with these people. Even though they had gone through bad times, been foreclosed on, the record showed they were good people. They were honest, even to lenders. We checked."

On Monday, January 1, 1989, Bob Schmidt called Ross House and made his offer: They would pay $350,000 cash for the 685 acres, including the hog barn, that Travelers had on the market for $525,000. And they would pay $90,000, secured by a two-year note, for the 200-acre south farm that Travelers then was renting out separately. That was a total of $440,000 for 885 acres.

"I don't think they'll do it," House responded. "The price is low, and I don't think they'll finance that ninety thousand dollars. Maybe they'll go on the price. But not the financing."

"Well . . . ," Schmidt said. "See what they'll do."

"Yep, I'll call them tomorrow."

A day later, Tuesday, January 2, the phone rang in the Schmidt farmhouse.

"Bob, are you sitting down?" House began.

"Yeah, I guess."

"First of all," House said, "they wouldn't accept your offer. I was right. They don't want to finance a note. But they have made a counteroffer. They'll sell everything for three hundred ninety-five thousand dollars cash. The whole eight hundred eighty-five acres. You take it all."

Schmidt was nonplussed. Travelers's price was $45,000 less than what his family had offered. It came to a rock bottom $446 an acre. He could barely choke out his assent.

"The Schmidts bought back their farm at what now appears to be a ridiculously low price," their banker Laughlin said recently. "But it was the bottom of the market. The insurance company got a little excited. They really took some baths they didn't have to take. It was good fortune for the Schmidts to be able to buy it back."

The deal closed in March 1989. Bob and Sheri Schmidt put their White Bear Lake home up for sale and moved back to the farm that June, days after their son Morgan was graduated from high school. Sheri kept her job in St. Paul, so took over from Bob the role of com muter. In November, after a series of family conferences, they bought out Billy and Wendy's share of the farm, and formed a new partnership with Schmidt's father.

Combined with 120 privately financed acres they'd managed to keep through the years, the Fox Den Farm holdings totaled 1,005 acres, the shank of the original farm. Where there once had been a $1.4 million mortgage, though, there now was a $395,000 obligation. And where there was once a $1.2 million short-term debt, there now was a $150,000 line of credit, only $30,000 of it being used.

Fox Den Farm sent six thousand hogs to market in 1990, 250 every two weeks, and produced thirty thousand bushels of corn. The cow herd climbed back up to 114 head. Total revenue in 1990, $850,000, was not much different from what it was in 1984, but the cost of operations dropped from $793,000 to $654,850, and interest payments shrank even more, from $345,000 to $59,210. The farm, consequently, yielded an operating profit of more than $100,000. Livestock prices have gone sky high, making the Schmidts' current projections if anything look overly conservative. Independent appraisers now value Fox Den Farm at a thousand dollars an acre, more than twice what the Schmidts paid Travelers in early 1989.

Meanwhile, the Schmidts' past lenders, First Bank and Travelers, have not fared nearly as well as their former borrower.

First Bank System's decision in the mid-1980s to bet on interest rates in the bond market proved highly profitable for a while but then turned disastrous when interest rates unexpectedly headed higher in April 1987. After holding on to its $8 billion portfolio for months, vainly hoping for rates to fall, the bank finally bailed out and took a $506 million loss in the fourth quarter of 1988, which resulted in a $310 million net loss for the year and one of the worst interest-rate fiascos in modern banking history.

Travelers's mid-1980s foray into commercial real estate proved an even worse investment. With $17.3 billion—a third of its assets—tied up in hotels, office buildings, apartments and shopping centers, the company set aside $415 million for real estate losses in the second quarter of 1988, then added $650 million in October 1990. Travelers reported a record $500 million loss in the third quarter and a net loss of $178 million for 1990.

Heads have rolled at both institutions—Travelers's entire real estate operation has been restaffed in the past two years, and First Bank System's president and chairman have departed. The new First Bank chairman, John F. Grundhofer, recently expressed regret that his predecessors had sold off the company's smaller rural branches to rid itself of exposure to the farm economy. Agriculture is once again profitable, after all—institutional investors such as pension and mutual funds are rediscovering the heartland, and even supply and seed companies are now competing with banks for the right to lend farmers money. No wonder—overall, at 10.7 percent a year, farmers in southern Minnesota have matched Wall Street and mutual funds on annual rate of return from 1960 to 1988. "In hindsight," Grundhofer told a reporter in the spring of 1990, "First Bank would be even more valuable if we still had those rural branches."

Bob Schmidt cannot avoid feeling bemused when reflecting on such a turn of events, but in the end his thoughts about what has happened are more conflicted and shaded than triumphant, and weighted by a sense of his own responsibility. He still believes there were good reasons for their rapid expansion and heavy debt burden, not the least being tax laws that allowed large writeoffs and government policies that encouraged growth. But the laws and policies have changed, and so has his outlook.

He operates more carefully now. He sends some hogs to feed at a neighboring farmer's facilities rather than pay to expand his physical plant. He spends much of his time in the upstairs office adjacent to his bedroom, studying cash flow sheets, reading consultants' reports and hedging both corn and hog prices by playing the commodities market. Current grain and livestock prices roll continuously across a computer screen linked to his recently leased satellite dish. He still hankers to expand, and means to do so, with a new breeding barn and a remodeled hog barn that will increase annual hog production from six to ten thousand. But he's going to move slowly, in stages, paying his way through cash flow.

"I look back at stupid things we did," he said one recent evening, sitting on his porch and gazing at all the land he has regained. "Yeah, we did stupid things. So did the lenders and the government. I think the basic idea behind what we did was reasonable, though. Maybe we would have needed some restructuring, but there was money there. Consider this—twelve months after the forced selling of our calves for fifty cents a pound, the going market price was eighty cents. I can't help wondering—what would have happened if First Bank and Travelers just hadn't changed their investment direction? What would have happened if they just hadn't pulled out of agriculture?"

A Perfect Machine

August 1983
Callao, Peru

When it began, the sea change was not recognized for what it was. Northwest of this port town, the isolated reach of the eastern Pacific Ocean along the equator remained misleadingly benign. The few who sailed near at the time remember an eerie, beautiful stillness—a flat sea of glassy waters and little wind. The sun blazed from a crystal-blue sky, interrupted only occasionally by a towering cumulus cloud. But during May 1982, the temperature of the sea surface had risen slightly, less than one degree Fahrenheit.

Reports of the subtle warming, measured by weather satellites and drifting buoys deployed by the United States' National Oceanographic and Atmospheric Administration, flowed that month into the suburban Camp Springs, Maryland, office of Gene Rasmusson, chief of the diagnostics branch of the NOAA's Climate Analysis Center. Rasmusson thought the readings odd, particularly because the Southern Hemisphere was entering its winter season, but he figured the satellite data probably were faulty.

Then in June, the chronically low atmospheric pressure at a measuring station in Darwin, Australia, on the western side of the Pacific, suddenly rose sharply, while the chronically high pressure at another station in Tahiti, in the central Pacific, fell dramatically. Rasmusson made a passing reference to the abnormal figures that month at a gathering of American meteorologists and oceanographers in Seattle. A few eyebrows were raised. Then the scientists went on to other business.

"In retrospect, we should have been able to figure what was happening," Oregon State University oceanographer William Quinn said a year later. "The signs were there."

What was happening was the beginning of a natural catastrophe unequaled in this century, associated with the warm ocean current called *El Niño*. In the year that followed, disrupted weather patterns wreaked havoc across three-fourths of the globe, causing more than eight hundred deaths and eight billion dollars in damage. For months, the vast natural world appeared to veer from the laws of rational order. Perennial winds and currents died or reversed direction. Normal sea levels and temperatures soared or plummeted. Millions of fish and seabirds disappeared. Weather systems were displaced by thousands of miles, withering normally lush lands and turning deserts into lakes. California, the Rocky Mountain states, the Gulf Coast, Peru, Ecuador and Bolivia staggered under torrential rains, flooding, mud slides and destructive tides, while Australia, Indonesia and southern Africa gasped through record droughts. Some areas accustomed to six inches of rain received twelve feet.

"This warm episode will go down in the records as one of the strongest and in some respects one of the more unusual events of the past century," Rasmusson concluded in the fall of 1982. "Things unheard of were happening. From a human and economic standpoint, it may also have been one of the most costly. The major socio-economic problems which have been created in many areas of the world can only be completely evaluated after the event has passed into history."

The *El Niño* of 1982–83 also encouraged modesty rather than arrogance in those usually accustomed to understanding and mastering the natural world. Armed with the finest instruments modern technology could provide, some of the premier scientists in meteorology and oceanography failed to predict what was to happen, did not believe it when it began, thought it was ending when it was reaching a new peak and announced it was over when it was still lingering. In the end, some of them joined the laymen staring heavenward, pondering man's vulnerability to the unfathomable dynamics of the natural world. Their learned conversations became dotted with words such as *awesome* and *overwhelming*. Some conceded that they simply did not understand what was happening.

"When you see what can happen, how a quirk in the wind can do all this, it's humbling," said Alan Strong of NOAA's National Environmental Satellite, Data and Information Service. "It reminds us what mother nature can do. . . . It is fascinating that what happens in one area can affect the whole world. As to why this happens, that's the question of the century. Scientists are trying to make order out of chaos."

Finally, in the face of the frightening destruction, the scientists still admired and appreciated what was unfolding. The wondrous, vast dynamics before them conjured up thoughts of beauty and elegance side by side with their sense of confusion. If only they had more data, they asserted, or grasped more securely the physical laws of the world, they could understand. When questioned, they insisted they still believed there was a rational order where others saw only random chaos or an angry God. Scientists who give in to theological tendencies, they noted wryly, tend to have limited credibility.

"Those of us in climatology do not believe that changes in the climate are completely random, that God is playing dice with us," said Jerome Namias, the renowned oceanographer at the Scripps Institution of Oceanography in La Jolla. "It is not a gull flapping its wings somewhere or a grasshopper jumping in the Sahara that twists the whole atmosphere around."

Peruvian fishermen knew long before scientists arrived with sophisticated instruments that the waters off Peru and Ecuador warmed almost every year, usually around Christmas. For this reason, legend has it, they named the warm current *El Niño,* in reference to the Christ child. Another version says the fishermen originally called it *el corrienta del niño,* the little warm current, because it confronted the more powerful cold Humboldt Current that usually flows north up the South American coast. In recent times, scientists and journalists have come to use the term *El Niño* broadly to describe the more unusual and powerful major warming events in the equatorial Pacific. These warmings have been felt globally seven times in the past hundred years, in 1891, 1925, 1931, 1941–42, 1957–58, 1972 and—the largest of them all—1982–83.

El Niño in this broader sense is literally a sea change.

Normally, the eastern equatorial Pacific is a region of high atmospheric pressure, while the western equatorial Pacific is one of lower pressure. Just as water runs only downhill, winds blow only from high pressure to low, so trade winds usually flow from the South American coast westward toward Australia and Indonesia. These trade winds drag the eastern Pacific's warm surface water to the west with them. This allows cold, nutrient-rich water to well up off the coasts of Peru and Ecuador, making that area one of the most abundant fisheries in the world. It also leaves a thick mass of warm water in the western Pacific. Along the coast of Australia sea levels are not only warmer but often are six feet higher than along the coast of South America.

During *El Niño,* however, this condition inexplicably seesaws. The normal low pressure zone in the western Pacific switches places with the usual high pressure in the eastern Pacific. Scientists call this event the "southern oscillation," but they can't explain why it happens. They do know what it causes.

The normal trade winds to the west die, and sometimes actually reverse direction, flowing east toward South America. Without the winds pushing toward the west, the huge mass of warm water sloshes back toward South America in a mammoth surge called a Kelvin Wave. The front of this surge crosses six thousand miles of the vast Pacific at the rate of five knots, or 125 miles a day. When the warm water reaches South America, it hooks south along the coasts of Ecuador and Peru and, because warm water is less dense than cold water, overrides the cold Humboldt Current. This blocks the upwelling of cold, nutrient-rich water from the ocean bottom. With nothing to feed on, many species of fish disappear, along with fish-eating seabirds. The Peruvian anchovy industry, which had accounted for thirty-eight percent of the world's supply, was devastated by an earlier *El Niño* in 1972, cutting the catch from 10.3 to 1.8 million metric tons.

The weather is also affected. Through evaporation the warm *El Niño* water along the South American coast sends enormous amounts of heat and moisture into the atmosphere. The warm moist air condenses, and heavy rains fall. Meanwhile, Australia and Indonesia, which usually get the warm waters and rains, stay cool and dry. The two sides of the Pacific literally swap systems.

Although these regions feel the most intense results of *El Niño,* its effects spread much farther. The warm equatorial sea also forces unusual heat energy into the northern Pacific's atmosphere, and this energy increases the contrast in air pressure between the equator and the Arctic. The heightened contrast in air pressure, in turn, affects both the subtropical and polar jet streams in North America. The eastbound tropical jet stream, which usually dies out by the time it reaches Baja

California, continues to roar eastward instead, bringing abnormal rain and storms to California, the Southwest, the Gulf Coast, Florida and Cuba. The polar jet stream is displaced hundreds of miles to the south, bringing additional torrential rains, winds and high tides to California coastal regions.

It is misleading, though, to talk quite so directly of causes and effects when describing this process, for there can be no unique, simple source for weather or climate. Scientists instead talk of "multiple causes" and the constant "interaction" between two "nonlinear systems"—the atmosphere and the ocean—that takes place simultaneously in the dimensions of both space and time. By this they mean that the atmosphere is volatile, changes rapidly, and lacks an internal mechanism that could dictate long-term weather patterns, while the ocean is a large, dense mass that changes only sluggishly. Where the atmosphere has a "short memory," the ocean has a "long memory"—once it undergoes a change, such as a rise in water temperature, that change is likely to remain in place and affect weather for a long time.

"There is no universal starting point," says Jerome Namias at the Scripps Institution. "It's quite arbitrary, but that doesn't mean random —where you break into the scene is the starting place. The chicken-or-egg question is not pertinent. In large-scale air-sea interactions, it is presently almost impossible to prove cause and effect. Probably the sea is both slave and master of the atmosphere—a complexly coupled system."

Gene Rasmusson, putting it in simpler terms, says, "When you add one effect to another, it can add up to more than two. Effects multiply. A small perturbation can make much more of an effect than it seems. . . . When one part of the atmosphere moves, another part feels the kick."

Historical accounts suggest that *El Niños* have affected man for many hundreds of years.

Eighteenth-century British pirate ship log books recorded the blood-red patches of plankton that are linked to *El Niño*. Other accounts cite unusual sharks, alligators and yellow-bellied sea snakes in Peruvian warm waters. Tristan Jones, a veteran sailor and author of *The Incredible Voyage,* concluded, after researching the topic everywhere from the Maritime Museum in Barcelona, Spain, to the British Museum and Lima University, that one *El Niño* had even helped shape the history of the modern world. Jones believes that Francisco Pizarro, the conqueror of the Incas, prevailed only because he inadvertently happened to find himself sailing down the coast of South America from Panama during an *El Niño* condition. Instead of bucking a powerful northbound Humboldt Current, he was pushed by the warm southbound *El Niño.* "Had this not been the case," Jones argues, "it would have taken the Spaniards much, much longer to reach the Inca Empire. Atahualpa, the emperor, would have been forewarned by their slow approach and would have been ready for them. The Spaniards would probably have been massacred and the history of the world would have taken a completely different course. More than likely, the Spanish would not have gained access to the treasures of the Andes with which to finance their conquests, and the nations of Northern Europe would probably not have been spurred into colonial conquest in order to counter the growing threat of Spanish domination of Europe."

Whatever future seers may make of its political import, the *El Niño* of 1982–83 physically was the largest and most intense in recorded history. Scientists never before saw so much warm water, at such high temperatures—surface readings at the Equator reached an astounding ninety degrees Fahrenheit. But the 1982 *El Niño* also baffled the scientists for other reasons. It began at the wrong time of year; *El Niño* usually starts about December, during the Southern Hemisphere's summer, but this one began in June, during winter. *El Niño* is supposed to be preceded by a year of heavy buildup of waters and winds in the western Pacific, but this cne began without any buildup.

The first signs could be seen in the far western Pacific. In Australia, air pressure rose at Darwin in June 1982. The westbound trade winds died and reversed direction. The drought began that month in Australia, Indonesia and New Guinea. Sea levels rose at Nauru and a deep blanket of clouds settled over the equatorial central Pacific as the great warm ocean surge began its inexorable eastward movement.

The evidence first became overwhelming in the central Pacific. By July, sea levels at Fanning and Christmas islands were up six to ten inches. The rains began. The amount of precipitation in July at Tarawa was four times the norm. By August, the normal low pressure station at Darwin was recording its highest pressures in a century, and Tahiti was reporting its lowest pressures in fifty years. The current that normally flows westward along the equator was moving strongly to the east. Five cyclones formed in the eastern Pacific. It started to rain at Christmas Island during what is usually the beginning of the dry season. Deluges were reported from the Gilbert Islands (now the independent nation of Kiribati) to the Line Islands.

In September, Rasmusson issued the first of what would become a series of special climate diagnostics bulletins. A genial, bemused, sometimes self-deprecating man of fifty-four years, he was trained in meteorology by the Air Force and later earned a doctorate from the Massachusetts Institute of Technology. He had been studying *El Niño* since the late 1970s, and helped to found NOAA's diagnostics branch in 1979. In this first bulletin, he stopped short of announcing an *El Niño,* saying that the situation "is as yet unclear." The scientists simply could not believe their own information. The figures were too bizarre. In fact, the data flowing into NOAA's Climate Analysis Center from satellites, buoys and merchant ships were actually being rejected. The NOAA computer system was programmed to regard numbers too far from the norm as being the result of faulty instruments.

But at the same time, in the equatorial Pacific, a small expedition on board *The Conrad,* a research vessel financed by the National Science Foundation, had fewer doubts. Unintentionally, expedition members found themselves in the middle of the fiercest *El Niño* of the century, just as it was springing to full life. *The Conrad* left Honolulu on September 10 and steamed eastward along or near the equator to Panama, reaching the canal October 13, 1982. The ship's scientists, conducting a large-scale study of current, surface and subsurface temperatures, were not in the region because of *El Niño* and had not known it existed. But the chief scientist on the cruise, John Toole, a physical oceanographer from the Woods Hole Oceanographic Institution, soon began noticing something strange. Surface temperatures were seven to nine degrees warmer than normal, and even more important, the warm water continued deep below the surface. Normally, the ocean in this region cools to fifty-nine degrees Fahrenheit (fifteen degrees Celsius) at a depth of 165 feet. Toole could not find water that cool above 726 feet. What is called by oceanographers the "fifteen-degree isotherm" had been pushed an astounding 561 feet deeper than its normal level. "I'd never been in water that warm," Toole said later.

The oddities continued. Normally, a force called the "equatorial counter current" (EUC) runs eastward deep below the surface, under the main westward flow. Toole could not locate the EUC—it had simply disappeared. "The currents just weren't acting right," said Vicky Thayer, a Duke University marine biology researcher on board. "Everything was out of kilter. We couldn't find the mammals and birds normally seen in hordes in this area. The stormy petrels were gone. We fished for a long time off the stern, and had Fijians on board who really know how to fish. They caught nothing." Toole was in a bad mood, worrying that *The Conrad* might be behind schedule because one of the ship's engines was broken. Then he took a reading of the ship's position. "I was amazed," he later recalled. "We were traveling much faster than I expected. You usually figure to be going against the current when you're heading east. But we were being pushed one knot. The current was going in the wrong direction."

When he realized that he was watching the birth of *El Niño,* Toole told Thayer, "We're in it." From the ship, Thayer radioed the news to her supervisor, Richard Barber, director of Duke University's Marine Laboratory. "You're right out there on the edge of scientific history," Barber radioed back. Thayer, recollecting later, said, "It was awesome. We didn't have control. Nature was more powerful than us, going its own way." Unbeknownst to Toole and Thayer, however, the NOAA's computers in Washington still would not believe what was happening. *The Conrad*'s data, so far from the norm, were also being rejected.

In October, *El Niño*'s warm surge reached the South American coast. Record rains and flooding far beyond historic levels struck Ecuador and northern Peru and continued unabated for eight months. Rasmusson later called it "part of the most catastrophic and prolonged *El Niño* visitation of record." On October 18, the NOAA's own scientific research vessel, *The Researcher,* left Rodman Naval Base on the Pacific side of the Panama Canal, cruising west as far as the Galápagos Islands, then south to Callao, just north of Lima, reaching there November 16. Chief scientist Stan Hayes found surface temperatures up to six and a half degrees Fahrenheit warmer than the norm. The normal westward equatorial current was "virtually nonexistent. . . . Essentially all surface flow . . . was to the east." In Washington, though, the NOAA's computers still were not convinced—*The Researcher*'s initial data were also discarded.

At the same time, a renowned physical oceanographer at the University of Hawaii, then considered in scientific circles to be "Mr. *El Niño,*" was being misled by his own theoretical model of how *El Niño* is supposed to act. At the seventh annual Climate Diagnostics Workshop, sponsored by the NOAA from October 18 to 22 in Boulder, Colorado, Klaus Wyrtki flatly insisted there could not be an *El Niño* brewing. It was Wyrtki's theory, much respected and accepted, that *El Niño* is preceded by unusually strong westbound winds and a huge buildup of water on the western side of the Pacific, which then sloshes back to the eastern Pacific when the winds die. There had been no such prior buildup this time—so Wyrtki argued, in a written paper, that there could be no *El Niño.*

"Yes, some in Boulder were saying there was no *El Niño* at the same time people in Peru were getting heavy rain and staring at water eleven degrees warmer than normal," Rasmusson said later, chuckling at the contrast. "It was happening. But people just got locked into their theories and models."

Looking back months later, Wyrtki said, "I never did think that an *El Niño* could develop from a state of rest. I would not have thought the wind field could collapse without a buildup. . . . If I were a politician, I'd be embarrassed, but as a scientist, I'm not. We are always learning. That's what we do. We can't go in the lab and alter a situation and experiment. Nature is doing the experimenting. We can only observe."

In late October 1982, the NOAA finally decided it was losing too much data through computer rejection. "We started realizing we were throwing the baby out with the bath water," Rasmusson said. "We went back and started to look again at the data from *The Conrad* and the buoys. We decided that this was good data after all." The computer was reprogrammed to accept the abnormal figures and Rasmusson redrew the September map of the region before its release. With the new figures, it became clear to Rasmusson that *El Niño* was under way. In November, he issued his second special climate diagnostics bulletin, for the first time announcing an *El Niño.* The current situation, he reported, "has now reached the dimensions of a major warm episode. . . . There seems little doubt that the [current *El Niño* conditions] are of major proportions, rivaling or possibly even exceeding the events of 1972 and 1976."

In the equatorial Pacific, there was no doubt at all. Chaos reigned.

In November, 4.32 inches of rain fell at Guayaquil, Ecuador, compared to a norm of 0.32 inches. The Line Islands reeled under powerful eastbound winds. Fanning and Washington islands suffered extensive erosion and damage to vegetation on their western shores because of heavy clouds of salt spray blowing inland from the surf. A plantation manager on Washington reported that fifty-year-old trees had been undermined and had fallen into the sea. A rare, devastating northeasterly hurricane, Iwa, slammed into Hawaii, causing $230 million in crop and property damage and killing one. Soon after, French Polynesia was devastated by the first of what would turn out to be six major tropical cyclones. The captain of *The Machias,* a research vessel traveling along the equator at the time, reported seeing tree trunks, plastic bottles and rubber slippers streaming by in the open sea.

On Christmas Island, Ralph Schreiber, the curator of the ornithology section of Los Angeles County's Museum of Natural History, and his wife Elizabeth, a researcher, found that the entire bird population of seventeen million, which usually reproduces on the island, had disappeared, abandoning their nestlings. The Schreibers saw an island eerily transformed from the hospitable spot they had visited often before. Harsh eastbound winds, heavy rain, solid cloud cover and high sea levels prevailed. Roads in many areas were impassable for the first time in the memory of inhabitants. A pilot salt pond enterprise was completely underwater, dikes and all. Most striking, though, was the absence of those birds, on an island renowned as a breeding sanctuary. Where they were accustomed to seeing thousands of blue-faced boobies, the Schreibers found only one nestling and three adults. They saw just six great frigates—and nineteen carcasses. There were hundreds of dead lesser frigate nestlings. Where there normally was a population of fourteen million sooty terns, the Schreibers in November neither saw nor heard a single one. Christmas Island was devastated.

"We believe that the food supply (fish and squid) has disappeared for the majority of the birds," Schreiber reported. "The result is that adults abandoned the island and the nestlings then starved. Ecological theory indicates . . . it is evolutionarily best to abandon a nesting attempt rather than place undue stress on the adult, who can return to breed again when the food situation improves. We do not know where the adults have gone or if they have survived."

On November 22, the NOAA's *Researcher* left Callao and conducted further tests as it steamed north along 85 west longitude, arriving in Panama December 6. Chief scientist Ants Leetmaa found that *El Niño* had altered the ocean to at least 3,300 feet, creating a remarkably deep mass of warm water. Near the equator, the fifteen-degree isotherm was down to 759 feet—594 feet deeper than normal. One day during the cruise, two hands who had left the ship in a small, motorized inflatable Zodiac raft to conduct tests were brushed by a shark, a creature that normally avoids outboard motor noise. The men caught it and a marine biologist aboard cut it open. The shark was starving. "You could eyeball it out there," said Jack Cutchins, *The Researcher*'s yeoman. "There were no fish or sea gulls. It was incredible. And the ship was hot. Normally the ocean cools us."

The effect of *El Niño* began to extend and appear over the northern Pacific parts of North America. Drought conditions developed from the Philippines eastward through the Hawaiian Islands. The tropical jet stream roared across California and the southern tier of the United States. The normal northern Pacific low around the Aleutian Islands reached record proportions, shifting more storms, winds and tides to California. By December, all measurements flowing into Rasmusson's Washington office were at record levels—for atmospheric pressure, sea temperature, precipitation, isotherms. "It just kept building and building. I was in awe," Rasmusson said.

Then, just as the existence of *El Niño* had finally been universally recognized, it played another bizarre trick on its observers. In January and February 1983 all the statistical indicators started to decline. Water temperatures dropped nine degrees. Drifting buoys near the equator that had previously been moving eastward, changed direction and headed west, indicating a return of the current to its normal flow toward Australia. Wind measurements indicated a beginning shift back to the normal westbound flow. The pressure readings at Darwin began to assume normal levels. Rasmusson, in his third special bulletin, announced on February 14 that "it is now clear that the 1982–83 event will go down in the records as one of the strongest, and in many respects one of the more unusual warm episodes of the century." He also said that observations and statistics now "indicate that this *El Niño* event may have passed its peak."

He was wrong. In March, sea temperatures inexplicably surged upward again. Along the coasts of Peru and Ecuador, the waters warmed to a staggering twelve to thirteen degrees above normal. The drifting buoys that in mid-January had turned back to the west once more reversed direction and headed eastward. All measurements in April and May exceeded the previous December peaks.

By June *El Niño* had become a media celebrity, carrying on its shirttails the meteorologists and oceanographers studying its bizarre pattern. Worldwide, newspapers and magazines devoted articles, columns, editorials and multicolored graphs to the topic. In Washington, scientists such as Rasmusson and J. Murray Mitchell, Jr., senior research climatologist for the NOAA, were besieged with dozens of calls daily from persons hoping for predictions. During one hour in mid-June, Rasmusson fielded calls from a TV station in Minnesota, a magazine writer in Toronto, and an aide to the prime minister of Australia—who was encamped at Washington's Mayflower Hotel and wanted to know the future of his country's drought. *The Researcher*, docking at Callao on one leg of its journey, was greeted by Peru's president, Pernando Belaunde Terry. Returning in mid-July, it was met by television cameras on the pier.

The attention was understandable. By then, the effect of *El Niño* had reached epic, global proportions.

In desert areas of Peru, Ecuador and Bolivia, where the climate is normally so arid that roofs are not built watertight, twelve feet of rain had fallen, compared to a norm of four to five inches in a full year. Meanwhile, in agricultural regions of northern Bolivia and southern Peru, there had been no rain in eight months. Only ten percent of Bolivia's staple, the potato crop, had survived. Roads, including the Pan American Highway, ended in lakes several miles long. Some forty thousand adobe homes had melted. Urban sewer systems had burst. The Galápagos saw more rain in one six-week period than it normally sees in six years. Mexico and Central America lost $600 million, all from drought. Cuba suffered fifteen deaths and $170 million in property and sugar crop damage because of heavy rains and flooding. The United States, fearing that the disruption caused by the natural catastrophes was serious enough to threaten the stability of the Andean democracies of Peru, Ecuador and Bolivia, pledged $48.6 million worth of food as part of a support program.

On the other side of the Pacific, Australia had endured the driest summer in two centuries. Huge brush fires had ravaged the countryside. Crop, livestock and property damage approached three billion dollars. Nineteen African countries, many in the southern portion of the continent, had endured property and crop damage of $1.2 billion. The corn and wheat crops were decimated, rivers were dry, lakes too low for irrigation. Cattle, sheep and goats died by the thousands. Zimbabwe, a major beef producer, was contemplating the need to relocate one million head of cattle. In Micronesia, where a quarter of the food crops and half the critical coconut harvest were lost, countries were running out of drinking water and facing serious public health problems, including an outbreak of infectious hepatitis. Between January and June, Ponape and Yap, which usually get 180 inches and 110 inches of rain respectively, received just seven inches and five and a half inches. Water for Yap's capital of Colonia had to be pumped from a swamp, trucked to town and chlorinated. India, Sri Lanka and Indonesia endured 340 deaths and $650 million in crop damage.

It was the wettest spring on record for much of the United States, from the Deep South to Chicago and across New England. Many areas of the Northeast got twice their normal rainfall; Los Angeles had nearly triple its norm. California and other Pacific and Rocky Mountain states suffered $1.1 billion of damage from beach erosion, landslides, floods, tornadoes, crop and livestock losses. Heavy snowpacks in the Sierra Nevada and Utah mountains triggered destructive mud slides and flooding in Utah and Nevada and, ultimately, along the Colorado River. A severe blizzard slammed into Denver in late May. The Gulf Coast states suffered fifty deaths and more than one billion dollars of damage, with rain-bloated rivers cresting at record highs in Texas, Arkansas, Mississippi and Louisiana.

Marine life off the coast of California dumbfounded veteran fishermen—they found species that did not belong and couldn't find those that did. Millions of tiny red crabs washed ashore in southern California, clogging pipes at the San Onofre nuclear plant. On Monterey Bay, the sardine, which had disappeared after World War II, reappeared, conjuring dreams of a return to the world of John Steinbeck's Cannery Row. Seahorses and marlin were spotted off Huntington Beach. Giant squid and anchovies were spawning.

To the north, on the Farallon Islands near San Francisco, the Christmas Island disaster was replayed. Some three hundred thousand birds normally congregated there during spring and early summer, making it the largest breeding ground for seabirds in the continental United States. But they feed on shrimplike krill, anchovies and young rockfish that flourish in upwelling cold water, so without the cold water, the food chain was disrupted and the birds disappeared.

Sitting in Washington in June 1983, a frustrated Gene Rasmusson could not answer many of the questions he was hearing. The pressure readings at Darwin and Tahiti had returned to normal, but *The Researcher* had traversed the equatorial Pacific twice more that month and found no upwelling of cold water. Temperatures had stayed warm. "There's a hell of a lot of things we can't explain," he said. "How does this thing end? What shuts it off? The SOI [southern oscillation index] has dropped, but the sea surface temperatures are still historically high. There's no resolution. It's still gigantic. It ought to go away, but it hasn't. I don't know what will happen this year."

Rasmusson issued another bulletin in June summarizing the past year's events, but he could not just yet put an end to his story. "The future course of the warm episode," he concluded, "was still in doubt at the time of this writing."

Then, finally, in the first week of July, Rasmusson received the news he'd been expecting to hear many months before. Sea surface temperatures along the coast of Peru and Ecuador had suddenly fallen ten to eleven degrees. Cool water was rising closer to the surface. The U.S. government's drifting buoys were heading westward, indicating that the ocean current had resumed its customary flow toward Australia.

The temperatures were still almost eleven degrees above normal, but Rasmusson felt certain he now was looking at the final stage of *El Niño.* On July 15, he issued his sixth special bulletin since *El Niño* began. "*El Niño* is finally entering its decay phase," he said flatly. "This will be the last of our series of special climate diagnostics bulletins."

All that remained for the scientists was the urge to understand. What had caused the historic, catastrophic *El Niño* of 1982–83 in the first place? Was it part of an ordered, rational system that could be predicted and understood, or was it a product of random chaos in the natural world?

That question, scientists allowed, was not an easy one. In fact, Jerome Namias at the Scripps Institution ventured to suggest that "the cause of weather is probably the second most difficult problem in the world to understand—after human behavior." J. Murray Mitchell, Jr., the NOAA senior climatologist, said, "At the lowest level, we can try our best to describe. At the higher level, we can try to predict. To understand is the hardest." Even the scientists who had been most stymied and awed by its sweeping, irrational power, however, were far from willing to say that the 1982–83 *El Niño* was the product of an angry God or anarchy in the skies and seas. There is purpose, they insisted, even if we can't grasp all the causes.

They could say nothing else, of course, for in the end they know too much about the grander order of which *El Niño* is just one puzzling part. They know that because of the shape of the earth and its rotation, an excessive amount of the sun's heat is absorbed at the equator, and that the sea there gets the largest share—there is as much heat in the top meter of ocean as in the entire atmosphere. They know this heat must be distributed across the earth. They know that is what weather—from storms to drought—accomplishes. They know that is why what happens in the equatorial Pacific is so influential worldwide—scientists call the equatorial Pacific the crucial "flywheel" of the heat engine that drives the world's weather.

"The weather, climate and atmosphere are part of our environment,"

J. Murray Mitchell likes to point out. "They do not have a life or destiny of their own. When I look at the jet stream, clouds, heat, storms and all that, I see a perfect machine. The overall system is constantly working to convey heat and cold from where there is too much to where there is too little. Without that system, most of the earth would be broiling or freezing, and would be as uninhabitable as other planets. The weather out the window now, today, is just a detail. It's the climate system that's the being, the organism. It may not be comfortable that there's a thunderstorm out there, but it's a necessary byproduct of a larger process."

For this reason, Gene Rasmusson contemplates with distinct ambivalence the now slowly decaying natural force that he has watched wreak global havoc for more than a year.

"I feel like Robert E. Lee at Fredericksburg," the meteorologist confessed one morning in mid-July 1983. "I think Lee said there, 'It is well that war is so terrible, or we should get too fond of it.' That's sort of how I feel about *El Niño*. Very seldom do you see the entire global system linked. It's always happening, but it's rare that we can see it so clearly. I know it's caused great destruction, and I don't have all the answers. But it's just an elegant physical system. It's just beautiful."

Grateful acknowledgment is made for permission to reprint the following:

"Making the Leap" (originally appeared as "Eggs, Prizes, on the Line for Scientists" and "Desire to be First Colors Gene Studies") by Barry Siegel. Copyright © December 13 and 14, 1987, *Los Angeles Times.* Reprinted by permission. "Unborn Patients" (originally appeared as "Fetal Doctors—They Scan for Defects," "A Decision to Wrestle with Nature," "Why Not Try to Fix What is Wrong?" and "You Have to Individualize These Cases") by Barry Siegel. Copyright © November 16, 17, 18 and 19, 1986, *Los Angeles Times.* Reprinted by permission. "Could This Be Murder?" (originally appeared as "Murder Case a Corporate Landmark" and "Trial Makes History, Stirs Controversy") by Barry Siegel. Copyright © September 15 and 16, 1985, *Los Angeles Times.* Reprinted by permission. "A Perfect Machine" (originally appeared as "El Niño: the World Turns Topsy Turvy" and "El Niño Still Lingers After Scientists Predict Demise") by Barry Siegel. Copyright © August 17 and 18, 1983, *Los Angeles Times.* Reprinted by permission. "A Crafty Purpose (originally appeared as "Cold Virus: An Image of the Unseen") by Barry Siegel. Copyright © December 25, 1985, *Los Angeles Times.* Reprinted by permission. "Lobstermen and Weathermen" (originally appeared as "Weather: Accuracy Put to the Test") by Barry Siegel. Copyright © March 28, 1985, *Los Angeles Times.* Reprinted by permission. "You Got to Know Your People" (originally appeared as "Ruling Casts Shadow on Jury System") by Barry Siegel. Copyright © March 20, 1986, *Los Angeles Times.* Reprinted by permission. "A Little Excitement" (originally appeared as "Sentencing the Wrong Man to Die") by Barry Siegel. Copyright © March 10, 1987, *Los Angeles Times.* Reprinted by permission. "A Time to Die" (originally appeared as "Law Versus the Right Not To Suffer") by Barry Siegel. Copyright © January 12, 1983, *Los Angeles Times.* Reprinted by permission. "The Pendulum Swings" (originally appeared as "Child Abuse: Dilemma of Prevention") by Barry Siegel. Copyright © February 1, 1989, *Los Angeles Times.* Reprinted by permission. "Passing the Laugh Test" (originally appeared as "Managing Reists: Sense and Science") by Barry Siegel. Copyright © July 5, 1987, *Los Angeles Times.* Reprinted by permission. "Monstrous Mischief" (originally published as "Miles Lord: Champion or Zealot?") by Barry Siegel. Copyright © June 28, 1984, *Los Angeles Times.* Reprinted by permission. "Paper Games" (originally appeared as "Victims to Victors in Farming" and "Family Farm Reaped Gains From Economic Crunch") by Barry Siegel. Copyright © May 19 and 20, 1991, *Los Angeles Times.* Reprinted by permission. "An Easy Target in Adams County" (originally appeared as "Killing Forces Amish to Face Outside World") by Barry Siegel. Copyright © March 23, 1980, *Los Angeles Times.* Reprinted by permission. "Shadow of Doubt" by Barry Siegel. Copyright © November 19, 1989, *Los Angeles Times.* Reprinted by permission. "Portrait of a Dinosaur" (originally appeared as "The Disappearing Doctor") by Barry Siegel. Copyright © March 3, 1991, *Los Angeles Times.* Reprinted by permission.